Garden Apartments

Historical Studies of Urban America

EDITED BY LILIA FERNÁNDEZ, TIMOTHY J. GILFOYLE, AND AMANDA I. SELIGMAN

JAMES R. GROSSMAN, EDITOR EMERITUS

Recent titles in the series

Emily Lieb, *Road to Nowhere: How a Highway Map Wrecked Baltimore*

Ruby Oram, *Home Work: Gender, Child Labor, and Education for Girls in Urban America, 1870–1930*

Stephen M. Koeth, *Crabgrass Catholicism: How Suburbanization Transformed Faith and Politics in Postwar America*

Daniel Wortel-London, *The Menace of Prosperity: New York City and the Struggle for Economic Development, 1865–1981*

A. K. Sandoval-Strausz, ed., *Metropolitan Latinidad: Transforming American Urban History*

Alexander Wood, *Building the Metropolis: Architecture, Construction, and Labor in New York City, 1880–1935*

Leslie M. Harris, *In the Shadow of Slavery: African Americans in New York City, 1626–1863*, With a New Afterword by the Author

Tim Keogh, *In Levittown's Shadow: Poverty in America's Wealthiest Postwar Suburb*

Nicholas Dagen Bloom, *The Great American Transit Disaster: A Century of Austerity, Auto-Centric Planning, and White Flight*

Sean T. Dempsey, *City of Dignity: Christianity, Liberalism, and the Making of Global Los Angeles*

Claire Dunning, *Nonprofit Neighborhoods: An Urban History of Inequality and the American State*

Tracy E. K'Meyer, *To Live Peaceably Together: The American Friends Service Committee's Campaign for Open Housing*

Mike Amezcua, *Making Mexican Chicago: From Postwar Settlement to the Age of Gentrification*

Arnold R. Hirsch, *Making the Second Ghetto: Race and Housing in Chicago, 1940–1960*, With a New Afterword by N. D. B. Connolly

William Sites, *Sun Ra's Chicago: Afrofuturism and the City*

David Schley, *Steam City: Railroads, Urban Space, and Corporate Capitalism in Nineteenth-Century Baltimore*

A complete list of series titles is available on the University of Chicago Press website.

Garden Apartments: The History of a Low-Rent Utopia

JOSHUA B. FREEMAN

The University of Chicago Press Chicago and London

Publication of this book has been aided by a grant from the Neil Harris Endowment Fund, which honors the innovative scholarship of Neil Harris, the Preston and Sterling Morton Professor Emeritus of History and Art History at the University of Chicago. The fund is supported by contributions from the students, colleagues, and friends of Neil Harris.

The University of Chicago Press, Chicago 60637
The University of Chicago Press, Ltd., London

Published 2026
Printed in the United States of America

35 34 33 32 31 30 29 28 27 26 1 2 3 4 5

ISBN-13: 978-0-226-84179-3 (cloth)
ISBN-13: 978-0-226-84181-6 (paper)
ISBN-13: 978-0-226-84180-9 (ebook)
DOI: https://doi.org/10.7208/chicago/9780226841809.001.0001

Library of Congress Cataloging-in-Publication Data

Names: Freeman, Joshua Benjamin author
Title: Garden apartments : the history of a low-rent utopia / Joshua B. Freeman.
Other titles: Historical studies of urban America
Description: Chicago ; London : The University of Chicago Press, 2026. | Series: Historical studies of urban America | Includes bibliographical references and index.
Identifiers: LCCN 2025015709 | ISBN 9780226841793 cloth | ISBN 9780226841816 paperback | ISBN 9780226841809 ebook
Subjects: LCSH: Garden apartments—United States—History | Garden apartments—Social aspects—United States | Housing policy—United States—History—20th century
Classification: LCC HD7287.6.U5 F74 2026 | DDC 333.33/80973—dc23/eng/20250602
LC record available at https://lccn.loc.gov/2025015709

♾ This paper meets the requirements of ANSI/NISO Z39.48-1992 (Permanence of Paper).

Authorized Representative for EU General Product Safety Regulation (GPSR) queries: **Easy Access System Europe**—Mustamäe tee 50, 10621 Tallinn, Estonia, gpsr.requests@easproject.com
Any other queries: https://press.uchicago.edu/press/contact.html

For Margo and Eleanor, and hope for a brighter future

CONTENTS

Introduction

When in 1948 Elvis Presley's family moved from Tupelo, Mississippi, to Memphis, Tennessee, they ended up in a one-room apartment, cooking on a hot plate and sharing a bathroom down the hall. The next year they moved to Lauderdale Courts, a 433-unit garden apartment complex run by the Memphis Housing Authority. Their apartment, with two bedrooms, a living room, a kitchen, and their own bathroom—quite a change from one room for everything—was in a building that formed one side of a shallow courtyard, a safe play area parents could monitor from inside. "For a kid growing up," wrote Presley's biographer, "there was a degree of comfort, a sense of place, a reassuring sense that everyone . . . was looking toward a bright new day."[1]

A year later and nearly a thousand miles away, former labor union journalist Betty Friedan moved into a privately owned garden apartment complex in Queens, New York, called Parkway Village. Though she would later become world-famous for chronicling the discontents of women in post–World War II America, she had nothing bad to say about her years living in a garden apartment. "I loved the concrete daily life of that community . . . the politics of it, the bonds we formed with other parents at the nursery school." She felt, she later wrote, that she "would never again, ever, be so happy as I was living in Queens."[2]

Kerry James Marshall moved with his family from Birmingham, Alabama, to Nickerson Gardens, a garden apartment complex in the Watts neighborhood of Los Angeles, in 1963. He later depicted his old home, the largest public housing project in the United States west of the Mississippi River, as part of his *Garden Project* paintings of public housing. (See plate 1.) Marshall wrote he "wanted to evoke some of the hope that the projects started with, but also to demonstrate a little bit of the despair."[3]

Garden apartments, the kind of dwelling Presley, Friedan, and Marshall lived in, are the Rodney Dangerfield of housing—they get no respect. Clusters of these low-rise, multifamily buildings, typically arrayed around courtyards or spread out over large sites with few streets, can be found

Figure I.1. 185 Winchester Avenue, Memphis. Elvis Presley lived in apartment 328.

all across the United States. Most were erected during the 1930s, '40s, or '50s, some as privately owned rental housing, some as government-owned public housing, and some as tenant-owned cooperatives. Together they provided decent, affordable housing to millions of Americans, and many still do. Yet most people would probably have no idea what you were talking about if you mentioned them.

Scholars and policy experts ignore them. Standard histories of housing and architecture focus on single-family homes and, to a lesser extent, large multistory apartment buildings. Grand estates, suburban subdivisions, and even vacation houses are examined, but garden apartments rarely merit even an aside.[4] Not, strictly speaking, a building form—the way architectural studies define their subject—garden apartments slip through disciplinary cracks. Even studies that focus on what is sometimes called "missing middle" housing, dwelling types that fall between single-family detached homes and large apartment buildings, such as bungalow courts, duplexes, triple-deckers, and townhouses, ignore garden apartments.[5] New York City has more garden apartments than any other city in the United States, but studies of its history, architecture, and housing generally ignore this common form of residence or give cursory attention to a few examples.[6]

The invisibility of the garden apartment is especially remarkable because it is a rare success story in the long, troubled effort to provide decent housing to Americans of modest means. These unpretentious developments, most of them thrown up quickly in the mid-twentieth century to meet acute housing needs, generally served their residents well. Many became vibrant communities. Typically, they incorporated design features and communal facilities that created environments that were superior, at least in some respects, to both denser urban neighborhoods and sprawling suburbs. Sixty, seventy, eighty years or more after they were built, hundreds of thousands of garden apartments remain occupied, functional, and often quite attractive.

Many residents and observers viewed garden apartments as almost idyllic, not simply affordable dwellings but model communities. One former resident of LeClaire Courts, a public housing project in Chicago, recalled, "The camaraderie was absolutely wonderful out there. We all took care of each other like a village." For children, garden apartments could be paradise. Marina Budhos, who grew up in Parkway Village, remembered that

Figure I.2. Betty Friedan, cutting the cake at her son's birthday party in Parkway Village, 1963.

"the general rule was that we could roam as far and wide as [we] wanted inside of the village, so long as we came home when the street lamps blinked on. Even then, in the spring and summer evenings, there were so many adult gatherings, that most of us would bolt outside again, comforted by the sound of tinkling and adult voices shifting through the trees."[7]

Critic Lewis Mumford waxed ecstatic in his assessment of Fresh Meadows, a postwar Queens, New York, complex built by New York Life Insurance Company that combined 137 garden apartment buildings with two taller residential structures and a shopping center. The design of the complex, Mumford wrote in *The New Yorker*, "provides for the comfort and the esthetic satisfaction of the inhabitants from the time they wake up, after a night of peaceful sleep, and put their small children on the lawn behind the houses—where they scamper about with reasonable safety on the grass while their mothers go shopping at the nearest marketing center—until everyone goes to bed again. Fresh Meadows is not just more housing; it is a slice of the City of Tomorrow."[8]

Figure I.3. Fresh Meadows, Queens, New York.

Multiple factors have contributed to the invisibility of garden apartments. Architecture is one. Very few garden apartments are architecturally distinguished. Most do not look like much. Generally, they are simple, unadorned, two- or three-story buildings. While their site layouts and settings can be quite attractive, the buildings themselves are mostly bland structures that seem to meld into the background. (See plates 2 and 3.) It is easy to walk or drive past them without giving them any attention. *Architectural Record* wrote of the buildings in Fresh Meadows, the community Mumford raved about, "their effect, aesthetically, is a great, timeless unobtrusiveness."[9]

The type of people who lived in garden apartments also contributed to their social oblivion. They, too, were a "missing middle," neither rich nor in the upper ranks of the middle class, but generally not impoverished either. Rather, they were families of bus drivers and clerks, schoolteachers and mechanics, factory workers and salesmen—people of modest means, though often on the ascent. Garden apartments were housing for the working class and the lower rungs of the middle class.

As architect and architectural historian Thomas C. Hubka has noted, most histories of housing ignore the kinds of buildings that most Americans lived in, focusing instead on the homes of a relatively small upper stratum. The dwellings of the middle 60 percent of Americans are all but absent in the literature. This is even more true of garden apartments than of other forms of what Hubka calls "middle-majority housing."[10]

History tends to be told from the point of view of elites—political, military, and business leaders; the wealthy; artistic and intellectual standouts. In the United States, this has become less so in recent decades, but the quotidian realities of ordinary people remain little-known territory. Inattention to garden apartments and their residents fits a general indifference to the circumstances, culture, and material history of working-class and lower-middle-class Americans.

Garden apartment residents did not command attention as a social problem, unlike some poorer populations. We know quite a bit about tenement dwellers in the nineteenth and early twentieth centuries and the buildings they lived in because, at the time, they were perceived by wealthy urbanites, political leaders, real estate investors, and reformers as a threat to public health, safety, and order. Accordingly, they were extensively investigated and documented by journalists, photographers, social workers, and sociologists. By contrast, there is no Jacob Riis of the garden apartment. Sociologists pumped out studies of post–World War II suburbs, but never entered the humble grounds of garden apartments.[11]

Garden apartments do not fit the dominant American narrative of what good housing is and how it is produced. For centuries, the United States has had a cult of homeownership, the material corollary of the deep individualism endemic, if not unchallenged, in the national history. In 1931 President Herbert Hoover proclaimed: "To possess one's own home is the hope and ambition of almost every individual in our country, whether he lives in hotel, apartment, or tenement. . . . Those immortal ballads, 'Home, Sweet Home'; 'My Old Kentucky Home'; and 'The Little Gray Home in the West,' were not written about tenements or apartments. . . . They never sing songs about a pile of rent receipts."[12]

The veneration of the owner-occupied single-family home reached even greater heights after World War II. By 1960, three out of five families owned their own homes. Homeownership was widely perceived as a mark of individual achievement. Most new homes were in the suburbs, which accounted for over 80 percent of population growth between 1950 and 1970. Suburban homeownership became linked to a national identity that embraced the nuclear family, car culture, and racial homogeneity.[13]

Garden apartments represented an alternative path. They did align with the mainstream in catering to nuclear families and in their typical—though not universal—racial uniformity. But most garden apartments were rented. If occupant owned, they were almost always owned collectively, as cooperative entities, not individually owned. Garden apartments were more communal than freestanding houses, sharing physical structures, recreational spaces, and amenities. Unlike the bulk of new postwar homes, most garden apartments were urban, often at the edges of cities but generally not in newly developed suburbs. In the usual, simplified telling of post–World War II United States history, garden apartments do not fit and do not appear.

Garden apartments were beneficiaries of what some scholars have called the "hidden" or "submerged" welfare state.[14] Without government support, garden apartments would not have existed as a form of mass housing. Some were built directly by the government and run as public housing. Many more were privately owned but made possible by advantageous government loans or mortgage insurance, and sometimes tax breaks, too.

While the American welfare state is often criticized for being meager, especially compared to many European countries, garden apartments suggest that the difference might not be as great as it seems. Garden apartments were a massive, successful experiment in state-sponsored housing that no one thinks about, at least in that way. To do so would contradict the widely shared, incorrect assumption that government involvement in housing (not counting assistance for single-family homes) primarily took the form of the development of high-rise public housing and was a disaster, proof of the superiority of the private sector and the market. Looking at garden apartments tells a very different story of the success—flawed, but a success—of government-promoted housing.

All these factors contribute to the same result. Garden apartments remain invisible because there is no shared context in which to place them. Acknowledging them forces us to rethink how we understand our history. But, hiding in plain sight, exist they did and exist they do.

There is no shared definition of a garden apartment, a somewhat amorphous term, used in different ways at different moments. The *Oxford English Dictionary* defines a garden apartment simply as "an apartment in a low-rise apartment complex with landscaped gardens or lawns."[15] In the 1910s and 1920s, the appellation was generally used to describe large apartment buildings set in extensive green space with many amenities for their residents. By the 1930s and 1940s, the term had come to be used for much humbler structures, simple two- or three-story buildings, with access to apartments through shared entranceways rather than internal public hallways, set on large, landscaped sites and aimed at low- or moderate-income families.[16]

It is the latter type of building on which this study focuses. Once you begin looking, they are easily recognized. A few characteristic designs account for the vast majority of complexes. Typically, garden apartment developments use modular plans, in which a handful of building types—or even just one—are repeated over and over. Brick, wood, and other common materials dominate. Ornamentation is usually minimal. Apartment layouts are similar. Most people would be hard-pressed to distinguish one garden apartment complex from another.

Some developments do not neatly fit the pattern of uniform, multifamily, two- or three- story buildings. There are projects that combine single-family or one-story structures with two- or three-story multifamily buildings. There are projects like Fresh Meadows that go the other way, joining high-rise structures with more typical garden apartments. And there are a few architecturally innovative complexes that have many of the characteristics of garden apartments but do not look at all like the usual specimens.

It is impossible to say precisely how many garden apartments were built during their heyday in the 1930s, '40s, and '50s because national housing data is not collected by building type. Even if it was possible to

Figure I.4. Baldwin Hills Village (now called The Village Green), Los Angeles.

do a national field survey, it would not be definitive, since a fair number of garden apartment complexes have been demolished over the years. Statistics about government housing programs provide clues, since most garden apartments received support from one federal program or another, but those programs supported other types of housing as well and usually did not disaggregate their data. It takes a great deal of detective work and some guessing to come up with even a broad estimate.

By the mid-1950s, there were probably well over a half-million privately owned garden apartments in the United States. In addition, there were several hundred thousand publicly owned garden apartments. Together they housed well over two million people. Given turnover, many more people than that lived in a garden apartment at some point. In a country with a 1955 population of 165 million, garden apartment residents represented a small minority, but in absolute terms they were a large group. As a percentage of those newly housed after World War II, they were substantial.[17] By 1970, the number of garden apartments had grown significantly—by one scholar's calculation, to 3.5 million rental units (public and private), along with a far smaller number of cooperatively owned residences. Living in a garden apartment, like living in a new suburban home, a decaying urban tenement, or a rural shack, was a defining postwar American experience.[18]

The history of the garden apartment would be important if all it did was fill in our understanding of the lives of the large number of mid-twentieth-century Americans, spread out across the country in big cities, inner suburbs, and modest-sized towns, who lived in them. Who wouldn't want to know more about Elvis Presley, Betty Friedan, Kerry James Marshall, and all their anonymous peers? On the humble grounds of garden apartment communities, the conflicting tendencies in American social, political, and cultural life played out: war and demobilization; racial separation, integration, and conflict; economic depression and boom; upward mobility and class barriers; individualism and mutuality; security and violence; changing gender roles; family togetherness and escape; fulfillment and disappointment.

This book tells that story. In part it is an architectural history, a narrative of design and construction. How and why did the characteristic form of garden apartments come to be? What were its strengths and weaknesses? Who designed and financed these oft-overlooked buildings? How was design meant to shape behavior and experience, and to what extent did it succeed? In part it is a social history, an account of who lived in garden apartments, what kinds of experiences they had, who stayed and who left, and why. But above all else, it is a political history.

In spite of its enormous wealth, the United States has struggled, over

Figure I.5. Children in the spray pool at Aliso Village, a public housing garden apartment complex in Los Angeles, 1944.

and over again, to fulfill what in 1944 President Franklin D. Roosevelt declared "the right of every family to a decent home." Even putting aside his now-jarring assumption that the right to shelter comes from family membership, this demand for what seems like a minimal social responsibility has been more than the United States has been able to achieve over its long history.

Since the late nineteenth century, critics and reformers have questioned whether mass affordable housing is even possible in a capitalist society. Very commonly, workers have received wages that have failed to match the cost of decent dwellings. Key players in the housing market have been driven by a quest for profit, not social need, with the highest rates of return coming from housing the well-off. In her 1934 report on European social housing, Catherine Bauer, arguably the most important twentieth-century American housing reformer, wrote, "The premises underlying the most successful and forward-pointing housing developments are not the premises of capitalism, of inviolate private property . . . of governments bent on preserving old interests rather than creating new values." Ultimately, she found herself agnostic about whether a successful modern housing program could be carried out under capitalist conditions.[19]

Garden apartments suggest that there were and are ways to decently house people of modest means within the framework of American capitalism, but with notable limitations in quantity and quality. At no point did garden apartments come anywhere near to plugging the gap in housing need. But they did help, and on a significant scale. Rather than a simple story of triumph or failure, the history of garden apartments suggests the possibilities for and constraints on affordable housing. At least sometimes, when progressive elements had sway within the state, real progress could be made.

While there are no comprehensive studies of garden apartments, the work of other scholars, who in one way or another touched on their history, makes this book possible. J. B. Jackson's essays on the landscapes of everyday life, from highways and garages to self-built homes and trailer parks, reveal the riches found in looking closely at structures normally taken for granted.[20] Robert Fishman, Eve Blau, Susan R. Henderson, Owen Hatherley, and Stanley Buder, among others, have written about efforts in Europe and the United States in the early twentieth century to build communities infused with the utopian spirit that characterized early garden apartment development.[21] Richard Plunz documented the first buildings in the United States to be called garden apartments, while providing a model of how to look at the broad range of urban housing types.[22]

Gail Radford's *Modern Housing for America: Policy Struggles in the New Deal Era* established a historical framework for this study. Radford delineated the ideas, forces, and conflicts that shaped mid-twentieth-century housing policy and raised many questions this study addresses. Kristin M. Szylvian extended Radford's work into the World War II era.[23]

Historians of public housing, including D. Bradford Hunt, Joseph Heathcott, Nicholas Dagen Bloom, Edward Goetz, and Lawrence W. Vale, have provided a wealth of information on the politics, economics, and design principles of the federal and local programs that built garden apartments as well as better-known high-rise projects.[24] Sylvie Murray's *The Progressive Housewife: Community Activism in Suburban Queens, 1945–1965* is a pioneering look at political and social life in garden apartment communities and proved invaluable for this study.[25] Finally, there is the work of Matthew Gordon Lasner, who has produced a rich literature on many forms of twentieth-century multifamily housing and profiled several garden apartment complexes.[26]

As valuable as the work of these scholars has been, this book differs in fundamental ways. First, and uniquely, it focuses exclusively on the garden apartment. It is the first history of this housing form. Second, it covers a longer time period than most histories of housing. By following the garden apartment from its early twentieth-century origins to recent neo-garden apartment developments, it reveals how changing economic, political, and social circumstances shaped the evolution of design. Third, because some garden apartments were publicly owned, some owned by commercial developers, and still others cooperatively owned by their residents, looking at this housing type allows an unusual natural experiment in comparing how different ownership forms shaped the lived experiences of residents and the differing fates of complexes with similar designs. It brings into question the standard view of the failure of public housing, which emphasizes design flaws and cheap construction, by showing how even well-designed, well-constructed public housing developments succumbed to problems, especially chronic underfunding, less likely to be found in similar, privately owned developments.

This study also departs from most histories of multifamily housing in its stress on politics and political ideas. In surprising ways, the history of the humble garden apartment reveals much about how change happens and does not happen. Garden apartments, like many social innovations, had roots in the political left, in radical efforts to transform relationships of power and wealth and construct a more democratic society. This book begins with late nineteenth- and early twentieth-century initiatives to build homes and whole communities for ill-housed European workers, the seed for what would become the garden apartment. Many of the first American efforts, drawing on European models, to build garden communities and garden apartments were imbued with a radical spirit. Though these transatlantic experiments have been discussed elsewhere, they are a necessary prerequisite to the main concern of this book, the garden apartment as an unacknowledged mass form of American housing.

During the New Deal, as part of a general movement for social reconstruction, government resources made it possible to begin fulfilling some of the promises of the garden apartment model on a large scale. After World War II, housing, including garden apartment construction, was one of the few policy areas where efforts to extend or expand New Deal programs succeeded. However, by then the political tides had already shifted away from the left. As a result, the possibilities for experimenting with new models of housing and community were severely limited. Garden apartments represented an example of accomplishment after defeat. Stripped of many of their most innovative features and their political cutting edge, they nonetheless represented a substantial social accomplishment.

Much of the recent literature on the New Deal and twentieth-century reform stresses their limitations and failings, including the perpetuation of racial and gender hierarchies.[27] Looking at garden apartments confirms the problematic nature of New Deal programs, but brings home a different message of how that moment of reform profoundly changed and improved the daily lives of ordinary Americans, white and black, Hispanic and Anglo, male and female. It suggests the danger of missing the achievements of reform by focusing too exclusively on its shortcomings.

Garden apartments, best thought of as a dumbed-down version of European social housing, became for many, as Lewis Mumford described them, a kind of low-rent utopia. Looking back from the present era—plagued with housing problems of its own, above all affordability, but also predatory sales and lending practices, poorly planned communities, dispiriting commutes, ecologically unsustainable practices, and racial discrimination—the garden apartment seems a historical experience and architectural model deserving of far more attention than it has received. From this plebian form of housing, we might learn something about how to move forward today. Its history deserves to be reclaimed.

1 *Utopian Roots*

The anodyne names of garden apartment complexes—Bell Park Manor and Terrace, Colonial Village, LeClaire Courts, Clearview Gardens—disguise their lineage. Rather than descending from upper-class English architecture, as their names might suggest, these seemingly commonplace developments have roots in European efforts to provide decent, affordable housing for urban, working-class families, efforts linked to socialist or social democratic movements to reform or replace the capitalist system.[1] Very few residents of American garden apartments have any idea that the conception and design of their dwellings derived, at least in part, from utopian ideas for reconstructing society. Still, as distant as a low-rise apartment complex in Houston or Poughkeepsie might seem from the European left of a century or more ago, to understand the successes and limitations of garden apartments we must go back to the circumstances, ideas, and experiments that ultimately led to their development.

The Garden City

The "garden" part of the term "garden apartment" derives from English reformer Ebenezer Howard's proposal, at the end of the nineteenth century, for what he called "garden cities." A solution to the ills of a depleted countryside, overcrowded cities, and exploitative social arrangements, Howard detailed a plan for self-contained small cities in rural settings, built on centrally owned and controlled land, with limits on profits from housing resales. Residential areas would have extensive park and public spaces, industry would be arrayed on the perimeters of the city, and each settlement would be surrounded by an agricultural greenbelt.

Howard's garden city vision proved enormously influential with architects, city planners, municipal officials, and even the general public in Europe and the United States. Howard skillfully synthesized various radical ideas about social organization and housing in a technocratic idiom that projected self-evident rationality and common sense and promised an existential improvement in daily life without directly challenging relationships of power. His 1898 book, *To-Morrow: A Peaceful Path to Real Reform*—revised and reprinted four years later as *Garden Cities of To-Morrow*—chock-full of details and diagrams, held forth the possibility of a kind of practical utopia, realizable not in some distant future but in the here and now.[2]

Like other housing reformers, Howard was appalled by the social misery and inequality brought on by rapid industrialization and urbanization. In nineteenth-century Manchester and London, New York and Boston, Paris and Vienna, grand public buildings and neighborhoods of the wealthy abutted dense, filthy, ramshackle quarters of the poor, with dark alleys, open sewage, and dangerous streets. For upper- and middle-class reformers, such conditions needed to be addressed because they threatened to spread disease, crime, and social rebellion to the areas where they had investments or themselves lived. For workers and their allies, deplorable housing presented a summons to transform society to better serve an ever-growing working class.[3]

Earlier reformers deeply influenced Howard. Born in London in 1850, he spent three years in the United States as a young man before settling down back in England, working as a stenographer for a company that published parliamentary records. Two American books, which he read after his return, profoundly shaped his thinking.

One of the best-selling books in the United States in the nineteenth century, Edward Bellamy's utopian novel *Looking Backward*, published in 1888, envisioned a path of escape from the ills of class conflict, poverty, and waste that threatened the stability and future of the country. Bellamy, horrified by the suffering and disparities produced by industrialization while fascinated by the technological and organizational advances that accompanied it, imagined a new type of society in which production and distribution systems would be owned by and serve the entire society through a powerful, benevolent national administration. Class conflict, and classes themselves, would disappear amid previously unknown abundance, made possible by the elimination of profit, competition, and exploitation. From Bellamy's fantasy society of the future (set in 2000), Howard drew the idea of a community organized along lines of rational planning and control, operating for collective good rather than individual advantage.[4]

From Henry George's *Progress and Poverty: An Inquiry into the Cause of Industrial Depressions and of Increase of Want with Increase of Wealth: The Remedy* (1879), Howard took the idea that speculative control of land and profiteering from rising land values was a central cause of inequality and suffering. In his proposal for garden cities, Howard embraced George's call to capture the rise in land values resulting from overall development for communities, not for private interests. His suggested mechanism was not George's single-tax on land. Instead, he proposed ground rents on community-owned building plots, which would rise when land values increased.[5]

Howard's plan reflected his distress not only at the condition of the urban poor but also at the hollowing out of the countryside as people moved to cities for employment, especially to London. Critiques of the emerging industrial system had long decried the growing divide between city and country. From the early nineteenth century on, various utopian schemes were proposed—and occasionally even attempted—to create new communities, set in the countryside, that combined manufacturing and agriculture on a communal, nonmarket basis. In France, Charles Fourier sketched out *phalanstères* or "phalanxes," small, self-contained settlements of craft workers and farmers living collectively in free association. In Great Britain, Robert Owen proposed small, cooperative settlements that combined agriculture with some manufacturing and featured communal domestic arrangements, including shared kitchens and dining halls (an idea Bellamy also promoted).[6]

Though Karl Marx and Friedrich Engels derided much of the thinking of "utopian socialists" like Fourier and Owen, they, too, criticized the growing separation of city from countryside. In a series of 1872 articles, Engels argued, "The housing question can be solved only when society has been sufficiently transformed for a start to be made toward abolishing the contrast between town and country which has been brought to its extreme point by present-day capitalist society." There simply was no way, he contended, to provide adequate housing to workers in large, modern, capitalist cities, because rising land values made decent working-class communities impossible to sustain.[7]

Howard's garden city provided a means to overcome the country-city division. First, it would draw people away from large, overcrowded cities to smaller communities that combined agriculture and industry, in the process repopulating and reanimating the countryside. Networks of these new settlements could take over most of the functions of giant cities like London. Then, as those cities depopulated, they could be redeveloped on a lower-density, more sustainable basis. (See plate 4.) Though inclined toward cooperative industry, Howard, unlike Engels, did not see the replacement of the capitalist mode of production as a prerequisite to creating a new type of community that combined rural and urban life. In fact, not long after publishing *Garden Cities of To-Morrow*, Howard set out to do precisely that.

In 1903, Howard and a group of colleagues established the First Garden City Company to create a settlement embodying his ideas. For financing, Howard turned to well-off philanthropists, including George Cadbury,

Figure 1.1. Aerial photograph of Letchworth Garden City, 1930s.

from the chocolate company, and W. H. Lever, from the soap company, both of whom had built model towns for their workers. (See plate 5.) The new company purchased a large block of land thirty-three miles north of London. The manifesto for what was named Letchworth Garden City, channeling Henry George, declared it "an attempt to secure social justice for the people by constitutional means, by diverting the increment of values attached to the land into the pockets of those who created that value."

Two architects associated with the arts and crafts movement, Raymond Unwin and Barry Parker, won a competition to lay out the new town, broadly following Howard's guidelines. From a central town square surrounded by municipal buildings, broad boulevards would radiate out. Separate residential and industrial areas were delimited—in an era before zoning was common—with a greenbelt surrounding both.

Within a year, the first residents moved into Letchworth. A 1905 census found most to be from the middle class with independent means (some accompanied by servants) or skilled artisans. Unwin and Parker designed a variety of house types to accommodate the newcomers, adopting an architectural style meant to evoke traditional British villages, with brick and stucco, gables, and tile roofs. Though Letchworth social arrangements were generally quite conventional, the town did include one "cooperative quadrangle," Homesgarth, into which Howard and his wife moved in 1913. It had private apartments without kitchens, with food served in a central dining hall. A nursery and recreation room further communized domestic life.

Most houses in Letchworth were built by commercial developers or individual homeowners. Originally, the town planned to provide ten-year leases on building lots, with the option to raise the rates upon lease renewals to reflect the increased value of land as Letchworth grew. But its leaders quickly discovered that no one would invest in construction if they were unable to know their future costs. So Letchworth switched to offering renewable ninety-nine-year land leases, abandoning the effort to capture the fruits of rising land values for the entire community. When a few factories set up shop in Letchworth, a cooperative building society was formed to construct houses for their employees. Without rent subsidies, though, only skilled workers could afford the small, attached houses with private gardens. Less skilled factory workers ended up having to live out of town, in cheaper, less attractive dwellings.[8]

Figure 1.2. The dining room at Homesgarth.

In 1939, after thirty-five years, Letchworth had an estimated population of only 17,500. The cooperative manufacturing and retail enterprises that Howard hoped it would attract never materialized. A second garden city, Welwyn Garden City, not far from Letchworth, was launched in 1919, but it, too, only slowly developed. The rather nostalgic designs of Letchworth and Welwyn left even sympathetic observers like Lewis Mumford cold; he judged their overall architectural effect "mediocre." Still, the mere creation and survival of these communities is impressive; most utopian schemes never got off the ground or, like Robert Owen's "New Harmony" colony in Indiana, lasted only briefly.[9]

While garden cities developed only limited traction as a way to redistribute population and create more equitable communities, as Howard intended, some of the design features associated with them appeared over and over again in "garden suburbs" created across Europe and North America. These were planned neighborhoods on the outskirts of cities, characterized by low-rise housing (generally single-family homes), extensive landscaping, and nearby recreational and commercial facilities. The first of these efforts, Hampstead Garden Suburb, was designed by Raymond Unwin. Located on the north side of London, it had strong ties to the garden city movement, which tended to fudge the difference between garden cities, with their grand social ambitions, and garden suburbs, with their more limited brief.

Like Letchworth and Welwyn, Hampstead Garden Suburb was planned as a totality on a large tract of land purchased for the development. Through a trust, a central administrative body retained control over land use and even external building appearance. By carefully laying out building sites and avoiding a grid, Unwin dramatically reduced the amount of land needed for roads. This lowered costs and allowed for the creation of far more green space than typical in communities of similar density, making for a very attractive ambience. Hampstead tried to accommodate residents from a variety of economic strata, including workers, and some of the housing was cooperatively built, but gentrification eventually drove up the cost of even tiny worker cottages.[10]

The success of Hampstead Garden Suburb inspired the spread of lush, well-ordered communities to house economically comfortable families on urban outskirts in North America, Europe, and South Africa. Most garden suburbs did not have pretensions of social uplift or reform. Instead, they were simply attractive and often financially lucrative developments for middle- and upper-class residents who commuted into nearby cities for their jobs. Such communities are familiar to us today, with their cul-de-sac or curvilinear streets, extensive greenery and park space, and zoning or regulations to keep industry—and usually poor people, too—at a distance.[11]

Ebenezer Howard, who was knighted in 1927 and died the next year, lived long enough to see his most obvious legacy was not in the realm of social reform, his initial motivation, but in the arena of design. In the end, the importance of the garden city lay not in its alleviation of urban misery or a radical restructuring of society—it did neither—but in its role as an inspiration for other efforts to address the shortage and wretched quality of housing for working people that plagued the industrial world.

Social Housing

At roughly the same time that the garden city was being experimented with in England, various European initiatives began to rehouse workers and the poor through the creation of what came to be known as social housing. While there is no strict definition of the term, or its equivalent in other languages (*Sozialwohnungen* in German, *logement social* in French, *sociale huisvesting* in Dutch), social housing generally meant subsidized rental dwellings for working-class residents priced below commercial rates. This was a different, if sometimes overlapping, project than English garden cities and suburbs, where a lack of subsidies made housing too expensive for most workers.

The first attempts to provide improved worker homes usually took the form of model dwellings built by philanthropists or company housing built by large industrial employers. Part of their motive was to reduce the possibility of dangerous or threatening worker behavior, with extensive rules and surveillance designed to instill new social norms in residents. Industry required a steady, stable workforce, which these developments—aimed not at the very poor but at employed blue-collar workers—could help ensure. In addition, in some countries, like Denmark and the Netherlands, worker organizations built a significant amount of cooperative housing. From the start, social housing had two faces: It was both an effort to stabilize capitalism and a way to circumvent, supplement, or supersede it.

By the early twentieth century, in an effort to accelerate rehousing workers, most European countries passed some sort of national law to regulate housing and permit the allocation of public money for construction.[12] During World War I, the need for housing for workers in arms-related industries led to new government initiatives. So did growing fear of radicalism. The Russian Revolution and the left-wing surge right after the war led even conservative governments to seek to ameliorate unrest through social benefit programs, including subsidized housing. "All the noxious weeds, from tuberculosis to Bolshevism . . . flourish where housing conditions are bad," one writer reported as the view of Belgian housing officials. After the war, as socialist or social democratic parties came to power, or at least influence, locally and nationally, they became leading sponsors of social housing. The virtual collapse of commercial house building in many European countries in the face of material shortages, inflation, and economic uncertainty added to popular support for their efforts. The result was a massive wave of social housing construction from World War I through the early 1930s.[13]

Catherine Bauer, whose 1934 book *Modern Housing* surveyed developments in Europe, calculated that in the five countries and selected urban districts of six more that she studied, four-and-a-half million state-assisted housing units had been erected since the war. These dwellings constituted 70 percent of all residential construction during the period. In Europe as a whole, she estimated, there were about seven million state-assisted homes.[14]

In Great Britain, much of the postwar social housing was directly government-built, justified by the sacrifices of soldiers who, when the war ended, found few if any decent dwellings they could afford. "Homes fit for heroes," Liberal Party Prime Minister Lloyd George proclaimed. Many conservatives bought into the notion, fearing that veterans might turn to the left; *The Spectator* wrote of slum clearance, "This we believe is the way to fight communism." Some "council houses," built by local authorities with funding from the national government, were erected on cleared inner-city sites. Others were constructed on less expensive land on urban outskirts. In Vienna, Oslo, and Zurich, as well, local authorities built social housing.[15]

In most of Europe, by contrast, governments helped finance and promote social housing, but a variety of independent entities undertook construction and management: cooperatives, nonprofit housing agencies (in some cases linked to unions or with particular political or denominational identities), and philanthropies. State assistance included low-cost loans, leased public land, tax reductions, capital grants, and rent subsidies. In Germany, the large social insurance funds also provided financing. Some of the Continental social housing was aimed at the very poor, but the focus tended to be on housing the employed working class, speaking to both political imperatives and the manpower needs of industry.[16]

European social housing took many physical forms, from single-family homes to large apartment blocks, designed in a wide variety of styles and layouts. Very little of this housing received any attention in the United States, either at the time or since, except among a small number of reformers, architects, and planners. The one effort that did achieve modest renown in the United States was in some ways atypical: the apartment buildings of Red Vienna.[17]

When World War I ended, the bulk of the population of Vienna lived in miserable circumstances. Most people occupied single-room tenement apartments, often without kitchens, gas, or electricity. Toilets almost always were outside. To upgrade living standards, between 1919 and 1934 the social democratic government of Vienna built some 64,000 units of *Gemeindebauten* (municipal housing). By the latter year, 200,000 people—a tenth of the population of the city—lived in these projects. The massive building program was financed by a highly progressive tax on housing, various luxury taxes, and general municipal funds, with no expectation that capital costs would be repaid. The city was able to buy land cheaply because a combination of rent control and inflation all but eliminated any prospects for profitable commercial development. Since *Gemeindebauten* rents were used only for maintenance and administration, they could be kept very low. Viennese leaders saw municipal housing as a step toward and prefigurative of socialism, which they believed could be achieved incrementally, rather than through a Bolshevik-style revolution.

Most of the four hundred municipal apartment buildings were tucked into the existing urban fabric, adopting a traditional Viennese design of four- to six-story structures arrayed along the perimeters of a block, with internal courtyards that housed playgrounds and gardens. Some of the housing openly embraced modernism, most famously the massive Karl-Marx-Hof, with its large semicircular entries and geometrical facade. (See plate 6.) Mostly, however, the outward appearance of the new municipal structures did not radically deviate from established norms.

While often externally grand, the apartments within the municipal buildings were very modest. Most had only two rooms: a combined living room and kitchen (some later-built apartments had a small separate kitchen) and a bedroom. Some apartments had a small additional bedroom as well. The apartments had toilets, cold water, electricity, and gas for cooking but lacked central heating and running hot water. Compensating residents for their modest apartments, municipal buildings offered numerous communal facilities, including bathhouses (individual apartments did not have showers or tubs), laundry rooms, cooperative stores, kindergartens, medical and dental clinics, libraries, theaters, and workshops.

In 1923, Vienna set the size for new municipal apartments at 409 square feet for two rooms and 517 square feet for three. (By comparison, in 2012, the average size of a newly built apartment in the United States was 941 square feet; in 2022, 887 square feet.) The small apartment sizes meant that the *Gemeindebauten* could only house nuclear families, not extended families, which were common in the tenements. The use of physical design to promote the nuclear family would be adopted in American garden apartments as well.[18]

Social housing elsewhere adopted elements of the Viennese designs. The London County Council built several inner-city projects influenced

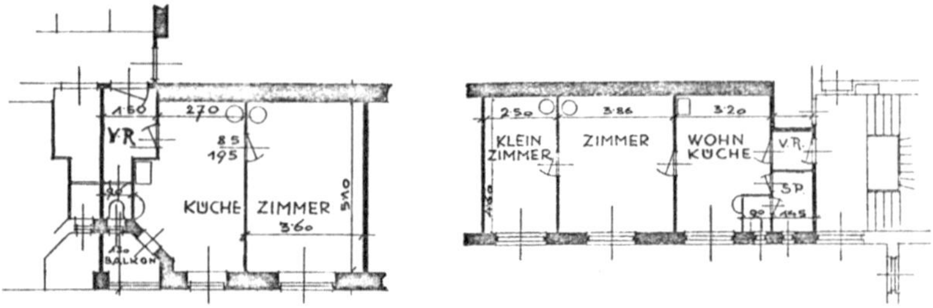

Figure 1.3. Floor plans for two- and three-room Vienna municipal apartments. Note the absence of hallways in the apartments.

Figure 1.4. Amalgamated Dwellings, Manhattan, New York.

by Austrian municipal housing, most notably the Ossulston Estate, with arches echoing Karl-Marx-Hof. In New York, the 1930 Amalgamated Dwellings, a union-sponsored cooperative on the Lower East Side, adopted the Karl-Marx-Hof model, too, though on a much smaller scale. Roland Wank, the principal architect, had lived in Vienna before emigrating to the United States. (He went on to be the chief architect for the Tennessee Valley Authority.) The six-story brick building, with art deco touches, is arrayed along the perimeter of a block, with a parabolic archway entrance to an inner courtyard from which apartments are accessed. Communal facilities included a library, nursery, roof deck, gymnasium, and auditorium.[19]

While large, multistory, inner-city apartment buildings represented one model of social housing, another, probably more prevalent, drew on the garden city/garden suburb model in constructing low-rise projects set amid extensive greenery, often on urban outskirts. These developments were precursors to and inspirations for garden apartments in the United States, though they were, and are, all but unknown to the American public.

Ebenezer Howard's ideas and Raymond Unwin's design approaches proved remarkably influential among social housing builders across Europe. In Great Britain, many council house developments were designed along garden city lines, though few were actually new satellite communities. Belgium and the Netherlands, which built some of the finest interwar social housing, also employed garden city approaches. Many of these projects combined traditional architecture with innovative site layouts and financing.[20]

In Germany, a substantial number of social housing projects melded garden city thinking with architectural modernism. The Deutsche Gartenstadt-Gesellschaft (German Garden City Association) was founded in 1902, just three years after Howard launched its British equivalent. In its early years, the group embraced a comprehensive socialist vision of urban reform, encompassing not only housing but also politics, education, fashion, the arts, and even sexuality. Rather than actual garden cities, it focused on building garden suburbs. Many German cities had acquired substantial tracts of underutilized land on their outskirts at low prices even before World War I, allowing them to build large-scale housing developments without facing huge land acquisition costs or the need to wedge them into an existing cityscape. A robust infrastructure of social benefit funds, cooperatives, nonprofit housing organizations, labor unions, and socialist-led local governments, as well as a cadre of able civil servants, facilitated development. So did substantial state funding.[21]

Some of the best projects, which pointed toward the American-style garden apartment, were constructed in Frankfurt and Berlin. Compared to later projects in the United States, they had greater aesthetic flair, more numerous communal facilities, and notable socialist overtones. But the family resemblance is clear.

In 1925, the city of Frankfurt, under a left-liberal coalition government, hired architect Ernst May to head a powerful, well-funded housing department. While studying architecture, May had spent two years in the office of Unwin and Parker at the time they were designing Hampstead Garden

Figure 1.5. Siedlung Römerstadt, Frankfurt.

Suburb. The experience made the Frankfurt native a lifelong believer in garden cities. From Unwin, May adopted a holistic approach to planning, as he witnessed the British architect not only lay out the new suburb and design many of its buildings but also take charge of all the accompanying details, from lighting and pavement to benches and letter boxes.[22]

Between 1925 and 1933, Frankfurt built 15,000 units of social housing. May originally sought to create a garden city some fifteen or twenty miles outside of Frankfurt proper, but facing political opposition, he instead settled on developing what might be termed working-class garden suburbs, new settlements separated from the existing city by narrow greenbelts and parks. Having large tracts to work with, May and his colleagues designed sizable housing clusters or, as they are called in German, *Siedlungen* (settlements), including Siedlung Römerstadt, with 1,182 units, and Siedlung Praunheim, with 1,441 units, perhaps the best-known projects. The settlements included schools, kindergartens, playgrounds, garden plots, and parks. As was the case with the Vienna *Gemeindebauten*, the Frankfurt *Siedlungen* became strongholds of socialist culture and identity.

While in broad conception the Frankfurt projects resembled Unwin and Parker's garden cities and suburbs, the design and layout of the buildings and the methods of construction were radically different. May favored low-rise buildings—sometimes one story high, sometimes two or three—that were almost always designed with flat roofs, sometimes equipped

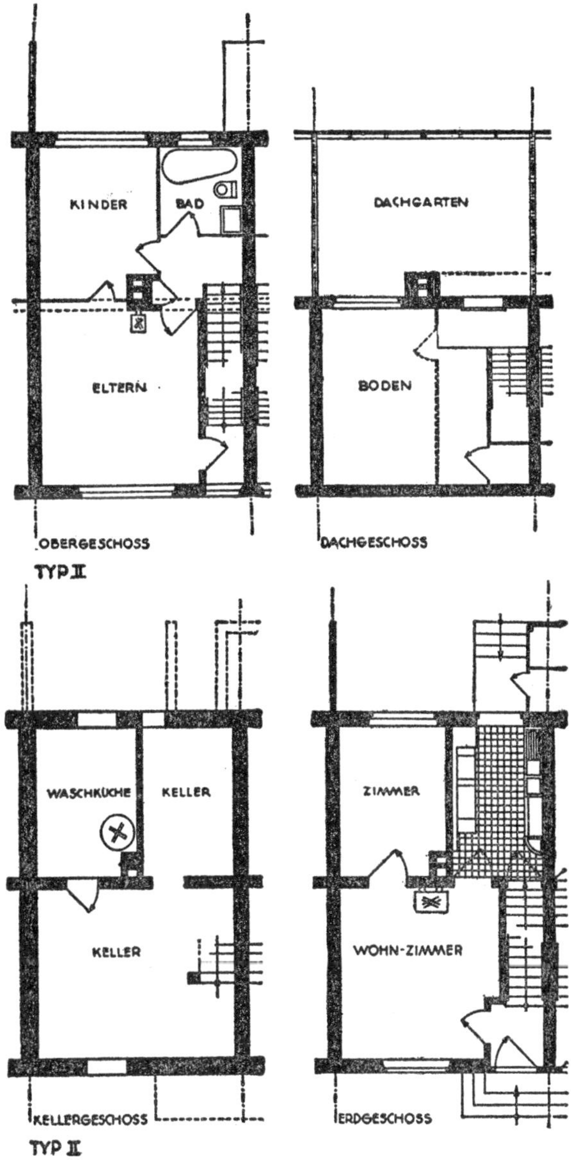

Figure 1.6. The floor plan for a four-room house in a Frankfurt *Siedlung*, with a roof garden and cellar.

with rooftop gardens. With little if any ornamentation, May's modernist designs represented a clean break from traditional German home designs.

The typical Frankfurt apartment was larger than a Vienna unit and included central heating, hot water, and a private bathroom. In 1926, four-room units averaged 1,011 square feet. After careful studies of the best way to economically provide light and air, May settled on long parallel lines of attached buildings, with green space on both sides. As would be the case with garden apartments in the United States, the May buildings had no internal hallways. This allowed light and air to enter apartments from two sides.

European social housing designers were captivated by industrial developments in the United States, particularly "scientific management," as promoted by Frederick Winslow Taylor, and the mass production techniques of the Ford Motor Company. To reduce costs, May and his team designed standardized components, experimented with new materials, and used prefabrication. Austrian architect Margarete Schütte-Lihotzky, who worked with May, conducted interviews and time-motion studies of kitchen use, then designed several versions of a built-in kitchen meant to improve the efficiency and ease of domestic tasks. It included a gas or electric stove (as opposed to then-common wood-burning stoves), a sink, wrap-around counters, storage spaces, special bins for flour and other staples, a fold-down ironing board, a swivel stool, a ceiling light, and a window. Her kitchen represented a major departure from the working-class norm of minimal kitchen appliances in a room that also served as a living, dining, and working space (an arrangement continued in many Vienna *Gemeindebauten*). A "Frankfurt kitchen" was installed in 10,000 Frankfurt dwellings. As Catherine Bauer noted in *Modern Housing*, large-scale planning, mass production techniques, reduced financing charges, and community control of land use—all in place in Frankfurt—could drastically reduce the cost of housing, in her estimation by a cumulative 35 percent compared to traditional methods.[23]

Siedlung construction, heavily influenced by the garden city movement, began in Berlin even earlier than in Frankfurt. Through World War I, 90 percent of the Berlin population lived in four- or five-story tenements, nearly half of which were rear buildings away from a street. Nine out of ten lacked bathrooms. Work started in 1913 on Gartenstadt Falkenberg (Falkenberg Garden City), a project of eighty single-family homes, mostly row houses or semidetached, and six apartment buildings. Sponsored by a nonprofit building cooperative created by the German Garden City Association, and designed by Bruno Taut, it was located on the southeastern edge of the city. At first glance, the two-story buildings from the first

Figure 1.7. A Frankfurt kitchen, designed by Margarete Schütte-Lihotzky.

phase of construction, clustered around a landscaped cul-de-sac, might be confused with an American garden apartment courtyard from decades later, except for the colorful palette Taut used on the building exteriors. (See plate 7.) Houses in the estates included gardens so that families could grow some of their own food. Communal life was rich, with a nursery and kindergarten, clubs of all kinds, bulk purchases of appliances and consumer goods, and health services, including a physician, infirmary, and insurance plan.

In 1920 the city limits of Berlin were expanded to include former agricultural land, providing inexpensive sites for new housing. Five more social housing settlements were completed by 1934. The earlier projects benefited from a tax on mortgage interest while the later ones received direct municipal allocations. Siedlung Schillerpark, with three-story red-brick buildings and a courtyard layout, seems to directly anticipate Fresh Meadows (though the buildings are more handsome). (See plate 8.)

Großsiedlung Britz, designed by Taut and Martin Wagner, housed some 5,000 people on the south side of Berlin. Its centerpiece was a huge, three-story, horseshoe-shaped ring of attached buildings surrounding a natural lake. Outside it lay block after block of two- and three-story row houses. (See plate 9.)

Like May, Wagner, the socialist chief city planner for Berlin, tried to apply Fordist mass production techniques to housing. In practice, he was only partially successful. Though standardization and prefabrication were employed, building the *Siedlungen* still required considerable on-site manual labor. With apartments somewhat larger than those in the Frankfurt *Siedlungen*, rents in Berlin projects like the Großsiedlung Britz proved too high for many workers, even with cost-saving approaches and various state subsidies, so tenants were heavily middle class.[24]

The View from America

During the 1920s and early 1930s, housing reformers in the United States looked enviously at developments in Europe. In 1923, after touring European social housing, Edith Elmer Wood felt confident that, unlike the United States, the Continent was well on its way to solving the problem of working-class housing through government efforts and public-nonprofit partnerships. She took to task politicians who extolled the "American workingman's standard of living," arguing that compared to Western Europe "our leadership in that respect has already passed from us," most importantly in the realm of housing. "We have more automobiles, it is true. But which will profit a nation more in the long run—to have 100 per cent of its people living in good wholesome homes, or to have 50 per cent rushing up and down in Fords?" Five years later, Louis Pink (who one day would have a New York City public housing project named for him) concurred in *The New Day in Housing*: "The splendid accomplishment of the London County Council in slum clearance and the erection of new dwellings for the workers forcibly emphasizes the amazing lack of similar effort in the United States. By comparison, New York and Chicago have done nothing!"[25]

Catherine Bauer, after inspecting European dwellings in 1930 and 1932, dubbed much of what she saw "modern housing." With such housing, she wrote, "the economical unit for construction and administration, and the social unit for living, is the complete neighborhood, designed and equipped as such. . . . Modern housing provides certain minimum amenities for every dwelling: cross-ventilation, for one thing; sunlight, quiet, and a pleasant outlook from every window; adequate privacy, space, and sanitary facilities; children's play space adjacent. And finally it will be available at a price which citizens of average income or less can afford." By her calculation, some six million units of housing that met these criteria had been constructed in Europe since World War I. The United States had almost none, perhaps five or ten thousand such units.[26]

Some of the difference between North America and Europe reflected the status of their real estate industries. The European real estate industry had been weakened by World War I and postwar developments. Wood noted that there was very little European opposition to social housing. "The owner of slum property . . . knows he will receive compensation when it is expropriated. . . . The speculative builder will continue to build for the only classes he has ever built for—those who can afford to pay him a profit."[27] By contrast, US realtors, developers, home builders, and their financial and political allies proved to be powerful, tenacious opponents of social housing and government intervention in the housing market. Furthermore, at least until the Great Depression, industrial and political leaders in the United States, unlike their European equivalents, felt little need to build housing to prevent working-class revolts. As a result, mass, government-supported social housing simply did not exist in the United States before the New Deal, nor did the architectural innovations that came with it.

But the very existence of the books by Wood, Pink, and Bauer surveying European housing, the authors' close connections with political leaders and other reformers, and their efforts to figure out how European models might be emulated in the United States reflected the growth since the First World War of a small but lively housing movement. Its activists sought to radically rethink American housing in order to make it more attractive and affordable to ordinary people and to use it as a vehicle for broader social change. Out of their efforts, deeply influenced by developments in Europe, would come the garden apartment, a kind of dumbed-down but nonetheless genuinely progressive form of social housing.

2 *The Garden City Comes to America*

The first buildings in the United States called garden apartments were built in Jackson Heights, Queens, during and soon after World War I. Their development reflected the influence of the garden city movement and European social housing. These complexes had no aspirations of social reform; they were commercial projects aimed at well-off, middle-class families. Nonetheless, they introduced city planning and architectural ideas that soon would be mobilized to house working-class families in more innovative projects with explicit reform or radical agendas.[1]

Garden Living for the Well-To-Do

The construction of the first garden apartments reflected substantial American interest in European housing innovations among commercial developers as well as reformers. In 1906, Christian socialist William Dwight Porter Bliss founded the Garden Cities Association of America in New York after visiting Letchworth and meeting the leaders of the British garden cities movement. Along with other reform and religious leaders, prominent businessmen signed on. Reformers saw the garden city as a way to disperse the poor from overcrowded inner-city districts. Doing so, they believed, would upgrade their living conditions while removing them from a corrupting environment. For businessmen and developers with investments in outer-city land or transit systems, garden cities presented a recipe for profit clothed in social good.[2]

Though the Garden Cities Association had a short life, undermined by the 1907 financial panic, the garden city ideal retained its appeal in business, philanthropic, and architectural circles. In 1909, the Russell Sage Foundation bought a large tract of land in Queens, which, though not far from Manhattan, still had lots of open countryside, to create a garden suburb, Forest Hills Gardens. It aimed to show that new European planning ideas could be used to profitably develop middle-class housing.[3]

The Queensboro Corporation, a large developer founded in 1909, built the first garden apartments not far away. In 1914, the directors of the company visited Germany to study new developments in housing. They were particularly impressed by the buildings they saw in newer Berlin suburbs like Charlottenburg. Architectural historian Richard Plunz speculates that the Americans visited the apartment buildings designed by Erich Kohn and Paul Mebes for the Berlin Civil Servants Dwellings Association, large five- and six-story buildings, arrayed along block perimeters, with substantial internal courtyards. It is possible they also visited the nearby worker housing constructed by the Siemens electric company, similarly scaled buildings likewise laid out around courtyards.[4]

Four years later, Queensboro erected what it called the Garden Apartments, which lined the two sides of 80th Street, between 35th and 37th Avenues, in Jackson Heights. Designed by architect George H. Well, the five-story buildings had small gardens in front and larger green spaces behind them. This apparently was the first time the term "garden apartment" was applied to a specific building in the United States.

Queensboro's next projects took advantage of developing whole blocks at one time, rather than individual building lots, by arraying buildings along two adjacent streets, with their rears facing shared gardens. Initially the company left the short sides of the rectangular blocks open, so that the internal gardens formed landscaped promenades. At Linden Court, designed by Andrew J. Thomas and opened in 1919, the company experimented with garages on the backside of the apartment buildings, accessed by an inner-block passageway. Subsequent developments became increasingly elaborate, like the Chateau Gardens and The Towers, both also designed by Thomas. These projects consisted of U-shaped buildings (with self-service elevators) with small courtyards facing mid-block greenways. The extensive open space and greenery differed markedly from typical tightly packed Manhattan apartment buildings.

Besides their extensive green space, the Queensboro buildings were distinguished by the many amenities provided for residents. With most of the land surrounding the projects still empty, the company was able to offer tennis courts, a skating rink, a riding academy, garden plots, and a nine-hole golf course, facilities associated with suburban living, not city apartments. Aimed at middle- or upper-middle-class families, these Queens complexes used restrictive covenants and other devices to bar African Americans, Catholics, and Jews. Other developers soon began building similar apartment buildings in Washington, DC, Chicago, and elsewhere in the New York region.[5]

Cooperative Housing

In 1925 the Garden Apartments were renamed Greystones (as the complex is still called) when the rental buildings were converted to cooperative

Figure 2.1. Chateau Gardens, Queens, New York, 1925.

ownership. Residential co-ops already had a long history in New York, starting with The Rembrandt on West 57th Street in 1881. Typically, residents in co-ops buy shares in a company that owns a building, getting the right to occupy a particular apartment while charged a proportional part of the mortgage and maintenance costs. For a developer, co-ops allowed a quicker return of capital and profits than collecting rent over an extended period. Also, many residents preferred to be owners rather than renters. Cooperatives would be an important ownership form throughout the history of garden apartments.

Though first adopted by developers for high-end apartments, cooperative residential ownership also came to be embraced by workers adverse to capitalism, who drew on European experiences. Their projects had the same basic ownership structure as commercial co-ops, but they kept share prices low and required residents, when they moved away, to sell their shares back to the cooperative at cost, rather than on the open market, preserving affordability. In New York, which ultimately became the national center for working-class cooperative housing, Finnish immigrants, modeling their effort on housing in Helsinki, established the city's first nonprofit cooperative residence in 1916, a small, four-story apartment building in Brooklyn.[6]

Not long afterward, a cooperative development was built in Milwaukee that in some respects closely paralleled European social housing. A large German-speaking immigrant community helped make Milwaukee a stronghold for socialism. In 1910, socialists, running on a platform that promised city-built, low-cost worker housing to meet a severe housing shortage, elected mayor Emil Seidel and won most of the aldermanic seats. Seidel lost office two years later, before producing any new homes. But when Daniel W. Hoan recaptured city hall for the socialists in 1916, he began a renewed effort. The upshot was a plan for city-supported cooperative housing along garden city lines.

As a first step, Milwaukee officials convinced the state legislature to allow the creation of public housing corporations with stock owned by local governments and private investors. The Garden Homes Company, incorporated in 1921, received its initial capital from the Milwaukee city and county governments, which controlled it through their ownership of a majority of the preferred stock. Thirty-eight local businessmen provided additional funds through smaller stock purchases. Under the company scheme, residents of the houses to be built would gradually buy out the government and private investors with their down payments and monthly rents, until they fully controlled the cooperative.

The Garden Homes Company bought a twenty-nine-acre site surrounded by farmland, just outside of the northern city limits of Milwaukee, for its new community. Its architect, William Schuchardt, a local journeyman, was deeply influenced by the garden city settlements he had visited in England and Germany in 1911. The layout of what came to be called the Garden Homes district closely followed, in miniature, the garden city/garden suburb model, with tree-lined curving streets around a central, two-acre park. In an explicit homage, the streets were named after model English housing developments, including Letchworth and Hampstead.

The suburban location of the new community allowed low-density development; of the ninety-three freestanding, two-story houses, eleven were for two families and the rest were for just one. Though the houses Schuchardt designed looked like conventional, small, colonial revival buildings, they used a new kind of sheathing called flaxolinum (made of

Figure 2.2. Milwaukee Garden Homes Historic District, as it appeared in 1988.

treated flax) under their stucco exteriors and spruce wood fiber for interior wall and ceiling sheathing, both of which promised superior insulation. To save costs, the cooperative used new mass production methods during the construction. Crews of workers went from house to house, each undertaking a specific task, rather than one crew building an entire structure, an approach that anticipated methods used in Frankfurt and later in Levittown and other large post–World War II commercial suburban developments.

The combination of cooperative ownership, garden city design, and experimental construction techniques made the Milwaukee project truer to Ebenezer Howard's vision than anything else built in the United States. But the project quickly became troubled. Insufficient funding stopped construction far short of the initial plan to build 3,500 homes. In the post–World War I atmosphere of antiradicalism, local business, real estate, and conservative elements attacked the cooperative as un-American, even Bolshevik. Meanwhile, many of the initial residents soured on the cooperative arrangement when faced with unexpected sewer and street assessments and the realization that any improvements that they made to their houses would accrue not to themselves but to the cooperative company, to which they were obligated to sell back their shares at par value if they chose to move. So in 1925, just two years after construction wound down, the Garden Homes cooperative began selling off houses to individual residents. In the 1940s, there were efforts to revive the combination of single-family homes and cooperative ownership, but the arrangement never proved very successful.[7]

A more fruitful model combined cooperative ownership for working people with the physical design of the Jackson Heights apartments. During the 1920s, three radical Jewish groups and the Amalgamated Clothing Workers Union sponsored nonprofit cooperative housing developments in the Bronx. Perhaps because in New York cooperative residences were first associated with upper-class living, their embrace by left-wing workers never provoked much backlash, despite the sometimes explicit anticapitalist thrust that accompanied it.

Like the Queensboro Corporation buildings, the Bronx cooperatives were sited to take advantage of the expanding New York subway system, which made commuting to Manhattan jobs practical. They all were either built around courtyards or widely spaced on large sites that preserved considerable open space. The first phase of the United Workers' Cooperative Colony (almost universally known as "the Coops") along Bronx Park East—the first of the projects to be completed—covered only 56 percent of its site, and its second phase only 46 percent. The Coops and the other nearby cooperatives—the Amalgamated Houses, the Sholem Aleichem Houses, and the Farband Houses—embraced conventionality in their exterior design (much like the typical Vienna *Gemeindebauten*), mimicking the neo-Tudor style then in fashion. At the Coops, though, the hammers and sickles and factory designs over several entranceways let it be known that something else was going on inside.

Most of the Bronx cooperative buildings were five- or six-story walkups. At the Coops, residents gained access to their homes through entranceways and staircases off the courtyards, each serving only a few apartments. Some of the Vienna municipal houses and the Queensboro buildings used the same arrangement. So did the courtyard apartment buildings going up at the time in Chicago and other cities.

The use of separate entranceways for small clusters of living units would become a defining feature of garden apartments. The device went all the way back to medieval monasteries and the quads at Cambridge and Oxford. In the early 1850s, Henry Roberts designed a series of model apartment buildings for charitable organizations that similarly avoided internal public hallways. For the 1850 "Model Home for Families" on Streatham Street in London, he used a central staircase that accessed outdoor galleries from which individual apartments were entered (a design that still can be seen on some surviving high-rise US public housing buildings). Two-story model "cottages" that Roberts built under the sponsorship of Prince Albert for the 1851 Great Exhibition had a central entryway

Figure 2.3. The Amalgamated Houses, Bronx, New York.

and staircase providing access to apartments on each side of the building, what became the most common arrangement of mid-twentieth-century American garden apartments.[8]

Multiple-entranceway designs eliminated the need for long, internal corridors, which saved the expense of building lightly used spaces and provided residents with greater privacy. Also, without internal public hallways, apartments could get light and air from both the front and the back of buildings. Along with extensive landscaping, direct access to apartments from the outside brought some of the attractions of single-family homes to apartment living.

Though the Bronx cooperatives resembled the commercial Queens developments in some ways, they differed profoundly in others. Rather than middle-class residents, these projects targeted working-class families. Their nonprofit status helped keep purchase and maintenance costs low. So did the tax exemptions offered by New York State under its 1926 Limited Dividend Housing Companies Act to affordable housing developers that agreed to cap their profits at 6 percent. (This device, of offering tax breaks and other government assistance to housing groups that limit their profits, dates back to mid-nineteenth-century England and is still in use today.)

Instead of providing golf and tennis, the Bronx co-ops offered day care centers, cooperative stores and cafeterias, libraries, auditoriums, summer camps, and spaces for resident artists. An early plan for the Coops proposed collective kitchens on every floor rather than individual facilities—shades of Edward Bellamy and Ebenezer Howard. Though in the end that arrangement was abandoned, the Coops did include fifty-seven kitchenless apartments for single men and women or couples without children, organized into clusters with shared kitchens.[9]

Philanthropic Housing

In both Europe and America, before World War I, philanthropic projects were an important component of the efforts to provide decent housing to people of modest means. After the war, philanthropy faded in significance in Europe, as government involvement became increasingly important. By contrast, in the United States, where affordable housing efforts remained very modest and the government's role in them minimal, philanthropy still played a leading part. Wealthy housing patrons hoped to show that private efforts could provide good affordable homes while generating modest profits.

Many of their projects adopted design approaches pioneered in the Queens garden apartments. A porous line separated commercial and philanthropic housing, as some developers, financiers, and architects engaged in both. Andrew Thomas played a key role in the transmission of ideas from one realm to the other. When in 1924 New York's *The Evening World*, a populist Pulitzer paper, ran a multipart series, "Garden Apartments to Replace Slums," which purported to show "How New York Can Profitably Build Low Rental Homes on High Priced Land," it recruited Thomas as its expert and effectively became a platform for his views. The paper argued that six-story walk-up buildings, covering only half their sites, could provide apartments renting for ten dollars or less a room ($184 in 2025 currency), even on expensive land, if they were erected on large areas, using economical designs, with limited dividends for investors. A proposed site layout closely mimicked the U-shaped Jackson Heights buildings that had courtyards facing block interiors.[10]

John D. Rockefeller Jr. took the lead in trying to carry out Thomas's vision, hoping to show that affordable housing could be constructed without government involvement. When a union-sponsored cooperative housing effort in the Bronx ran into financial difficulty, Rockefeller assumed control and hired Thomas as his architect. Thomas designed a full-block complex of five-story walk-up buildings. Occupants accessed their apartments via entryways reached through an internal garden and courtyards.

Figure 2.4. Bird's-eye view of Rosenwald Court Apartments, Chicago.

Rockefeller restricted the complex—named Thomas Garden Apartments after its architect—to white residents.

To accommodate African Americans, Rockefeller sponsored a companion project in Harlem, the Paul Laurence Dunbar Apartments, again designed by Thomas, with internal courtyards and gardens. With very few good housing options open to them because of discrimination, some of the most prominent black New Yorkers bought into the Dunbar cooperative, including W. E. B. Du Bois, Paul Robeson, and A. Philip Randolph. (Though in theory the Rockefeller projects were resident-owned, the philanthropist used retained preferred stock to tightly control them.)[11]

In Chicago, two philanthropists with money from pioneer department stores picked up the limited-profit garden apartment model. Marshall Field III, using funds from his grandfather's estate, bought two city blocks on the Near North Side and hired Thomas to design a large residential complex. Ten red-brick, four- and five-story buildings, arrayed along the perimeter of the site, contained 628 apartments. Amenities included laundry rooms, an activity room, a playground, and rooftop gardens. Built in a run-down Italian working-class neighborhood, costs proved greater than expected and rents too high for most area residents. The project only accepted white tenants.[12]

On the city's South Side, Sears, Roebuck and Co. president Julius Rosenwald built a similar project for African Americans, the Michigan Boulevard Garden Apartments (later renamed the Rosenwald Court Apartments) in Bronzeville. On a 1926 visit to Vienna, Rosenwald had visited the *Gemeindebauten*. He knew, too, about the garden apartments in New York.

One of the architects Rosenwald hired, his nephew Ernest A. Grunsfeld Jr., had worked for Thomas as a draftsman. The other, Eugene Klaber, had practiced in New York, where he frequented housing reform circles.

The Michigan Boulevard Garden Apartments resembled a Thomas project, with the buildings covering only half the six-acre site, surrounding gardens and courtyards. From the landscaped central area, more than two dozen entryways provided access to 421 apartments in the five-story walk-ups. Apartments were small; living rooms averaged just 168 square feet, bedrooms 120 square feet, and kitchens 75 square feet. But the complex had extensive communal space, including a half-mile rooftop promenade, two playgrounds, two nursery schools, and a "social room."

Figure 2.5. A typical Rosenwald Court kitchen, not that different than the Frankfurt kitchens being constructed at the same time. Note the dumbwaiter on the left, used for what proved to be an expensive system of garbage disposal.

Like the Dunbar Apartments, the Michigan Boulevard Garden Apartments housed many prominent African Americans. Gwendolyn Brooks, Joe Louis, Nat King Cole, and, as a child, Quincy Jones lived there. But an occupational breakdown of residents from 1934 indicated the largest group consisted of "railroad employees," probably mostly Pullman porters, followed by post office workers and local government employees, jobs at the top of the black working-class hierarchy.[13]

Toward the Future of the Garden Apartment

The four-to-six-story perimeter garden apartment ended up as a brief episode in the effort to build affordable housing for working people. Far more important, over time, would be lower-rise buildings that adopted some aspects of the earlier garden apartment model but with different site layouts and lower densities. The path toward those types of buildings, which became extremely common after World War II, began even as the Andrew Thomas–type garden apartments were being built.

A project in Queens, Sunnyside Gardens, pointed the way. Built between 1924 and 1928, the 1,202-unit low-rise complex was the brainchild of a group of architects, planners, reformers, intellectuals, and businessmen clustered in the Regional Planning Association of America (RPAA), founded in 1923. The stellar RPAA crew included architects Frederick L. Ackerman, Henry Wright, Clarence Stein, Charles Harris Whitaker, Robert D. Kohn, Eugene Klaber, and Frederick Bigger; writers Lewis Mumford and Stuart Chase; regional planner Benton MacKaye (who conceived of the Appalachian Trail); and real estate developer Alexander Bing. In their efforts to come up with solutions to urban overcrowding, low-quality buildings, unaffordable dwellings, and unhealthy, unattractive environs, the RPAA reformers were deeply influenced by the brief World War I experience in government-built housing, in which several were involved.[14]

The rapid US military buildup during World War I resulted in a lack of housing for workers at shipyards and other defense production facilities. To meet the emergency, the federal government undertook large-scale housing construction for civilians for the first time. In 1917 Frederick Ackerman traveled to Britain to study wartime housing there, in which Raymond Unwin was heavily involved, and returned a disciple of Ebenezer Howard. As the head of Housing and Town Planning for the Emergency Fleet Corporation (EFC), charged with housing shipyard workers, Ackerman spearheaded the construction of garden suburb–type communities. Ackerman hoped that wartime projects might serve as models for postwar working-class housing. Henry Wright worked with Ackerman and Robert D. Kohn at the EFC, gaining experience in community planning and the design of row houses and other low-rise worker homes.[15]

When the war ended, the attention of public officials and the nascent city planning movement shifted to the long-term housing needs of working people. In New York State, various schemes were proposed, including direct government construction of housing and low-cost government loans, common approaches in Europe, but neither was adopted. Instead, Governor Alfred E. Smith created a Commission of Housing and Regional Planning for Permanent Housing Relief, chaired by Clarence Stein. That in turn led to the passage of the 1926 housing law. In the meantime, Stein's trip to England and the Netherlands to see housing developments deepened his commitment to the ideas of Howard and Unwin.[16]

Hoping to create a garden city in the New York area, Stein recruited the semiretired Bing, who had extensive experience in commercial development, as his collaborator. Bing created a limited-dividend company, the City Housing Corporation (CHC), and, like Howard, succeeded in attracting rich and prominent investors and patrons. John D. Rockefeller Jr. bought $150,000 worth of stock ($2.8 million in 2025 dollars). Eleanor Roosevelt and Felix Adler (the founder of the New York Society for Ethical Culture) served on an advisory board. Herbert Hoover and the Russell Sage Foundation provided mortgage money. The CHC aspired not simply to build housing but "to create a setting in which a democratic community might grow." With the goal of ultimately building "an American Garden City," it viewed Sunnyside Gardens as a modest first step, "a laboratory" for experimenting with architectural, financial, and social arrangements.[17]

For the development, the CHC purchased seventy-seven acres of inexpensive land—a former railroad yard—in western Queens, adjacent to a subway stop. Most of the area still consisted of open, undeveloped fields. Wright, who began his career as a landscape architect, took the lead in laying out the site. Influenced by Unwin's idea of "nothing gained by overcrowding," but constrained by the city street grid, Wright and Stein experimented with various layouts of row houses, with shared green spaces, courtyards, playgrounds, and private gardens filling the interiors of blocks. They located garages in a separate area at some distance from the dwellings.

Though Stein later designed large apartment complexes, RPAA members generally preferred low-rise, low-density dwellings. Most of the defense-worker housing built under Ackerman's supervision consisted of single-family homes, which he believed Americans preferred. Wright, after doing elaborate calculations on costs for the Michigan Boulevard Garden Apartments (for which he served as a consultant) and other buildings, came to believe that, even in dense urban areas, buildings taller than four

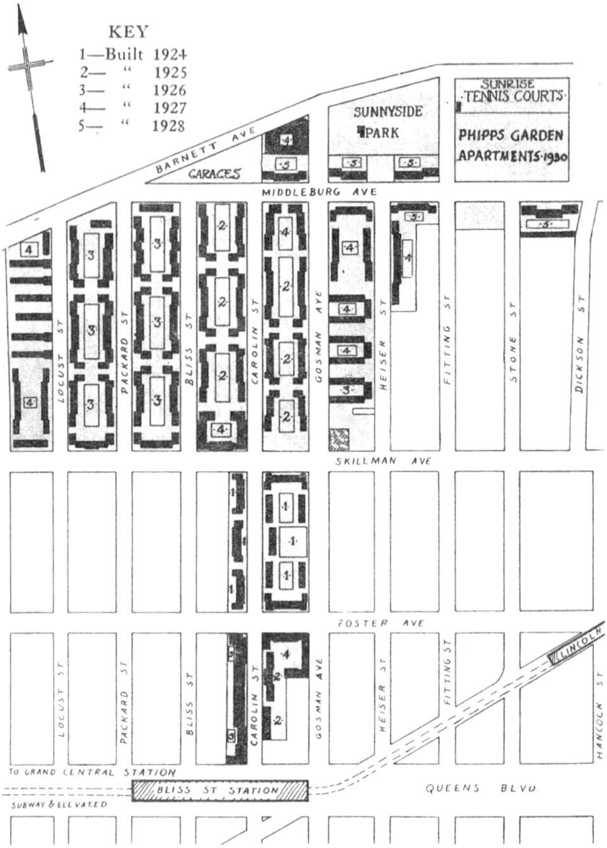

Figure 2.6. Site plan for Sunnyside Gardens, Queens, New York.

stories rarely bought savings in unit costs. He argued that even dwellings with fewer floors could financially work.[18]

The Sunnyside Gardens buildings covered an exceptionally small portion of their site. Eliminating the narrow side alleys that typically separated low-cost single-family homes and clustering the garages allowed for larger shared spaces and reduced costs. Marjorie Sewell Cautley created the extensive landscaping, while Stein and Ackerman designed the variety of one-, two-, and three-family homes, all two stories high, and the three-story apartment buildings that made up the complex. The garden-like block interiors and the attention to detail throughout, such as staggering row houses to create variety and visually break up the long sides of the blocks and using Hudson River brick for the exteriors, made the whole complex visually pleasing, then and now.[19]

Stein and Wright tried to contain costs, in both their designs and building practices. They kept living units small. The most common apartment model measured 700 square feet, occupying one story of a two-story row house. These apartments, though substantially bigger than the municipal apartments being built at the time in Vienna and the later Rosenwald apartments, are 21 percent smaller than the average apartment built in the United States in 2022.[20]

The CHC houses ended up costing somewhat more than commercially built homes, even with fewer marketing expenses than other developers. Early on the company tried to sell some of the dwellings to newly organized cooperative entities, but the idea failed to catch on. The company sold some buildings on an individual basis (with the CHC itself providing mortgages on very favorable terms), before beginning to rent as well.[21]

Sunnyside Gardens attracted a heterogeneous group of tenants, economically and occupationally. Half of the first group of residents moved out of tenements on the Lower East Side. For them, the change must have been startling. At the time Sunnyside Gardens opened, tenements built during the Civil War were still being occupied, like the one at 97 Orchard Street, now home to the Tenement Museum. Its apartments had only three rooms, together measuring 350 square feet or less. Apartments in later tenements typically had more rooms and more total space, but still were far more cramped and less pleasant than the Sunnyside Gardens units. Many tenement apartments looked out only on airshafts or back courts, dreary vistas providing little light or air. By contrast, apartments in Sunnyside Gardens were surrounded by greenery and open space. On some blocks on the project periphery, to avoid having residents look out at what Stein described as "outside builders' monotonous rows," the CHC arrayed buildings in U-shaped configurations surrounding courtyards that opened onto a street within the complex, a layout that would become extremely common for later garden apartments.[22]

Better-off families moved to Sunnyside Gardens as well. A 1928 survey found about twice as many white-collar workers as blue-collar workers, with a mix ranging from lawyers, doctors, teachers, and actors to mechanics, chauffeurs, salesmen, and restaurant workers. Lewis Mumford lived in the complex for eleven years, as did, more briefly, Henry Wright. (By contrast, Stein, a wealthy man who had trained at the École des Beaux-Arts in Paris, resided in a penthouse overlooking Central Park.) Though ethnically mixed, with many liberal and left-wing residents, Sunnyside Gardens, like the Queensboro Corporation buildings, had no black residents, as the originators of the project consciously decided not to encourage racial integration.[23]

Sunnyside Gardens attracted considerable attention over the years. It

Figure 2.7. Woman sunbathing on a Sunnyside Gardens lawn, ca. 1966.

must have been highly satisfying to Bing, Stein, and Wright when Howard and Unwin, who were in New York for a 1925 convention of the International Federation of Town and Country Planning and Garden Cities, toured Sunnyside Gardens. But the project ended up being something of a one-off, an effort in some ways very successful yet never repeated, at least not in quite that way. Its key planners, drawn to the garden city model, saw Sunnyside Gardens as compromised by its in-city location and necessary conformity to the existing pattern of rectilinear streets and modest-sized blocks. Many residents faced financial disaster and even eviction when the Great Depression began, just a year after the project was completed, rending the sense of community the project had strived for. Furthermore, the combination of private ownership and communal space ultimately proved problematic. The interior land behind the Sunnyside Gardens buildings legally belonged to particular owners, who agreed to forty-year easements allowing communal use. When the easements expired, most of the shared space was claimed and fenced off by its owners.[24]

The significance of Sunnyside Gardens, in the end, did not lie in serving as a template for future developments. Only many decades later, in the attached home "condo" developments that sprang up in California and elsewhere, did a spatial organization of dwellings somewhat resembling Sunnyside Gardens become common, with a very indirect genealogy connecting them. Instead, its significance was much what its creators hoped it would be, as an experiment, a laboratory for working out ideas about housing and community that could be applied elsewhere. At the forefront of doing so were Stein and Wright, who, together and apart, emerged as the foremost theoreticians and practitioners of garden apartment design.

Even before Sunnyside Gardens was completed, the CHC and RPAA began a follow-up project in Radburn, New Jersey, intended to be a more fully realized version of a garden city, accommodating 25,000 residents. Built on 640 acres, sixteen miles from New York City, Radburn was planned to be a self-contained community, with housing, schools, shopping areas, industry, and parks. It included some garden apartments, but the bulk of the dwellings were one- or two-family detached houses. Nonetheless, the project proved influential on future garden apartment planning in its conception of community and its treatment of the automobile.[25]

Radburn embodied an idea then gaining currency among city planners and progressive architects, the "neighborhood unit." As codified by its leading advocate, the Russell Sage Foundation's Clarence Arthur Perry, its underlying principle was "that an urban neighborhood should be regarded both as a unit of a larger whole and as a distinct entity in itself." Aimed specifically at families with children at home, it called for each neighborhood unit to have its own school, playground, green space, small shops, and other facilities, preferably within easy walking distance from every home within it. (Anyone who has played the video game *SimCity* will be familiar with the idea.) Such organization, with each neighborhood unit no larger than the number of houses needed to fill an elementary school, would provide not only convenience but also foster community association. Coming out of a Progressive Era mindset that believed that overcrowded slums caused social pathologies, Perry, Stein, and many of their colleagues believed that cohesive communities fostered by neighborhood unit planning would prevent social ills such as youth gangs and, as Perry put it, hold "a man in place morally."[26]

The neighborhood unit idea overlapped with approaches to social housing adopted in Frankfurt and elsewhere in Europe. In the United States it would animate some, though certainly not all, future garden apartment developments. Its reach proved wide, as it gained influence in the development of new towns in Latin America, the Soviet Union, Eastern and Western Europe, and South Asia.[27]

The neighborhood unit sometimes was held forth as the basis for grassroots democracy but, like the broader idea of community, it could be exclusionary and discriminatory. Perry himself wrote, "the great foe to community life is heterogeneity." Parents, he claimed, "want their children to associate with children from homes which hold standards similar to their own."[28] In Radburn, that meant trying to keep out everyone but white Christians. A survey of the community reported, "To create what they saw as a congenial environment, realtors hired by the CHC discouraged

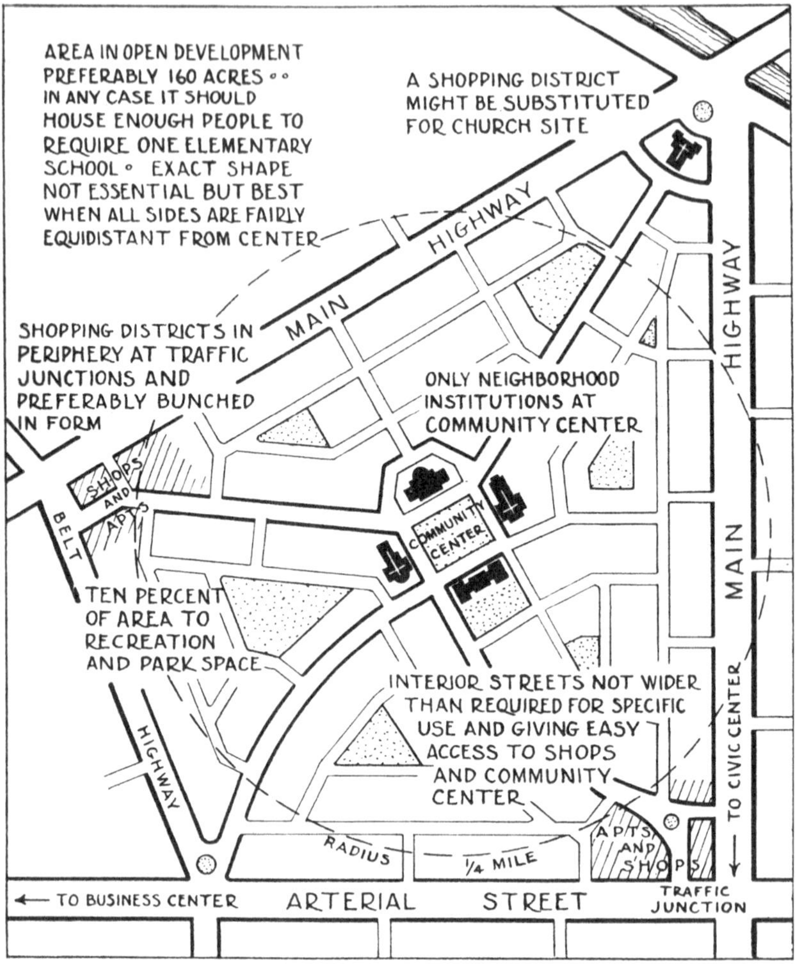

Figure 2.8. Clarence Arthur Perry's 1927 representation of a neighborhood unit.

Jews—as well as blacks—from moving into Radburn, a policy which met with approval or indifference from the town's financiers, administrators, and residents alike. Shared values and experience, not economic and ethnic diversity, were considered important attributes for a smoothly functioning, attractive community." This attitude, accepted by many in the RPAA circle, formed part of its heritage.[29]

For the designers of Radburn, who consulted with Perry, the neighborhood unit meant a walking neighborhood. Stein and Wright, like Perry, were attuned to the growing importance of the automobile. The RPAA crowd did not dislike automobiles—to the contrary they saw them as enabling population dispersion, which was central to the garden city idea—but they believed that careful planning was required to keep vehicle traffic from disrupting family and neighborhood life.

The key, Wright and Stein decided, lay in what they called "the superblock." Wright, in a detailed "Study of Application of Sunnyside Planning Principles to a Larger City Area," compared various configurations, including eliminating streets to create larger blocks. That allowed for the inclusion of community facilities and potential cost savings. Before laying out Radburn, he and Stein visited Britain to look at the use of large blocks at Letchworth, Welwyn, and Hampstead Garden Suburb. For Radburn, they decided to use even larger blocks of thirty to fifty acres. Surrounded

Figure 2.9. Site plan for two superblocks at Radburn, New Jersey.

by perimeter roads for through traffic, superblock residential areas were designed with curving roadways and cul-de-sacs that limited vehicle presence and speed. Houses faced away from roadways, toward interior green spaces, with a network of pathways and underpasses beneath roads that provided safe pedestrian passage.[30]

Radburn ended up as a white-collar commuter suburb, rather than a self-contained garden city. No industry moved to Radburn. Over 70 percent of job holders traveled for work into New York City. As Stein freely admitted, even if blue-collar jobs had materialized, without government subsidies there was no way to make the Radburn houses affordable to workers. It was, he later said, "more of a country club without a golf course." Like many of the communities influenced by Howard and Unwin, it had no real social reform component, only some innovative elements of good design.[31]

Wright and Stein's last collaboration before the Depression halted most private residential construction was a small development in the Mt. Washington area of Pittsburgh, Chatham Village. Even more than their previous projects, it established principles and templates for the larger-scale garden apartment complexes to come. Chatham Village came about when Pittsburgh department store owner Henry Buhl Jr. died in 1929, leaving behind a large sum to create a foundation dedicated to local improvements. As its first substantial project, the Buhl Foundation, like Rockefeller and Field, set out to demonstrate that decent, affordable housing could be built on a commercial basis, buying a former estate just across the Monongahela River from downtown Pittsburgh.

To guide the project, the Buhl Foundation commissioned reports from Wright and Stein and from Frederick Bigger, an RPAA member practicing architecture in Pittsburgh. Originally the foundation envisioned freestanding houses to sell to low-income residents. But Wright, Stein, and Bigger were convinced that doing so would not be financially viable. Instead, the foundation agreed with their recommendation for row housing aimed at middle-class residents, to be rented rather than sold.

Wright laid out the streets and house locations on the hilly site and, along with Stein, served as a consulting architect. Their design perfected various devices they had tried out in Sunnyside and Radburn. The complex consisted entirely of two-story row houses, in groups of two to seven, surrounded by greenery. The houses had service entrances facing perimeter streets, but their main entrances faced interior spaces. Separate pathways kept pedestrians and cars apart. Some houses had garages beneath them while others had assigned parking in nearby clusters of garages, an arrangement later widely replicated in garden apartment complexes.

Local architects William Boyd and Charles Ingham designed the buildings with simple but attractive ornamentation that combined elements of

Figure 2.10. Chatham Village, Pittsburgh, 1936.

the colonial revival and arts and crafts styles. Ralph E. Griswold, who had recently landscaped Colonial Williamsburg, designed the grounds. Chatham Village's hilly setting, the small greenbelt that was preserved around it, its curving streets, the well-designed buildings, the courtyards, and the sensitive landscaping combined to make for a physically attractive, almost bucolic settlement just a few miles from downtown Pittsburgh. Few later garden apartments matched its quality of design, though some, like Parkway Village in Queens, would markedly resemble it.

Setting a pattern other garden apartments would follow, Chatham Village cloaked its innovations and its departure from the tradition of freestanding, single-family houses in nostalgic garb. Its very name suggested something different from what it actually was, a neighborhood of a major industrial city in an area once known as Coal Hill. Ingham, explicitly rejecting German modernist residential architecture, which he was well aware of, declared that at Chatham Village "there was no impulse to express the machine age in its design, but rather to create a retreat from the machine age." For all its design inventiveness, Chatham Village was as much backward looking as forward looking.

The middle-class constituency it was aimed at seemed pleased by the combination. Almost immediately the project was fully occupied by a variety of white-collar workers, professionals, and junior executives. The Buhl Foundation used tenant selection procedures to keep out Jews, Catholics, and African Americans.[32]

Architects, planners, housing reformers, commercial developers, and government officials praised Chatham Village. Catherine Bauer called it "probably the best example of modern planned housing in the country." But not everyone admired it. Critic Jane Jacobs hated just about everything about Chatham Village. In her landmark 1961 book *The Death and Life of Great American Cities*, she described the settlement as operating "according to . . . provincial premises of social insularity," disdaining "the degree of chumminess that neighborliness in Chatham Village entails." The genius of the city, for Jacobs, lay in its diversity and in unexpected encounters with people different from oneself, something the demographic makeup and design of Chatham Village all but precluded. For Jacobs, in Chatham Village there was "no public life . . . in any city sense." Even the physical design of Chatham Village irked Jacobs. Fetishizing the street, much like Howard, Unwin, Stein, and Wright fetishized the garden, Jacobs criticized the orientation of houses toward protected internal green spaces, which she believed suitable only for young children: "no child of enterprise or spirit will willingly stay in such a boring place after he reaches the age of six." Like garden city advocates, Jacobs moralized what were in part aesthetic issues. Still, the issue of insularity versus integration into the cityscape would hover over garden apartments for decades to come.[33]

Cul-de-Sac

Chatham Village, like Sunnyside Gardens, had few immediate imitators, not because of criticism along the lines Jacobs would later make but because of economic circumstances. In the late 1920s, around the time Chatham Village was being planned, some commercial builders experimented with small, low-rise garden apartment complexes.[34] But the stock market crash halted their development, along with most other residential construction.[35]

The Great Depression effectively ended the first phase of garden apartment development. Cooperative and philanthropic efforts had led to the development of some promising models for affordable garden apartments, though on a very modest scale. The economic collapse that began in 1929 not only halted further advances, but it also revealed the weakness and limitations of existing projects.

Cooperatives, including those backed by philanthropy, did not fare well during the Depression. The Bronx Coops, with so many residents out of work and unable to pay the charges for their apartments, could not meet its mortgage payments. Lenders eventually foreclosed and turned it into a commercial rental project. The same woes hit the Rockefeller cooperatives. When the Thomas Garden and Dunbar projects went into arrears on the mortgages Rockefeller had provided, he sold them off, the former to a commercial entity and the latter, ultimately, to the Methodist-Episcopal Church.[36]

The economic meltdown devastated Sunnyside Gardens and Radburn as well. More than half the Sunnyside Gardens homeowners, unable to pay their mortgages, suffered foreclosure and eviction, as a tenacious community campaign to renegotiate mortgage terms with the CHC and other lenders proved unsuccessful. At Radburn, only a small part of the originally planned community could be completed before the CHC ran out of money. With so many Sunnyside Gardens and Radburn residents with mortgages from the CHC stopping their payments, the CHC itself went into bankruptcy within a few years.[37]

The leading backers of philanthropic affordable housing realized that their model simply did not work. Rockefeller, who had launched his involvement in housing in part to show that government intervention was unnecessary, not only pulled out of his enterprises but even tried, unsuccessfully, to sell the Dunbar Apartments to the newly formed New York City Housing Authority. In Chicago, where the Marshall Field Garden Apartments struggled with high costs and many vacancies—in part because of its refusal to rent to African Americans—Marshall Field III came to believe that municipal government participation might be needed to make affordable housing work. The corporation that ran the Rosenwald apartments, which fared better, dryly noted in a 1935 report, "Private capital can make a contribution to the solution of the housing problem, but its scope is definitely limited when it attempts to provide housing for the low wage earners." Clarence Stein came to believe that building communities like Radburn required "a certain amount of government cooperation," a polite call for public funding.[38]

The era when private entities, commercial or philanthropic, drove the development of the garden apartment proved short-lived. When garden apartment development resumed on a much larger scale, it was the state, primarily the federal government, that was responsible. But the pioneer projects of the 1920s shaped the government programs that would be responsible for the blossoming of garden apartments across the American landscape.

3 *New Deal Housing*

On November 29, 1935, President Franklin D. Roosevelt, who was in Atlanta, Georgia, to give a speech on national recovery, first stopped to inspect work on the Techwood Homes. Techwood was the first public housing project in the United States, a mixture of two- and three-story garden apartment buildings set on a twenty-two-acre site. Speaking to a crowd of 60,000 at the Georgia Tech football stadium, Roosevelt praised "the bright cheerful buildings of the Techwood Housing Project." Noting that "it is just around the corner," the president began to laugh, as he realized he had mouthed the oft-stated claim of his predecessor, Herbert Hoover, about prosperity. As the crowd roared, FDR added, "Now we know how to get around that corner." "Within a very short time," he continued, "people who never before could get a decent roof over their heads will live here in reasonable comfort amid healthy worthwhile surroundings; others will find similar homes in Atlanta's second slum clearance project, the University Project." Though the president did not say it, most people in the crowd probably knew that Techwood was being built for white residents and University for African Americans. Later he told students at Atlanta University that he was sorry he did not have time to visit the University housing project, "but when it is finished, I hope to come back and see it because, as you know, we are all working to provide better homes for the American people to live in." The following year, for the formal dedication of Techwood Homes, Eleanor Roosevelt sent a rose bush from the president's home in Hyde Park, New York.[1]

The New Deal was a moment in US history of seemingly sudden change, when the established order tottered and previously marginal or unthinkable ideas became the new common sense. That was true for housing as for so many other realms. In 1935, longtime housing activist Edith Elmer Wood wrote, "The provision of housing in this country up to now has been exclusively the field of private enterprise. The disgraceful living conditions of a third of our population are the result. . . . If lower-wage earners are to have adequate homes . . . at least a fourth of our urban housing will have to be . . . rebuilt by public agencies of some sort on a no-profit basis." What a few years earlier would have been seen as a radical, fringe view now was the policy of the United States government, for which Wood worked as a consultant.[2]

The massive entrance of government into housing during the Roosevelt administration forever changed how Americans lived and what their homes looked like. The garden apartment was an important element of that transformation. Government action took the garden apartment from a small-scale experimental form of living, heavily influenced by European precedents, to a distinctively American type of mass affordable housing. Federal initiatives led to the creation of a variety of garden apartment forms, some built by the government, others privately built with government aid. By the time World War II brought their construction to a temporary halt, a template for the garden apartment had been developed that would be the basis for a massive postwar proliferation of these low-rise dwellings for the common man.

As built, garden apartments were not all that their advocates had hoped for; some of the more radical and innovative aspects of their design were abandoned. Instead, an architecturally and socially stripped-down version of social housing emerged. Nonetheless, these dwellings provided a vast improvement in living conditions for those who moved into them. Without government action, the garden apartment would never have emerged as a major, mid-twentieth-century type of housing. In a broad sense, it constituted a physical embodiment of the New Deal order that arose from the wreckage of the Great Depression. It is one example of how much the New Deal, for all its shortcomings and limitations, accomplished for ordinary Americans.

The Public Works Administration

The Roosevelt administration, from its start, set out to stimulate residential construction and develop new models for housing and community. New Deal leaders were sensitive to the miserable housing conditions in much of the country. But even more pressing, in their eyes, was the need to provide employment for construction workers and building material producers, who were among the hardest hit by unemployment, and to bail out mortgage holders and lenders facing financial ruin. In typical New Deal fashion, Congress and the administration set up several different housing programs, which evolved and multiplied over time as housing reformers, the real estate industry, financial interests, organized labor, and others jockeyed for influence.

The first major New Deal recovery program, the National Industrial

Recovery Act, passed in June 1933, set up a modest housing program within the much larger Public Works Administration (PWA). Its primary goal was to reduce joblessness in the construction industry, which at the time accounted for one-third of all unemployment in the country. The law gave broad authority to the PWA for slum clearance projects and the construction, repair, and alteration of low-cost housing. PWA administrator Harold Ickes, a veteran Chicago progressive who simultaneously served as Secretary of the Interior, appointed Robert D. Kohn, the RPAA member and World War I Emergency Fleet Corporation housing official, to head the PWA Housing Division. Kohn, in turn, brought in Wood, Henry Wright, and Rosenwald Court architect Eugene Klaber to help organize it.

Over the course of four years, the PWA was responsible for the construction of 22,000 residential units in fifty-nine housing projects. In terms of numbers, this was but a drop in the bucket of need, but the PWA effort proved highly influential, helping shape the long-term government approach to housing and establishing standards and models for future, larger-scale construction. Ickes and Roosevelt paid close attention to the housing program, genuinely concerned about housing conditions but also aware that PWA projects provided political benefits for the administration.[3]

Initially, the Housing Division expanded a program that had been started late in the Hoover administration by the Reconstruction Finance Corporation to finance housing construction by limited-dividend corporations. To participate in the program, which had barely gotten underway before Roosevelt took office, organizations had to agree to cap rents and profits and to supply 15 percent of project equity. In return, they would receive a favorable mortgage covering the rest of their costs. With the PWA program, the country seemingly embraced social housing very much along the lines of Continental Europe: nonprofit or limited-profit entities would do the building, with financial and other support from the state.

The limited-dividend program, however, proved to be a false start. The PWA received some five hundred project applications but approved only seven, determining that many lacked sufficient equity or had other problems. Without a national tradition of social housing, few architects or organizations had the know-how or wherewithal to quickly come up with fundable proposals. Still, the projects that did get approved included some of the most imaginative and successful housing efforts of the New Deal period.[4]

A sharp divide existed among housing advocates and within the PWA about priorities. Some veteran reformers, including Wood and Ickes, long concerned about urban poverty and deeply empathetic to the plight of slum dwellers, saw replacing slums with new housing as the most pressing need. Others—including Wright, Lewis Mumford, and Catherine Bauer, who came to housing from the perspective of planning and architecture

Figure 3.1. Neighborhood Gardens, St. Louis, ca. 1936.

rather than social reform, and who were more strongly influenced by the garden cities movement—favored concentrating on outlying areas, where land was inexpensive, the grid could be ignored, and construction might proceed more quickly. A court case that blocked the PWA from condemning land under the general welfare clause of the constitution for slum clearance purposes helped tip the balance away from expensive, inner-city sites. Only after the passage of the Housing Acts of 1937 and 1949 did extensive slum replacement occur.[5]

Just one of the PWA limited-dividend projects involved slum clearance. Neighborhood Gardens, built on a site cleared of old industrial buildings on the near north side of St. Louis, was directly inspired by European housing efforts. In 1932, J. A. Wolf, the director of a local social welfare organization, the Neighborhood Association, toured social housing developments in Austria and Germany. What he saw shaped the conception of Neighborhood Gardens as a community that would foster healthy family life for garment workers, who would be able to walk to their downtown jobs. The principals of the firm that designed it, Hoener, Baum & Froese, were conversant with modernist German architecture, which influenced the layout and look of the development. Twelve three-story buildings, containing 252 apartments, were arranged within a large city block to enclose courtyards and gardens. Each apartment had a balcony, while multiple

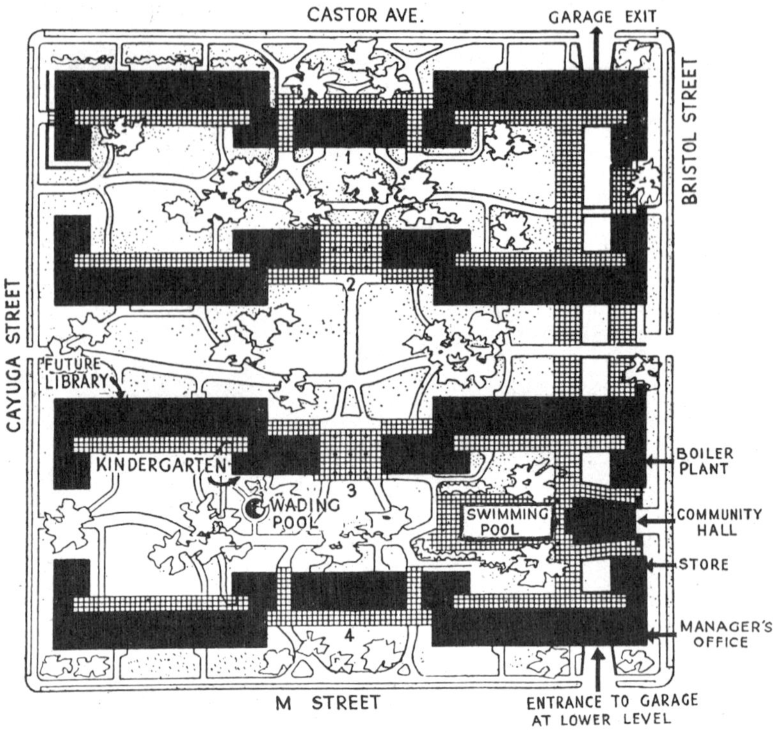

Figure 3.2. Site plan for Carl Mackley Houses in Philadelphia.

entrances obviated the need for hallways. Amenities included storage areas, a laundry room, a wading pool, play areas, and a community center equipped with club rooms, a library, a social hall, and a large communal kitchen. Frances Schutze, in a short story based on her time living in the project, described a "friendly cacophony," a jolly, very social atmosphere among young couples, many of them white-collar workers without much money but with plenty of spirit.[6]

Even more impressive was the Carl Mackley Houses in Philadelphia, sponsored by the American Federation of Hosiery Workers. The housing complex, named after a union member who had been killed in a strike, was designed by two German-born, European-trained architects, Oscar Stonorov and Alfred Kastner. Stonorov and Kastner had moved to Philadelphia because they were fired from their New York architectural firms after coming in second, ahead of Le Corbusier and Walter Gropius, in a competition to design the Palace of Soviets in Moscow. Their early designs for the Mackley Houses, to be built on vacant land in a semisuburban area, closely mimicked various German housing projects, with some influence from Le Corbusier as well. The completed project retained elements of that inspiration, with four three-story buildings, containing 284 apartments, enclosing two courtyards and a landscaped passageway. The arrangement distanced pedestrians from automobiles, which could be parked in an underground garage. A strong community life developed at the project, which included an on-site cooperative grocery store and a nursery school.

The innovative design of the Mackley Houses, its modernist sophistication, attention to detail, and extensive community facilities—including a large outdoor swimming pool—put it on a level far above most federally financed housing to come. However, as with many other attempts to build working-class housing without ongoing rent subsidies, the cost of living at the Mackley Houses proved greater than anticipated, making it too pricey for many working-class families. With no income limit for renters, the initial residents included professionals as well as blue-collar workers. For some housing reformers, the tenant profile represented a major failing. Others, including Kohn, never thought of PWA dwellings as for the poor but rather for the middle third of the market, as a way to upgrade the general benchmark for housing. This tension between quality and affordability would continue throughout the history of the garden apartment.[7]

Neighborhood Gardens and Carl Mackley Houses suggested the possibilities for nonprofit, in-city, low-rise housing that incorporated some of the principles of the garden suburb and the neighborhood unit. Both projects were idiosyncratic, more imaginative than what later became the standard design for garden apartments. Rather than fitting into the genealogy that ran through Sunnyside, Radburn, and Chatham Village, they related more closely to the German *Siedlungen.* Both are little-known landmarks in the history of American architecture, suggestive of what might have been as much as markers of what was to come.[8]

A few other PWA projects also directly reflected European modernism, like Lakeview Terrace in Cleveland, Ohio. But for the most part, the influence of European social housing on the New Deal did not manifest in modernist design. Rather, its main importance was in advancing the general notion of erecting large-scale, affordable housing tracts with government support, a departure from the long history of how Americans housed themselves.

Multiple interactions spread the European social housing gospel among New Dealers. Henry Wright, who many New Deal architects and planners looked up to, undertook an extended trip to Germany in 1932–33 to study recent housing. His influential 1935 book, *Rehousing Urban America,* included a chapter on "Evolution of Modern German Housing and Community Planning." Wright saw the "remarkable attainments" in Germany as a "source of inspiration." In 1934, Wright and Ernest J. Bohn, a Cleveland

Carl Mackley Houses, Philadelphia. Designed by Kastner & Stonorov, executed under the direction of W. Pope Barney.

Architecture in Government Housing

The Museum of Modern Art, New York

Figure 3.3. Carl Mackley Houses, as appearing on the cover of the catalog for a 1936 exhibition at the Museum of Modern Art in New York on "Architecture in Government Housing."

city council member who headed the National Association of Housing Officials, accompanied Raymond Unwin; Ernst Kahn, the former manager of public housing projects in Frankfurt; and Alice J. Samuel, a British housing manager, on a seven-week tour of the United States. Bohn sent to Roosevelt the report they wrote, recommending the construction by public authorities of low-rise housing on large empty sites, with space left for stores and community facilities. They presented slum clearance as a secondary option. In 1936, the PWA sent consultant William V. Reed to study housing in Great Britain and Continental Europe. The next year, Roosevelt related enjoying yet another report on European housing by administration representatives.[9]

The diminished influence of European architecture on New Deal housing, even as the impact of European ideas about planning and the need for social housing remained strong, in part stemmed from changes in the PWA housing program. In February 1934, Ickes announced a major restructuring. Having found the limited-dividend program impossible to scale up and seeking to avoid having the federal government simply react to outside initiatives, Ickes turned to direct government construction, ownership, and operation of housing units, either by the federal government alone or in partnership with local housing authorities. With this decision, the main channel of government investment in housing was redirected away from limited- or nonprofit entities to the state itself becoming a houser of last resort. It was the birth of what in the American lexicon came to be called public housing.[10]

Residences that the PWA built itself or with partners took a variety of physical forms, from the largest single project, the Williamsburg Houses in Brooklyn, New York, with 1,622 apartments in twenty four-story walk-up buildings situated on four superblocks, to low-rise projects in Caguas, Puerto Rico; Enid, Oklahoma; and Wayne, Pennsylvania, each with eighty or fewer apartments. Many PWA developments had the characteristics of garden apartments: low-rise buildings with multiple entranceways, taking up only a modest portion of large sites, with vehicular and pedestrian circulation kept separate.[11]

The PWA exerted much greater control over the design of what was called "direct-built" housing than over the limited-dividend projects. Central office staff and consultants were heavily involved in such issues as site location and layout, building design, and relations with local officials. The PWA created a "Sample Book" of unit plans, nominally for use by its staff to evaluate project proposals. In practice, this marked the beginning of the process of generating government templates and requirements for various kinds of housing developments. Such guidance ensured minimum standards while limiting the options of local authorities and their architects. Soon the agency had in place a recommendation for how much of a site should be covered with structures (25 to 30 percent), a policy of discouraging block perimeter building arrangements (as used in Sunnyside Gardens) because they limited cross-ventilation and vistas, and a list of minimum acceptable sizes for various kinds of rooms. Keeping in the tradition of housing reformers from the late nineteenth century on, and in line with modernist trends, the PWA adopted an aesthetic that minimized ornamentation: "Low rent housing demands mass design rather than expensive ornamentation in order to be successful in low rentals as well as in meritorious character of style," it pronounced. The PWA even adopted specifications for no-frills refrigerators, stoves, and heaters to install in its projects.[12]

The push toward design standardization reflected the circumstances under which the PWA operated. The United States had very few architects and planners familiar with social housing. It lacked the technically competent, experienced civil servants who, as Reed had noted in his report on European housing, provided continuity to British council house construction and who played such a large role in Germany. For New Deal officials, desperate to speed up housing production, developing templates and guidelines that could be used to quickly design or evaluate housing proposals seemed a logical step forward.

To develop standards and plans and approve or disapprove individual projects, Horatio B. Hackett, a Chicago developer whom Ickes brought in to replace Kohn as the head of the Housing Division, greatly increased the staff. At its peak, the housing unit employed 2,200 architects, engineers, draftsmen, and landscape architects in its central and field offices. For a program that, above all else, was meant to decrease unemployment in the building industry, that alone constituted a measure of success.

The new PWA approach, however, had serious drawbacks, as Oscar Stonorov wrote to the Housing Division. One was stigmatization; "a certain trivial standardization has taken hold of the interior arrangement and the exterior appearance which will definitely class these [PWA] buildings . . . as 'those buildings which the government built to house the poor people.'" Another was the discouragement of innovation: "The very fact which has made the project for the hosiery workers in Philadelphia so successful—its architectural novelty—is totally absent from nine-tenths of the projects being worked on now in the Housing Division. Every attempt at individuality is killed practically at conception by the staff, and only with the greatest pain can their bureaucratic attitude be won over to a new solution of the so-called minor details which . . . are major in housing problems."[13]

Figure 3.4. Techwood Homes, Atlanta, 1936.

The PWA's new emphasis on fast, standardized design of public housing did not yield many projects of the quality of the Mackley Houses. But the new "direct-built" dwellings brought a leap in the quality of life for their residents. Techwood Homes, built on a site cleared of dilapidated housing, included, in addition to 604 apartments, 6 stores, 2 gas stations, a health clinic, a library, free laundries, a small auditorium, playgrounds, a tennis court, park benches, and 182 garages. The apartments were well built if spare. Most had three or four rooms, without separate dining rooms. (The PWA frowned on dining rooms; they were used, it argued, "probably not much more than 1 hour a day. But you pay 24 hours a day.") Monthly rent, which included heat, hot water, electricity, and gas, averaged $7.39 a room, a bit less (adjusted for deflation) than what Andrew Thomas had said in 1924 would be the cost for rent alone in well-designed philanthropic housing. This was more than many residents of nearby or demolished slums could pay. But for those who could afford it, the project proved a boon. A photograph of Techwood residents in 1936 captures a seemingly very happy day in New Deal America, with neatly dressed families sitting on benches in front of their new homes, children on bicycles and tricycles, and newly planted trees leafing out.[14]

Or to be more precise, a very happy day in the Whitelandia division

Figure 3.5. University Homes, Atlanta, ca. 1940.

of the New Deal. The PWA was genuinely committed to improving housing for African Americans, reflecting the racial progressivism of Ickes, who had been president of the Chicago NAACP. Among other things, he desegregated the Interior Department and established its Office of Negro Affairs. Over one-third of the housing units the PWA financed were for black residents, and a PWA policy stated that half of all public housing projects in the South had to be for African Americans. The quality and cost of projects for blacks often matched, and in some cases exceeded, standards for whites. Extremely unusually, the PWA even required contractors on its projects to hire African American construction workers in proportion to their representation in the area workforce. But what the PWA did not insist on was that projects allow blacks and whites to live together, effectively giving federal sanction to Jim Crow. Almost all of the housing projects financed or built by the PWA were for one race only. The Logan Fontenelle Homes in Omaha, Nebraska, one of the few PWA-funded projects that accommodated both blacks and whites, housed them in separate sections.[15]

A common PWA practice was to pair a project for African Americans with one for whites. In Atlanta, at the very same time the proposal for

Techwood was submitted, the proposal for University Homes, near Atlanta University, was submitted as well. Because there was no federal rule formally establishing segregation in these projects, when a Georgia congressman raised "the question of the possibility of some colored applicant asking for an apartment" in Techwood, the issue went all the way up to the president. In the end, the head of the PWA Housing Division, by then A. R. Clas, asserted that "no man in Atlanta earnestly seeking to improve the living conditions of his family will ask for assignment to a project set up for occupancy by the opposite race." In the unlikely event that someone did, a local advisory committee would "be in a position to direct the assignment of white applicants to the white project and negro applicants to the negro project."[16]

While sometimes racially exclusionary projects were built in already segregated residential areas, that was not always the case. Neighborhood Gardens was built in an area with a substantial black population intermingled with white residents. Techwood Homes turned what had been an area of black population into one for whites. Black homeowners complained about being forced to sell (by eminent domain) and about the prices they were offered. Many of the displaced residents were domestic workers employed by white families living nearby. Building Techwood forced some to move far from their jobs or crowd into other slum areas. As Robert C. Weaver, hired by Ickes to advise him on racial issues, wrote in a memo, in this case "slum clearance would, in fact, create worse slums."[17]

The PWA's racial policies set the pattern for garden apartment development for decades to come. On the one hand, garden apartments became an important source of decent, affordable housing for Americans of diverse backgrounds. On the other hand, they also, generally speaking, sustained and even furthered the system of residential apartheid so characteristic of twentieth-century America and the many disadvantages it brought people of color.

By the late 1930s, garden apartment–style public housing projects, begun by the PWA, could be found all across the eastern half of the country. A May 1938 *Architectural Forum* survey of public housing profiled many of these developments, including Baker Homes in Lackawanna, New York; Kenfield Housing in Buffalo; Fairfield Court in Stamford, Connecticut; Stanley S. Holmes Village in Atlantic City, New Jersey; Hill Creek in Philadelphia; Lakeview Terrace in Cleveland; Lockefield Garden Apartments in Indianapolis; Cedar Springs Place in Dallas; Logan Fontenelle Homes in Omaha; Parklawn in Milwaukee; La Salle Place in Louisville; Chatham Place and Andrew Jackson Courts in Nashville; Smith Court in Birmingham; Meeting Street Manor and Cooper Village Court in Charleston, South

Figure 3.6. Lakeview Terrace, Cleveland, Ohio.

Figure 3.7. Andrew Jackson Courts, Nashville, Tennessee.

Carolina; and Liberty Square in Miami.[18] Garden apartments were beginning to become a mass form of housing.

Government Garden Cities

While the PWA pioneered garden apartment development and built the first public housing in the United States, a second, much smaller New

Figure 3.8. La Salle Place, Louisville, Kentucky.

Deal housing program, under the Resettlement Administration (RA) in the Department of Agriculture, also erected garden apartment–type housing. The agency, created in 1935 and headed by Rexford Tugwell, a New York economist who was perhaps the most radical of Roosevelt's close advisors, had as its main mission the creation of new communities for poor farmers who lost access to arable land or faced hardship from falling prices and other woes. But it also included a "Suburban Resettlement Division" intended to create new towns, along garden city lines, for poor city dwellers.

Tugwell and his allies had grand plans, initially envisioning as many as sixty new cities. Frederick Bigger, the RPAA member who had helped plan Chatham Village, headed Tugwell's planning staff. Clarence Stein, Henry Wright, and Catherine Bauer all worked with the agency. Tugwell thought of the suburban settlements in terms straight out of Ebenezer Howard: "My idea is to go just outside centers of population, pick up cheap land, build a whole community, and entice people into it. Then go back into the cities and tear down whole slums and make parks of them." It was, he wrote Roosevelt, "the most dramatic thing I've ever had to do with."[19]

As it turned out, the agency—renamed the Farm Security Administration (FSA) in 1937—only had a chance to plan four new towns, three of which were built: Greenbelt, Maryland (near Washington, DC); Greenhills, Ohio (near Cincinnati); and Greendale, Wisconsin (near Milwaukee). Buying large plots of land—3,411 acres for Greenbelt alone—the agency hoped to create what would be very substantial communities. Greendale had a target population of 12,000.

It was not to be. The proposed garden cities provoked ferocious opposition from business and real estate interests. The US Chamber of Commerce called the towns "an experiment in state control of far-reaching proportions." The National Association of Real Estate Boards declared them "undiluted socialism." Under the onslaught, the federal government began to retreat. When a lawsuit blocked the construction of what had been intended to be a fourth greenbelt town—Greenbrook, near New Brunswick, New Jersey, designed by Wright—on the grounds that it exceeded federal authority, the Roosevelt administration did not challenge the ruling. Instead, by the end of 1936, Tugwell, a lightning rod for criticism of the New Deal, left his position.

The FSA managed to carry on with its experiment, but on a much more modest scale. Facing budgetary limits and pressure to have something to show for public investment sooner rather than later, it switched gears. Working quickly and cheaply, using inexpensive building materials and workers off the Works Progress Administration (WPA) relief rolls, by mid-1938 the FSA completed 885 new housing units in Greenbelt, 676 in Greenhills, and 572 in Greendale.[20]

Stein, who designed Greenbelt, considered the three towns as the first time "the Garden City, the Radburn Idea, and the Neighborhood Unit" had been "amalgamated." Though there were variations among the projects, in all of them a town center was surrounded by low-rise residential buildings. Greenbelt had a mix of row houses and garden apartments and a few prefabricated single-family homes. Greenhills also consisted primarily of multifamily buildings. Under its chief architect, Roland Wank, who had designed the Amalgamated Dwellings in New York, some of its structures had a distinctly modernist air, with flat roofs reminiscent of German social housing, while others had more traditional designs, making for an odd mishmash. Most Greendale buildings were single-family homes. Combinations of superblocks, curving streets, cul-de-sacs, courtyards, green spaces, clustered garages, and pedestrian pathways kept vehicles at a distance from living and play spaces and allowed safe walking access to commercial, educational, and recreational facilities. Surrounding the towns were substantial greenbelts. Murals, bas-reliefs, and sculptures by artists employed by the WPA adorned settlement grounds and community buildings.

Tugwell and the FSA were strong supporters of cooperative enterprise. The original intent had been to turn over the new towns to cooperative associations. But their downsizing caused the agency to change plans, fearing insufficient economies of scale for the communities to handle maintenance and other costs. Instead, the federal government kept ownership

Figure 3.9. Children at play in Greenhills, Ohio.

Figure 3.10. Cooperatively owned movie theater in Greendale, Wisconsin.

of the land and buildings, renting out the living spaces. But for the stores that, along with schools and recreation facilities, formed the town centers, the FSA helped establish cooperative enterprises to which it leased space.

The FSA projects failed to attract either factories or offices, as originally intended (though sixty-five commercial farms operated within Greendale's greenbelt). The timing was not good; few factories or office buildings were built during the depths of the Depression. Also, the siting needs of factories and large office complexes did not necessarily correspond to what small garden settlements had to offer. So, like Radburn, the new federal towns became commuter suburbs.

The greenbelt cities served a particular slice of the population, far from the neediest. Strict income limits were used to keep out those seen as too poor to be able to reliably pay their rent, as well as those too well-off to need federally assisted housing. To move in, you had to be white; in the RPAA tradition, all the greenbelt cities excluded non-whites. Eligibility rules also were used to support the traditional, patriarchal nuclear family; families in which both husband and wife worked were not allowed to rent units in the government complexes.[21]

For Stein, looking back in 1950, the federal greenbelt cities were "three links in the experience that led . . . toward the future New Towns of America." But rather than steps toward the further blossoming of garden cities in the United States, Greenbelt, Greenhills, and Greendale more rightly should be seen as the sputtering out of a utopian quest, effectively the end of the line for Ebenezer Howard's vision brought to America. After World War II, there were a few commercial developments that in some respects carried on the garden city tradition, like Reston, Virginia; Columbia, Maryland; and Celebration, Florida, but they stand out more for their exceptionality than their influence. As a significant path for addressing housing and social inequality, even before the end of the 1930s, the garden city in the United States was dead.[22]

The end of the greenbelt program, and more broadly of garden city construction, reflected not only political opposition but also the lack of significant political pressure *for* their continuation. The garden city movement in the United States was a movement of elite reformers, architects, intellectuals, and the occasional businessperson. There was no problem finding people eager to move into Sunnyside Gardens, Radburn, Chatham Village, or the federal greenbelt cities, but neither was there a popular movement promoting the construction of more such communities. To the extent that there was mass mobilization around housing during the twentieth century, up to World War II it focused on fighting rent increases, evictions, and foreclosures, not constructing social housing or garden cities.[23]

In some ways, the whole impulse behind garden cities in the United States ran counter to dominant popular sentiment. A deep strain of anti-urbanism, from above not below, colored the movement for their construction, including the federal projects. Nowhere could it be more clearly seen than in the 1939 documentary film *The City*, the most important propaganda effort in the United States to promote the garden city idea.

The proposal for the film, by some accounts, came from Catherine Bauer, as housing reformers discussed how to present their ideas at the 1939–40 New York World's Fair. Clarence Stein took up the reins, organizing a group within the American Institute of Planners to produce a movie. Its board included RPAA members Robert Kohn, Frederick L. Ackerman, and Tracy Auger (then the chief town planner for the Tennessee Valley Authority). Funding came from the Carnegie Corporation. Pare Lorentz, who had directed two acclaimed films for the FSA, *The Plow That Broke the Plains* and *The River*, did the initial outline. Left-wing filmmakers Ralph Steiner and Willard Van Dyke codirected. Lewis Mumford wrote the narration. Aaron Copland composed the score. For two years, the film was shown at the World's Fair, garnering much attention.

Despite the progressive credentials and enormous talent behind it, *The City* is a surprisingly backward-looking, dyspeptic production. It opens with deeply nostalgic and almost comically romantic images of life in a traditional New England village, before cutting to depictions (filmed in Pittsburgh) of the industrial city as a demonic intrusion of smoke-blackened skies and urban squalor. New York City comes off no better, portrayed as overcrowded, dangerous, and alienating. The positive alternative comes in the last part of the film, with a portrait of "the new city," the garden city, filmed at Greenbelt and Radburn. As, once again, almost comically idyllic images are offered—boys on bicycles riding on pathways through the woods, a man fishing (while wearing a suit), a housewife happily working in her bright, well-organized kitchen—the garden city is presented as a return to the values of the old New England village through the application of the newest advances in science.[24]

The antiurbanism of *The City* is stunning. The cities portrayed do not have a single positive feature; audiences are given nothing at all to like about them. Virtue lay only in the New England village of yore or the so-called new cities featured at the end of the film (both racially exclusionary), which, in reality, had but a few thousand residents apiece, not cities at all.

But Americans liked cities. They flocked to cities. (The urban population of the United States grew from 39.6 percent of the total population in 1900 to 51.2 percent in 1920 and 56.5 percent in 1940.) They celebrated cities, in film and song and book. Cities were freedom, excitement, opportunity, fun. No one liked slums or smoke or dirt or danger, but to see existing cities as simply the sum of their problems represented an embrace of a reactionary antiurban streak in American life.

The New Deal at times embraced antiurbanism. It manifested not only in FSA housing but in such initiatives as the Civilian Conservation Corps, seen by Roosevelt as a way to reinvigorate the nation's young men by exposing them to healthy rural life, and the regionalist culture promoted by federal arts projects. But the New Deal also contained strong—if anything, stronger—urban impulses, from its mass base among big-city workers and immigrants to its many city-based relief, construction, and arts programs. *The City*, parochial and backward looking compared to the polyglot labor and radical movements that did so much to transform American life during the New Deal, garnered critical support but did little to advance the cause of the garden city, then grinding to a halt, even if its backers did not yet realize it.[25]

The end of garden city creation in the United States did not mean the end of all the ideas or design approaches associated with it. Long after the garden city, as a complete entity, was all but abandoned, the garden apartment flourished, generally not as an escape from the city but as a living mode within it. Here was a residential form much better suited to the circumstances and desires of Americans than the "new towns" so heavily promoted by the RPAA circle and its allies. Even as the federal government pulled back from garden city construction, it accelerated its commitment to garden apartments.

The United States Housing Authority

In 1937, the PWA and FSA housing efforts were superseded by the passage of the United States Housing Act, which established a new agency and framework for public housing. The PWA and FSA had been meant to be temporary relief measures. The new law encoded the outcome of a multiyear political battle over whether or not the country would adopt a permanent government housing program and, if so, what kind. New York Senator Robert Wagner, a key architect of New Deal legislation, introduced a housing bill in 1935 that focused on slum clearance and funding local authorities to build housing for the poor. Some housing reformers, including Catherine Bauer and Oscar Stonorov, dissatisfied with the narrow focus of his bill, drafted an alternative, introduced by Pennsylvania Representative Henry Ellenbogen (who had been born and educated in Vienna). Their bill would have empowered the federal government to continue to directly build housing, as well as to make loans and grants to regional, state, and local authorities and nonprofit housing groups, including cooperatives, to build dwellings for a broad range of income groups. Neither bill won passage.

Two years later, Wagner introduced a revised bill that incorporated elements of both approaches, winning support from housing activists, housing officials, and significant elements of the labor movement, including the building trades. But his proposal faced fierce opposition from congressional conservatives backed by the residential real estate industry, which wanted no government competition. Some elements of the Roosevelt administration also resisted the measure, including Harold Ickes, who did not want to lose control over housing to a new agency, and Treasury Secretary Henry Morgenthau Jr., who opposed new large-scale spending.[26]

Even within the PWA, the tide had turned away from a housing program meant to elevate living standards across the board. By the spring of 1937, the agency reverted to its roots in limiting projects to those "which have the greatest effect in the reduction of the number of employees on the relief rolls." An in-house survey of PWA architecture, listing "some of the principles learned," re-embraced Ickes's initial focus on housing for "those who now occupy slum areas." Such housing should promote "the maintenance of health, and the amenities of family life . . . but without luxury." Renouncing any desire to compete with the private sector, it declared "standards of construction and equipment should be lowered in the matter of technical perfection to conform to the standards used by private investment builders." Public housing for the nonpoor and as a way to raise the overall quality of housing had already gone out of fashion.[27]

Whittled down during the legislative process, the law that emerged in 1937 amounted to a less generous version of Wagner's 1935 proposal. The provisions for funding cooperative, nonprofit, and demonstration projects were eliminated, as was the ability of the federal government to directly build housing. Instead, the law only provided financing, through the newly created United States Housing Authority (USHA), for local housing authorities to build public housing for low-income residents. If a state decided not to authorize housing authorities—which as late as 1944 was the case in ten states—or a locality chose not to set one up, there simply would be no public housing in the area. Furthermore, the law linked public housing to slum clearance, requiring that for every new unit of public housing built, one "unsafe or unsanitary" unit had to be demolished or modernized (the latter usually impractical).[28]

The Housing Act of 1937 deliberately sought to lower the quality of government-funded housing so that it would not compete with or show up privately built residences. To do so, it capped the amount that could be spent to build each unit of housing and each room within those units at levels well below what the PWA had allocated. In its early years, the USHA spent even less than it legally could. As of February 1942, the average total development cost of a unit of USHA housing was $4,604, compared to the PWA average of $5,927. To keep down costs, rooms were made smaller, closets had no doors, kitchens were not separated from living areas (shades of early tenements and Viennese public housing), and elevators stopped only at every other floor.[29]

In its intent and effect, the 1937 act repositioned public housing from exemplary dwellings for working- and middle-class families to inferior living quarters only for the poor. The possibility for a capacious social housing program that used government funding to facilitate architecturally innovative communities for a broad public, sponsored not only by government entities but by all sorts of nonprofit, limited-dividend, and cooperative organizations, receded. But within narrowed confines, the garden apartment lived, and actually flourished, under the auspices of the USHA.

Unlike the PWA Housing Division, conceived of as a temporary work program, the USHA was intended to be a permanent housing program. The funding it provided for housing projects built and managed by local housing authorities took two forms. To cover capital expenses, the USHA could lend up to 90 percent of the cost of a housing development, with the sponsoring authority required to cover the remainder. Because the loans were of very long duration—up to sixty years—the carrying costs for sponsoring authorities were very low. (As a corollary, USHA-funded housing had to be built with an expected life of at least sixty years, which necessitated more solid construction than many commercial projects.) The 1937 law authorized an initial lending pool of $800 million—over $18 billion in 2025 currency—giving the USHA far greater capacity than its New Deal predecessors. In addition, and crucially, the USHA could offer annual operating subsidies to local authorities. Those authorities in turn had to provide subsidies of their own equal to 20 percent of the federal contribution. That usually took the form of a real estate tax exemption or the provision of free services to a housing project.

The combination of low-cost mortgages and ongoing operating subsidies meant that USHA-funded projects, unlike private endeavors such as Sunnyside and Chatham Village or the FSA and typical PWA developments, were genuinely affordable to poor families. As of early 1940, USHA projects on average were charging rents of $3 per room in the South and $4.25 in the North, compared to the typical $15 or more in new private housing and $11 to $12 in commercial developments receiving tax exemptions or other government benefits to increase affordability. If the 1937 housing act reduced the quality of public housing, the financial infrastructure it created, especially the ongoing subsidies, meant that for

Figure 3.11. Federal housing projects as of April 15, 1938. Black circles are PWA projects taken over by the USHA; white circles are USHA commitments; white squares are FSA greenbelt towns. There were no projects west of the map.

the first time social housing was available to the bottom economic strata of the population, to those who most needed it.[30]

Under the Housing Act of 1937, local authorities had the decision-making power regarding if and where to build public housing and what it would look like. The USHA, however, exerted considerable control through its power to accept or reject projects and set minimal standards for them. It had a stellar staff to do so, including general counsel Leon Keyserling, a close associate of both Tugwell and Wagner, who for the next two decades would be the quintessential New Deal liberal; Catherine Bauer, who served as director of research and information; Jacob Crane, director of project planning, who during World War I had been with the US Housing Corporation and later worked with the RA; Boris Shishkin, an American Federation of Labor economist who consulted on labor policy; and Robert C. Weaver, special assistant on racial relations.[31] (Weaver's 1966 appointment as Secretary of Housing and Urban Development would make him the first African American member of the cabinet.)

Like the PWA before it, the USHA published "recommendations" for projects it funded, though it insisted that they were "in no sense mandatory." The agency stressed economy: "The design, as well as the materials used, should reflect the lowest cost at which sound construction practices and low maintenance and operating expenses can be obtained." In addition to a table of recommended room sizes, it put forth such suggestions as "the arrangement of the principal bedroom should be such as to accommodate an infant's crib." Living units, the USHA recommended, should be grouped "into buildings having a maximum length of approximately 200 feet" to "decrease the number of buildings, thereby minimizing end walls and utility distribution lines." Local authorities were urged to consider having residents use existing, nearby social facilities to keep down costs, but the USHA did list appropriate sizes for meeting rooms, communal kitchens, and storage spaces if they had to be built.[32]

The PWA had favored low-rise developments, generally capping the height of projects it would fund at four stories. Initially, the USHA continued that inclination. The 1937 housing act prohibited high-rise construction except where low-rise projects were deemed impractical. As time went on, some public housing projects grew taller and taller, to the extent that the public came to associate public housing with projects like the eleven-story Pruitt-Igoe towers in St. Louis and the sixteen-story Robert Taylor Homes in Chicago, developments, rightly or wrongly, generally judged disastrous and eventually demolished. But most USHA-funded housing did not look anything like those projects. Rather, it consisted of low-rise projects with many of the characteristics of garden apartments. Bauer reported that of the projects in place or in the works three years after the passage of the law, "almost ninety per cent . . . consist of one- or two-story homes, built economically, in groups or rows, with private gardens." A scattering of USHA-funded projects had three-story buildings, but as of mid-1940, the only taller structures were in New York City.[33]

The first projects to start construction with USHA funds were two small, low-rise developments in Austin, Texas. After the passage of the 1937 law, Austin quickly set up a housing authority and applied for money for three projects: Rosewood Courts, for African Americans; Santa Rita Courts, for Mexican Americans; and Chalmers Courts, for whites (on which construction began after the others). First-term Congressman Lyndon B. Johnson, whose district included Austin, installed allies at the Austin Housing Authority and lobbied hard to get the city included in the first allocation of USHA money. Johnson directly confronted local business leaders who opposed the projects, calling the real estate interests among them "rent hogs."

Rosewood Courts initially consisted of sixty apartments in one-story buildings laid out on a superblock along what the Germans called *Zeilen-*

bau lines, parallel rows of buildings allowing for light and ventilation and defining courtyards between them, much like the housing in Frankfurt. The smaller Santa Rita project had a similar design. A second Rosewood Courts phase added seventy units in two-story buildings. The German design influence apparently came through USHA regional administrator Oliver Winston, a Texas architect who had worked at the PWA and became an advocate of Bauer's "modern housing." Her 1934 book included illustrations of *Zeilenbau* configurations.

The Austin Housing Authority located its first three projects in conformity with a 1928 city master plan that delineated segregated areas for the white, black, and Mexican American populations, furthering the program of racial separation. Early USHA projects typically were segregated, with tripartite segregation in the Southwest, though there were some integrated projects. (Though the USHA allowed racial discrimination in choosing tenants, it banned it in the employment of workers constructing housing it financed.) Ironically, Rosewood Courts was constructed on what had been Emancipation Park, the black-owned site of the most important Juneteenth parade ground in Austin, taken over by the city for the new project by eminent domain.[34]

Many low-rise public housing projects were modest in size and located in smaller cities, but some large, big-city projects also had garden apartment designs. Seth Boydon Court, the first public housing project in Newark, New Jersey, contained 503 apartments in three-story buildings situated on a superblock so as to create a series of semi-enclosed courtyards. Many of the early tenants were Jewish, while African American tenants later became predominant.[35]

The Lafitte Housing Project, one of six built by the Housing Authority of New Orleans (HANO) by 1942—four for black residents, including Lafitte, and two for white residents—had 896 units in garden apartment buildings, providing a home for some three thousand people. HANO, one of the most energetic housing authorities in the country, reported in 1938 that nearly half of all dwellings in New Orleans "may be described in a broad sense as 'indecent, unsafe and insanitary.'" At the sites for its new projects "a great majority of the homes . . . were without running hot water. Many hundreds of these homes had no facilities for bathing. Hundreds were without any arrangements for light or heat. In most cases the kitchens were only makeshift affairs at best." Not many families "had the use of a private indoor toilet. In nearly every case, this facility was shared with other families or was set apart from the dwelling proper." (Nationally, in 1940, only a little more than half of all households—and only a fifth of non-white households—had indoor toilets and bathing facilities.)[36]

The Lafitte project, located in New Orleans's Treme neighborhood,

Figure 3.12. Photomontage by the Housing Authority of New Orleans to illustrate "blight" in the area where the St. Thomas Project was to be constructed.

used garden city/garden suburb design devices, including courtyards and pedestrian paths away from roads. In 2006, *New York Times* architecture critic Nicolai Ouroussoff wrote of Lafitte, then threatened by demolition, "Solidly built, the buildings' detailed brickwork, tile roofs and wrought-iron balustrades represent a level of craft more likely found on an Ivy League campus than in a contemporary public housing complex." "Upon entering any of the buildings," according to one account, "families found sunny rooms with plenty of space, bedrooms with casement windows plus wood block floors, and bathrooms equipped with tile and porcelain. Kitchens had gas stoves and electric refrigerators and each family had their own private entrance." Outside lay play spaces, gardens, and large old oak trees. Through the 1950s, Lafitte had "a network of social services from nursery schools financed by the WPA to on-site medical care, adult education programs, Boy Scout groups, and gardening clubs." Rent varied by family income, with five levels of "graded rents" for each size apartment. Ouroussoff felt the New Orleans buildings did not "rise to the level, say, of the best Modernist workers housing built in Europe in the 1920s," but "certainly rank above the level of much of the conventional middle-class housing being churned out today."[37]

Even in New York City, then as now a center of public housing, there were low-rise projects. The first public housing built in the Bronx, the USHA-funded Clason Point Gardens, comprised four hundred apartments in two-story buildings covering just over a fifth of the site. The complex included four children's play areas, park areas for adults, and only one through street. Originally, the New York City Housing Authority hoped that its "first garden village" would consist of single-family houses, but that "proved uneconomical." But the garden city ideal remained, both in the reference to dwellings as "cottage-type buildings" and the provision for each family of a front lawn and a backyard with space for a private garden.[38] (See plate 10.) For most new residents, the project represented a jump in living standards, as nearly three-quarters came from homes without a private bathroom, three-fifths from homes without central heating, and nearly half from homes without a private toilet. New York City was not that different from New Orleans.

At the September 1941 dedication of Clason Point Gardens, USHA administrator Nathan Straus said: "I have always believed that men and women were not intended to live in tall, crowded buildings and that children can best enjoy a happy and healthy childhood if, instead of being crowded into even the best six, eight, and ten-story buildings, they are enabled to live amid the surroundings that you see as you look about you today." Straus's statement reflected a widespread conviction among housing reformers that the physical attributes of dwellings shaped the

Figure 3.13. Story time at Lafitte Housing Project, New Orleans.

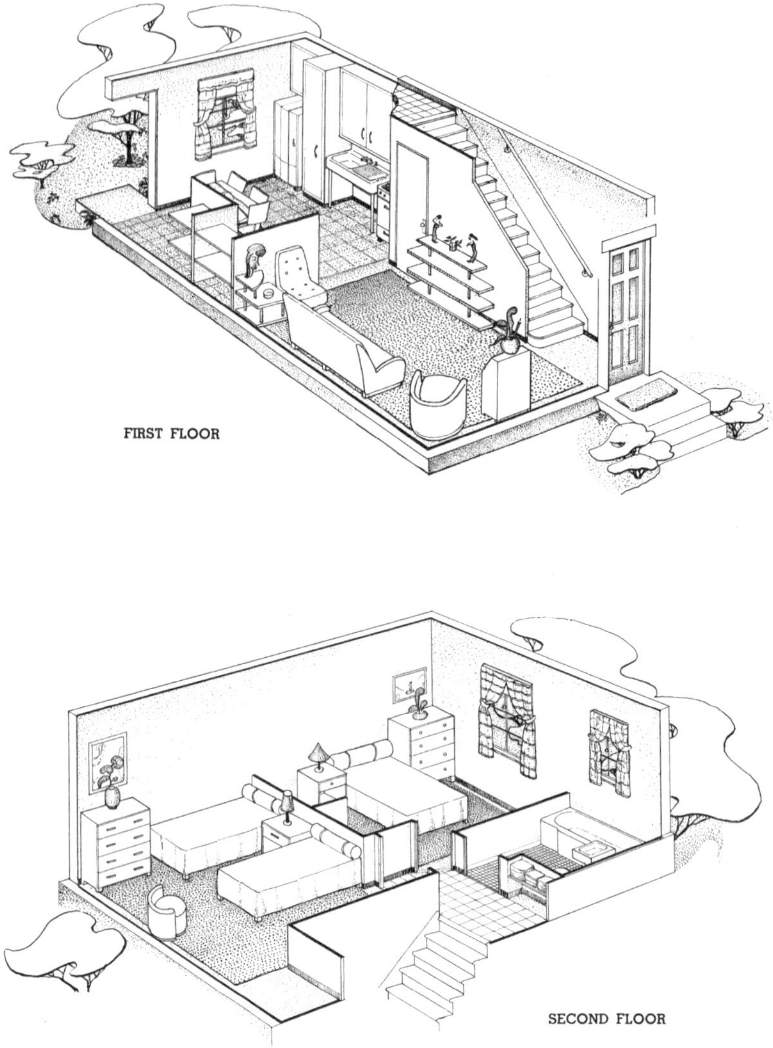

Figures 3.14a and 3.14b. Rendering of a "Typical 4½ Room Home" at Clason Point Gardens. The rent was $23.70 per month, including gas and electricity.

well-being and behavior of their residents. Better-designed housing would be a way not only to improve living standards but also to address a wide host of moral and social ills in the lower levels of society.

Some scholars have challenged the idea of design determinism, as you might call it, which characterized much of the thinking of housing reformers. They have suggested that problems like discrimination, lack of adequate income and job opportunities, poor building management, and crime were much more important in shaping the lives and problems of the poor than flawed housing design, such as the high-rise construction that eventually came to characterize public housing in Northeastern and Midwestern cities. Perhaps reformers *were* overconfident in the salutary effects of good design. Nonetheless many Clason Point Gardens tenants expressed their preference for the scale of their project compared to more typical New York public housing. (Clason Point Gardens eventually was overshadowed by the seven-story buildings of the Soundview public housing project built directly across the street, itself a modest size by post–World War II big-city public housing standards.) Sophie Schottler, who moved into Clason Point Gardens in 1942, fifty years later told a *New York Times* reporter, "I always loved it because it was like having your own little house."[39]

Not all the low-rise USHA projects were as well designed as Lafitte or Clason Point. In Macon, Georgia, the buildings in the Tindall Heights and Oglethorpe Homes projects, opened in 1940—the former for blacks, the latter for whites—resembled those at Clason Point, but with an inferior site design. (See plate 11.) Lined up in parallel rows, the two-story structures resembled army barracks as much as garden apartments. Still, when Otis Redding's family moved from the Georgia countryside into Tindall Heights in 1942, having "never enjoyed the benefits of electricity, much less gas heat and indoor plumbing, the place was a dream come true." Taking possession of a five-room apartment, with "a window in every room, glass in every window, and a solid roof overhead," wrote Redding's biographer, the family "hadn't just moved . . . into a new home. They had moved . . . into the twentieth century." Moving into the twentieth century cost $2.50 a week in rent when Tindall Heights opened, which included electricity, water, and natural gas.[40]

The Housing Act of 1937 constrained the possibilities for first-rate public housing for working people of varying income levels, which might have also set standards for the private sector. Still, within its parameters, good publicly owned garden apartments were produced on a large scale. At least for the initial generation or two, these projects brought a major improvement in living standards, providing the basis for a decent life. One Lafitte resident recalled, "I was the 2nd generation to live there—my mother's family were one of the first families to move into the new, pristine development in 1941. I remember it when it was a pleasure to live there; grounds were well kept, janitorial services available, neighbors took relative pride in keeping the Community clean and safe; we watched out for one another."[41] English garden city advocates, Continental social housers, and their disciples in the United States thought what they were doing was not only constructing collections of residences but creating democratic communities. In Lafitte and other locales across the country, public housing succeeded in doing just that.

Insuring Housing

The New Deal did more than introduce public housing to the United States. It also transformed private housing through massive intervention in the mortgage market. Ultimately, this proved to be the most important government housing program in the history of the United States, shaping not only residential patterns but also the very social structure of the country. During the fifty years that Sophie Schottler lived in public housing, the majority of Americans who managed to buy their "own little house" had the Federal Housing Administration (FHA) to thank.

Created in 1934, with strong support from the real estate industry, the FHA was designed to stimulate housing construction, after its catastrophic decline during the early years of the Depression, by opening the spigot of mortgage lending. To do so, the federal government embarked on a program of insuring home mortgages, all but eliminating the risk to lenders. By setting standards that mortgages and the dwellings they financed had to meet to be eligible for insurance, the FHA radically transformed the housing market and patterns of community settlement. Rather than short-term balloon loans that required very large down payments, the mortgage norm before the FHA, federal guidelines led to long-term loans, requiring small down payments, amortized so that both interest and principal were paid off in monthly installments. This opened borrowing and homeownership to millions of Americans previously unable to purchase houses. At the same time, by steering mortgage insurance to racially homogeneous neighborhoods, the FHA promoted racial segregation and inequality as the country expanded into the vast plains of suburban development.[42]

This is the FHA story most people know, but it is only one piece of the story. More than any other institution, it was the FHA that was responsible for scattering garden apartments across mid-twentieth-century America. Its role in housing hundreds of thousands of families in these undistinguished though highly functional dwellings has been largely forgotten because it goes against a common perception of the FHA as the dark agent of racially exclusive suburban sprawl, the enabler of the post–World War II pattern of single-family suburban homeownership that came to epitomize the United States at the height of its imperial glory.

Yet, in its early years, the FHA aggressively pursued the development of multiunit rental housing, much of it urban and in the form of garden apartments. During its first five years of operation, the Rental Housing Division of the FHA insured mortgages for 291 projects, containing more than 32,000 apartments, in thirty-eight states. Two hundred and twenty-eight of these projects were garden apartments. In 1940 *The Architectural Forum* declared that, fostered by the FHA, "in the past five years the garden apartment has come of age."[43]

The National Housing Act, which established the FHA, empowered it to insure mortgages for low-income rental projects built by public authorities or limited-dividend corporations. Later amendments added the authority to insure mortgages for commercial rental dwellings and replaced the restriction to "housing for persons of low income" with a cap on the mortgage value per room that it could insure. These changes broadened the income range of people the FHA could serve. In return for providing insurance, the agency had the right to regulate "rents, charges, capital structure, rate of return, and methods of operation" of covered properties.[44]

Consistent with the main thrust of New Deal housing policy, FHA leaders were at least as concerned with reviving the finance and construction industries as providing better homes for the ill-housed. With risks so low because of mortgage insurance, the agency believed that it could draw what it called "conservative capital" into the rental housing industry, even with a cap on profits, especially once it succeeded in amending the Housing Act to eliminate the language restricting insurance to low-income projects. The calculation proved correct; a 1938 list of FHA-insured rental projects included as lenders New York, Prudential, National, and Union Central life insurance companies, as well as Manufacturers Trust Co. and Marine Midland Trust Co., very substantial financial entities.[45]

The FHA rejected philanthropic and nonprofit organizations as significant vehicles for rehousing America—spurning that part of its original legislative mandate—preferring instead commercial developers. Nonetheless, it adopted and adapted many noncommercial design innovations, drawing on the American version of the garden city movement. Aiming to serve a population segment with significantly higher income than those living in public housing, FHA officials were particularly influenced by Chatham Village and the work of Henry Wright. In developing design manuals for the agency, key FHA officials drew heavily on Wright's analytic theories.[46]

The very first FHA-insured garden apartment complex, Colonial Village in Arlington, Virginia, incorporated lessons from earlier garden city

Figure 3.15. Colonial Village, Arlington, Virginia, 1995.

experiments and helped establish the template for hundreds of projects to come. It was the creation of developer Gustave Ring and architects Harvey H. Warwick Sr. and Francis Koening. Ring and Warwick previously had worked together on the Westchester, the largest luxury apartment complex in the District of Columbia. With the Depression having brought virtually all private construction to a halt, high-end architects and developers became interested in government-backed low- and moderate-income projects, if nothing else as a way to stay working.

Colonial Village consisted of forty-five two- and three-story buildings, the former containing four apartments apiece, the latter six. Spread out on large superblocks just ten minutes by bus from downtown Washington, the buildings, containing 1,189 units, covered only 18 percent of the site, leaving plenty of land for courtyards, forested areas, lawns, and walkways. The buildings themselves were simple brick structures with some colonial revival touches. A new shopping center was erected adjacent to the homes.[47]

The success of Colonial Village—the complex was swamped with applications—validated FHA support for garden apartment complexes and led to a growing number of similar projects. The Washington, DC, area, with the FHA headquartered right there, served as a proving ground. Over 5,000 units of FHA-backed garden apartments were built in the area between 1935 and 1940. These were New Deal projects not only in their facilitation by the FHA but also in their tenancy; many of their residents had moved to the Washington area to work for New Deal programs.[48]

Henry Wright prepared the site plan for the largest prewar FHA-insured rental development, the Buckingham Community in Arlington. Like many garden apartment complexes, it was built on what had been open land—in this case a one-hundred-acre farm—which kept down costs. Wright laid out angled streets and made extensive use of U-shaped courtyards to control vehicular traffic and create large, open areas near every apartment.

One building in the initial phase of the project, a three-story structure with a flat roof and recessed corner balconies, was designed to test the appeal of European-influenced modern architecture. Perhaps because of negative feedback (the building is not very attractive), the developer, Paramount Communities, Inc., in subsequent phases stuck to two-story, red-brick buildings. These were rapidly becoming the norm for garden apartments in most of the country and remained so for the next quarter century. Buckingham was Wright's last major project—he died in July 1936 at age 58—but his influence shaped the design of hundreds of thousands of garden apartments to come.[49]

Figure 3.16. A courtyard at Buckingham Community, Arlington, Virgina.

Figure 3.17. Modernist apartment building at Buckingham Community.

The Washington-area garden apartments, including Colonial Village and the Buckingham Community, became models for developments elsewhere, as the FHA Rental Housing Division exerted strong influence over the design of other projects. At first it did so through the review of each proposal to ensure it met FHA standards. Then, in 1937, like the PWA and USHA, it began issuing guidelines for future projects. Its standards were sometimes presented as merely preferences, but, given the ability of the agency to grant or deny insurance, such recommendations carried much weight. The FHA justified its intervention by the need to make sure that developments would be able to pay the mortgages it insured.

The FHA recommendations, often quite detailed, co-opted many elements of garden city design. For large projects, the agency required building coverage of only 20 to 25 percent of a contiguous site, with "minor residential streets . . . designed to discourage through-traffic." "Play areas for small children should be provided, largely hard-surfaced and protected with fencing, walls or heavy plantings." The FHA preferred buildings not over three stories high; it required elevators for taller structures, a significant financial disincentive. A multitude of diagrams put forth examples of favored and unfavored site and apartment layouts.

Rooms in FHA-insured rental projects were significantly larger than in USHA-funded public housing. Principal bedrooms averaged over 145 square feet, compared to a USHA recommendation of 120 to 130 square feet. FHA

Comparative Site Plans

THE FOLLOWING schemes illustrate revisions of typical site plans to develop project possibilities as fully as possible. Unit plans are not indicated because all are based on one or more of the types shown on page 33.

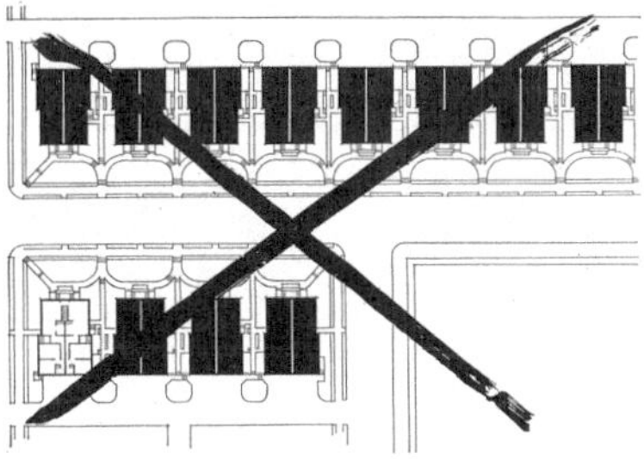

Four-family units on single lots—available open space is cut up and ineffective. Kitchens do not receive natural light; dining alcoves and bedrooms face adjacent units.

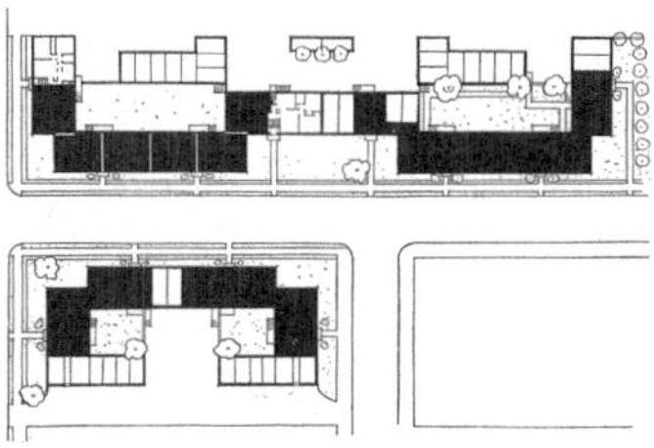

The same number of families are accommodated, all rooms having ample light and air. The group plan is not only more attractive, but also cheaper to build.

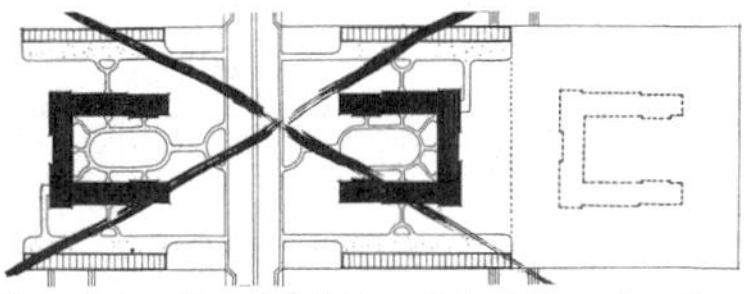

These 3-story U-court buildings, derived from plans for small urban lots, afford little protected garden area because most of the space opens to the street traffic. Access to garages requires twice the driveway it should.

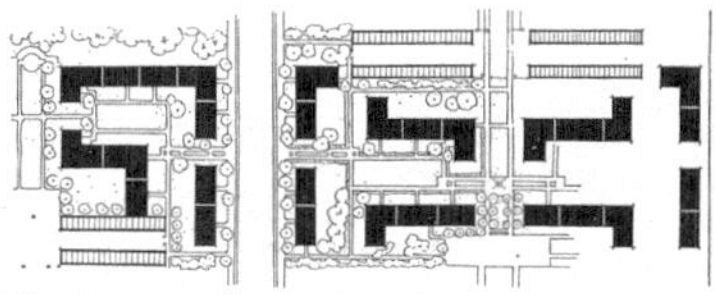

All major rooms face protected courts. Garage compounds are entered from dead-end streets with rear of garages forming a garden wall. No additional rental is required, since construction costs are not increased.

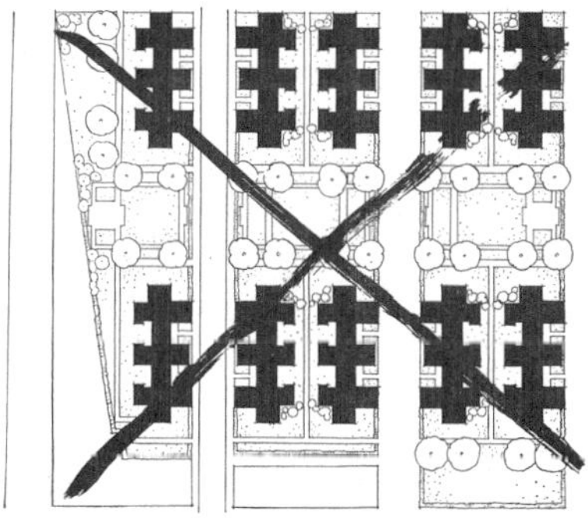

Elevator buildings with a central garden: this area can be seen from few apartments and crowds the buildings.

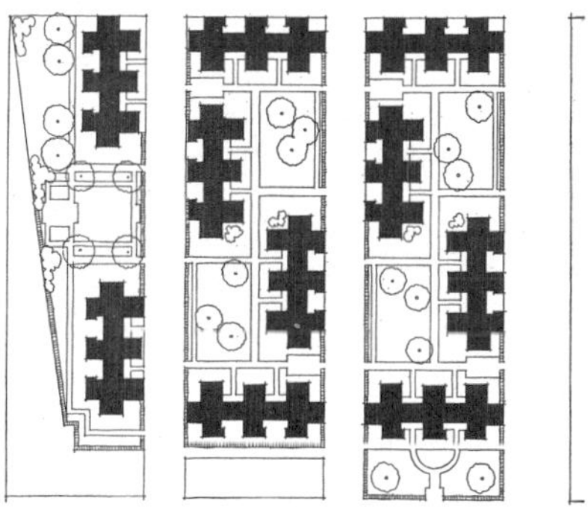

The same buildings rearranged with open space more adequately disposed—eliminating narrow courts.

Figure 3.18. Comparative site plans from an article by FHA deputy administrator Miles L. Colean.

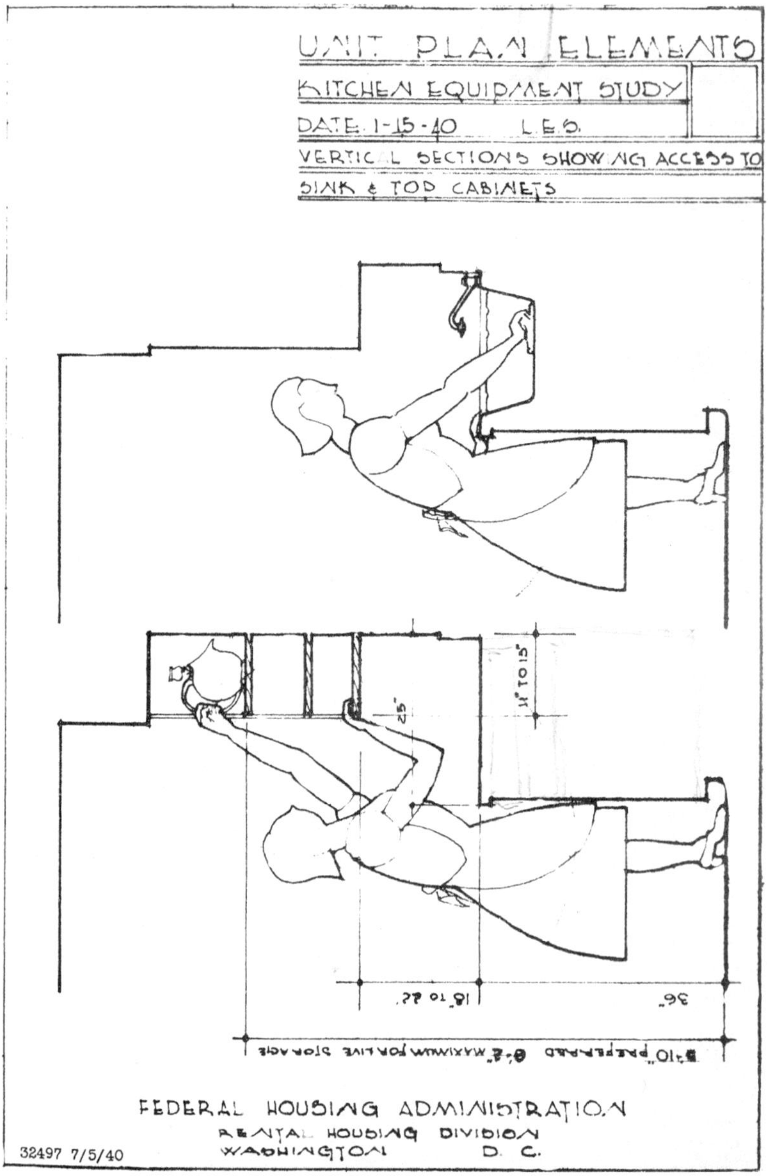

Figure 3.19. An FHA study for kitchen design, shades of Margarete Schütte-Lihotzky's studies for the Frankfurt kitchen.

guidelines recommended or required amenities that many middle-class apartment dwellers today would envy, including at least one closet of not less than five square feet in every bedroom, a linen closet not less than fourteen inches deep in each apartment, and a window in every bathroom "having not less than 10% of the floor area, not less than 3 sq. ft, and at least 50% of the required glass area openable." Eugene Klaber, who after leaving the PWA served as the Director of Architecture for the FHA Rental Division from 1934 to 1942, instructed FHA architects: "Except in the very lowest rental projects, the exposed heat riser is not an acceptable method of heating the bathroom or kitchen." (Anyone who has lived in a building with exposed heat risers can attest to the wisdom of his advice.) The FHA also called for individual apartment or communal laundry facilities and "garage service, or in some cases outdoor parking spaces." Bulletins on such issues as site planning, landscaping, bathrooms, and dining space helped FHA staff make quick judgments on the adequacy of submitted plans. Going beyond FHA recommendations, many government-insured garden apartments complexes provided such amenities as day care centers and meeting rooms and provided land for shopping centers, schools, and community buildings.[50]

FHA involvement continued after the design stage of projects, right through completion. Change orders had to be approved by the FHA and agency inspectors reported on work done and any possible deficiencies. The level of detail can be seen in a report of an FHA inspector on landscaping for the third phase of the Buckingham Community. It included appraisals and, in some cases, recommendations for additional plantings for each building, such as "Bldg. #67. Front planting satisfactory. Add 2 shrubs near corners on West rear between the end windows." This was truly intrusive government, for better or for worse.[51]

USHA housing, at least at first, was not well distributed across the country. Well over a third of its first seventy-three projects were in the North Atlantic region, with very few on the West Coast. By contrast, FHA-insured garden apartments quickly cropped up all across the country, with Los Angeles, along with the New York City and Washington, DC, areas, emerging as a center for such projects.[52] As architectural historian Katie Horak noted, garden apartments "were perfectly suited to Los Angeles" with its "abundance of open land." Moreover, the Southern California climate allowed residents to fully enjoy year-round the extensive outdoor public spaces in garden apartment developments.[53]

When Wyvernwood Garden Apartments, in the Boyle Heights neighborhood of Los Angeles, opened in 1939, it was the first large-scale rental housing complex in Southern California and one of the few in the entire Far West. With 1,102 apartments, it received the largest loan guarantee

Figure 3.20. Wyvernwood Garden Apartments, Los Angeles.

the FHA had yet offered. Built by developer John S. Griffith on a 72.7-acre site, the complex consisted of thirty-five two-story buildings, each generally containing four to six units. Its architects, Loyall F. Watson and David J. Witmer, hewed closely to the design principles Wright and Stein had used in Radburn. Streets curved through the large superblocks, with separate pedestrian walkways; buildings fronted on gardens, with service areas in the rear; and garages were grouped in nearby clusters.

Griffith aimed to house the families of workers employed in nearby downtown Los Angeles and close-by industrial areas. That required keeping costs and rents to a minimum, an approach the FHA encouraged as it sought to serve families with incomes below what was needed to live in many of the first projects it had insured. For housing intended for this income stratum, the agency lowered some of its standards. At Wyvernwood, prefabrication, innovative materials, and mass production techniques were employed to take advantage of economies of scale and reduce costs. Roof trusses were shop fabricated, reusable forms for concrete were created, and instead of tile, bathrooms had plystone, a glossy wall covering made by baking plastic onto asbestos-concrete backing. The building exteriors were of simple design, with little ornamentation. Through such measures, monthly rents were kept down to $29.50 to $46 a month for apartments that ranged from three to six rooms ($669 to $1,044 in 2025 dollars), the lowest rent level of any FHA-insured project.[54]

For two decades, because of discriminatory rental practices, only white renters were able to take advantage of the affordable housing Wyvernwood offered. (The initial residents were heavily Jewish.) Early FHA rental projects typically were segregated. The 1936 FHA *Underwriting Manual*, largely concerned with single-family homes but also applicable to multifamily rental properties, followed commercial industry practices in deeming the presence or likely inflow of "incompatible racial and social groups" a reason to lower valuations. A revision of the manual two years later explicitly advocated for the use of restrictive covenants prohibiting "the occupancy of properties except by the race for which they are intended." FHA administrator Stewart McDonald seemed to have little sympathy for the African American community. When FDR asked him if he had "one or two first class colored men in your Administration to look after your housing loans in Negro sections," he demurred. "The majority of lending institutions, even in the areas most thickly populated by Negroes, might be reluctant to cooperate if they were called upon by a Negro official," he replied. He added "that if any pronounced emphasis were placed upon Negro mortgage business, the free flow of money which is now coming . . . might be curtailed."[55]

While Wyvernwood marked the low end of FHA-insured rental housing, Baldwin Hills Village (now called The Village Green), located ten miles away between Crenshaw and Culver City, provided more expensive housing for middle- and upper-middle-class families. But the two projects shared many design approaches derived from earlier garden city experiments. In the case of Baldwin Hills, with Clarence Stein serving as consulting architect, the site layout represented something of a culmination of the effort that had begun in Sunnyside and ran through Radburn, Chatham Village, and the federal greenbelt towns.

Built on a very large superblock (1,100 feet by 2,750 feet), no through roads penetrated the Baldwin Hills site. Originally the project architects planned on building detached homes, but FHA guidelines pushed them to adopt the garden apartment model. Ninety-four residential buildings contained 627 apartments in a mixture of one-story bungalows, two-story apartments, and structures containing upper- and lower-level units. These buildings were positioned around a long central axis with three large greens. Apartment access came from "garage courts" behind the buildings, with a garage space and an additional outdoor parking space for each apartment, acknowledgment of the centrality of the automobile to Southern California living. A community clubhouse, where dances, art shows, lectures, and religious services were held, faced an administration

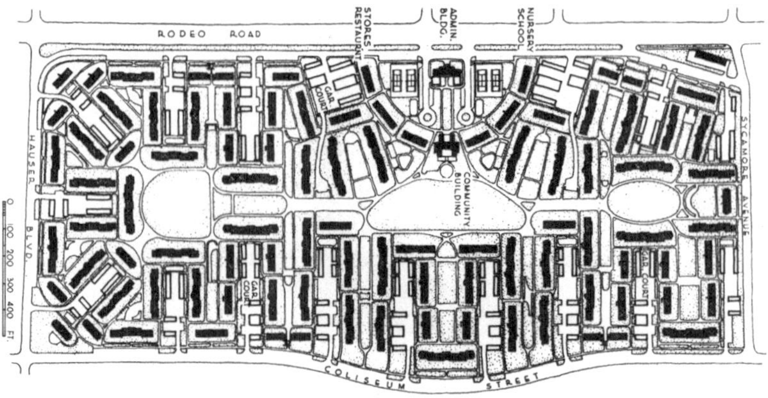

Figure 3.21. General plan for Baldwin Hills Village, Los Angeles.

building along an axis perpendicular to the greens. Rooms exceeded FHA size standards. Most apartments included a fenced outdoor patio, some had balconies, and a third had a working fireplace.

Architect Reginald D. Johnson and landscape architect Fred Barlow Jr. succeeded in giving Baldwin Hills a distinctive local feel. Rather than copying the East Coast norm of pseudo-colonial red-brick buildings, Baldwin Hills incorporated modernist elements using local building materials. The extensive landscaping made heavy use of native trees and plant species and ground coverings other than grass, which reduced the need for watering in a drought-prone region. (See plate 12.) Johnson and Barlow were so pleased with the results that both moved into the complex with their families when it opened.[56]

By the end of 1940, the FHA had insured mortgages for 317 rental projects for a total of nearly $127 million ($2.9 billion in 2025 currency). Over four-fifths of the units in these projects were in walk-up buildings—as opposed to elevator-equipped or detached structures—and in most cases they were garden apartments. The visible, well-documented success of the FHA-insured garden apartments led to the construction of at least one hundred garden apartment projects by private developers without FHA insurance, as builders and lenders saw the profit potential in the form.[57]

Private garden apartments without government mortgage insurance did not have to meet FHA standards nor were they subject to its power to limit rents and profits. Many aimed at families with incomes above those typical of residents in FHA projects. Developers even tried to return the garden apartment to its image from the period when it was aimed at well-off residents seeking semisuburban settings.

Westmoreland Gardens, a small 1940 garden apartment complex near the Little Neck station of the Long Island Rail Road in northeastern Queens, promoted itself as providing "a home life that would foster our great American ideal . . . freedom of the open spaces . . . surroundings of flowers, trees and playgrounds . . . and superb garden apartments." It was "for those people who could not afford to purchase a home in the suburbs and who desired the atmosphere, advantages, and appointments of a country residence without the expense or responsibility of maintaining such a home." William Hohauser, a well-known New York architect responsible for many office and apartment projects, including Tudor City, designed the complex for developer Conrad G. Glaser. With its buildings arrayed along the site perimeter, facing a landscaped internal courtyard, Westmoreland Gardens reincarnated Sunnyside Gardens without any of the social reform agenda associated with it.[58]

Garden Apartments for All

World War II ended the first phase of the mass production of garden apartments. As the defense buildup accelerated in 1940 and 1941, the federal government reoriented its housing programs from civilian residences

Figure 3.22. Sales brochure for Westmoreland Gardens, Queens, New York.

to dwellings for military personnel and war industry workers. Once the United States entered combat, virtually all non-defense-related housing construction came to a halt. By then, largely as a result of federal programs, the garden apartment had moved from a modest offshoot of the European garden city and social housing movements to a mass form of housing for a broad range of income groups, from the poor to the well-established middle class.

The New Deal proved the efficacy of state action to provide decent, affordable housing on a large scale. Its housing programs came as part of a broader effort to revive and reconstruct American capitalism in response to dire economic conditions and growing movements demanding change. In its push to use housing construction to provide jobs and stimulate the economy, the Roosevelt administration showed that a variety of approaches, from strictly government-built and -operated public housing to various kinds of public-private partnerships, could be used to create attractive, reasonably priced housing in settings from central cities to urban outskirts and satellite towns. The garden apartment proved well suited to the moment. Economical and quick to build, garden apartments provided modest but comfortable dwellings with privacy, light, ventilation, amenities, and green surroundings, features that were previously highly unusual for people of modest means to attain. Having demonstrated its value during the New Deal era, the garden apartment, after an interlude of war-related construction, would reach its heyday in the postwar years.

4 *The Garden Apartment Goes to War*

If you search on the internet for "Neutra" and "furniture," you will come across what is often called the Boomerang Chair, designed by architect Richard Neutra in 1942. The compact, low-slung chair has woven strips that form the seat and back, with wooden side pieces that look a bit like large boomerangs. The Los Angeles County Museum of Art has an original example in its collection, while modern reproductions can be bought for several thousand dollars. None of this is surprising, since Neutra was one of the greatest twentieth-century US architects, renowned for his beautiful, modernist houses built for wealthy Californians. What is surprising is that Neutra created the chair, along with other furniture, for shipyard and port workers who moved into a publicly owned garden apartment complex he designed near the Port of Los Angeles. The furniture, made of inexpensive materials like plywood and plastic, was meant to fit into small garden apartment rooms, providing comfort for working-class families that, in many cases, had come from far away for defense jobs, unable to bring furniture with them or not having any to bring.[1]

World War II was an interlude of sorts in the history of the garden apartment. Well before Pearl Harbor, virtually all non-war-oriented housing construction, public and private, came to a halt. With national defense an overwhelming priority, government agencies and private contractors concentrated on building residences for military personnel and workers in shipyards and armament plants, many of which were located in areas with woefully insufficient housing for the rapidly swelling workforces. More than a dozen different federal agencies—some preexisting entities that redirected their efforts toward military needs, others created specifically to build dwellings for war workers—built housing during the buildup to the war and during it. Private builders also constructed war-worker housing, taking advantage of federal mortgage insurance and other government support. By the time the war ended, some one-and-a-half million units of defense housing had been constructed. Ultimately, much of it ended up as part of the general pool of civilian housing.

Defense housing took many forms. Some of it was meant to be temporary, to be used only for the duration of the war. Trailers and dormitories were commonly constructed to that end. Of the housing built to be permanent, a great deal consisted of single-family homes, which the FHA and other federal agencies strived to make easier for defense workers to purchase. But across the country, garden apartments were erected as well.[2]

The exigencies of military necessity led to innovations in housing design and community development. For garden apartments, three stand out. One was the involvement in garden apartment design of some of the leading modernist architects in the country, including Neutra, Eliel and Eero Saarinen, Frank Lloyd Wright, Walter Gropius, Marcel Breuer, and Louis Kahn. Related was extensive experimentation with new building materials, prefabrication, and mass production techniques. Also striking was the increased involvement of organized labor in the advocacy and sponsorship of affordable housing. Taken together, these developments held forth the promise for a postwar leap in the quality and quantity of garden apartments. But even before the war ended, these new approaches to housing lost traction. World War II, rather than marking a suspension of politics, became a moment of intensified struggle over the fate of the New Deal and its social housing efforts, including one of its characteristic forms—the garden apartment.

Garden Apartments for Defense

In 1940 and 1941, as federal housing efforts shifted to national security needs, progressive housing reformers increased their sway within the federal government. This resulted from a reorganization of the agencies engaged with housing and an influx of money for defense-related construction. In July 1939, the Roosevelt administration created the Federal Works Agency (FWA) to consolidate and coordinate various government housing and infrastructure construction entities, including the USHA. To head the new umbrella agency, Roosevelt appointed John M. Carmody, a veteran New Dealer. Once war preparations were underway, Carmody sought to use defense projects, in his words, to "set a pattern for the future development of housing in America."

He was not starved for funds. In mid-1940 Congress authorized the USHA to use money originally appropriated for low-income housing projects for defense housing. It also sent $100 million (well over $2 billion in 2025 dollars) to the Navy and War Departments for defense-worker housing, nearly half of which they in turn transferred to the FWA. Just months later, in October 1940, Congress passed the Lanham Act, which authorized and funded public housing for defense workers in areas with

Figure 4.1. Gadsden Hall, a dormitory building, at McLean Gardens, Washington, DC, ca. 1950.

insufficient private construction underway. The administration also created the Defense Homes Corporation, under the Reconstruction Finance Corporation, to help finance private construction of defense housing in areas of military buildup.[3]

Before Pearl Harbor, many defense housing projects were designed with the intention of eventually recycling them to be used as permanent, civilian housing. The three largest projects undertaken by the Defense Homes Corporation were garden apartment complexes in the Washington, DC, area. To make sure that the apartments would be eligible after the war for federal mortgage insurance, the agency followed the FHA template in the design of the projects, which closely resembled prewar garden apartments. The generally high quality (and cost) of the construction had the intended effect. Today, for example, McLean Gardens, directly across Wisconsin Avenue from Sidwell Friends School, is an attractive, desirable, and not inexpensive home to more than one thousand Washingtonians. (Like many wartime projects, McLean Gardens originally included dormitories for workers living alone, but they were taken down after the war.)[4]

The explosion of the population of the Washington, DC, area as workers poured in for defense-related jobs resulted in an almost insatiable demand for housing and a proliferation of garden apartments. One strategy to quickly house defense workers was to build additional units at existing housing complexes with empty land. At Greenbelt, Maryland, in 1941, using Lanham Act funds, 1,000 new homes were added for defense-related workers. The new section of the town generally followed the design of the original settlement, though it was perhaps not quite of the same quality (or so thought Clarence Stein).[5]

In Arlington, Virginia—where in early 1943 the War Department opened its massive Pentagon headquarters—the population soared from

Figure 4.2. Parkfairfax, Arlington, Virginia, 1943.

57,000 in 1940 to 120,000 in 1944. To house the influx, forty-three garden apartment complexes were constructed between 1940 and 1945. Many of their builders took advantage of lowered FHA standards; in an effort to reduce the cost and rent of garden apartments it insured, the agency, for example, no longer required amenities such as garages or service walks. A lot of these wartime developments, like the Glenayr Apartments and the Kenmore Apartments, look like somewhat inferior versions of the pioneering Colonial Village, with red-brick colonial revival buildings but less attractive and more crowded site layouts and, in the case of Kenmore, more crudely designed structures.[6]

One of the largest Arlington garden apartment projects, Parkfairfax, was built by the Metropolitan Life Insurance Company at the request of President Franklin D. Roosevelt. The idea for it came from the army, which was worried about housing War Department workers. Metropolitan Life had recent experience with large-scale housing projects, having decided during the Depression that they would provide dependable long-term investments. Its massive project in the Bronx, Parkchester, begun in 1939, consisted of high-rise elevator buildings. But its large West Coast developments, Parklabrea in Los Angeles and Parkmerced in San Francisco, started before the war, consisted in their original phases of two-story buildings laid out in garden apartment fashion. (After the war, high-rise buildings were added to both projects.) Parkfairfax had 1,684 apartments in two- and three-story buildings, covering only a tenth of the 201-acre site not far from Washington and the Pentagon. In what had become the norm for suburban garden apartment developments, curving streets and cul-de-sacs controlled traffic, living and dining rooms faced green spaces, and community amenities were provided, including an elementary school built by the federal Works Progress Administration. The Defense Homes Corporation built an even larger adjacent garden apartment complex, Fairlington. (Its architects, Kenneth Franzheim and Alan B. Mills, also designed McLean Gardens.) That complex included more than 3,400 units by the time the war ended.[7]

Wartime Innovation

While the northern Virginia projects embraced what by then had become conventional garden apartment design, other wartime housing projects were more adventurous in their architecture, construction techniques, and ownership arrangements. The particular circumstances of the war buildup—the immediacy of the need for housing, the shortages and constraints on materials, and the uncertainty about the postwar fate of communities—made traditional design and construction techniques ill-suited to the scale of the challenge. The Lanham Act imposed a mandatory haste on construction: for projects funded under the law, the FWA had only fifty-nine days to select and purchase a site, design the buildings, prepare drawings, solicit bids, and award contracts. This breakneck timetable, along with the military necessity behind it, led to extensive experimentation with prefabrication, mass production techniques, and new materials like plywood and Plexiglas, echoing the efforts of social housing builders in Europe after World War I.[8]

The FWA, under Carmody, turned to some of the country's leading modernist architects to design housing that could be quickly erected. Many projects entailed single-family homes or dormitories, but a considerable number consisted of garden apartments or variations on the garden apartment idea. FWA leaders hoped that superior design would diminish the stigma associated with public housing, raise the housing expectations of industrial workers, and establish new templates for private construction.

Some of the architects they recruited had preexisting interest in worker housing or prefabrication. Many, no doubt, felt it their patriotic duty to participate in the defense housing program. But defense housing, more prosaically, also meant employment during a period when virtually all non-defense-related construction ground to a halt. Clarence Stein, who

Figure 4.3. Dessau-Törten Housing Estate, Dessau, Germany, 2015.

laid out a complex to house workers at a navy gunpowder plant in Indian Head, Maryland, as well as two defense housing projects near Pittsburgh, was delighted simply to be working. He wrote to his wife, "So we have a job and perhaps it will pay!" (The Indian Head site was used to test various types of prefabricated houses that could be later disassembled and rebuilt elsewhere.) Under these circumstances, the federal government proved able to hire a remarkable group of mostly young architects, many of whom were or would become world-renowned figures.[9]

To take the lead in innovation, the FWA set up the Division of Defense Housing (DDH), headed by Clark Foreman, a progressive Southerner who had worked under Harold Ickes in a variety of New Deal positions. Foreman, in turn, hired officials from other federal housing agencies to assemble a high-powered, reformist staff and recruited some of the most adventurous architects in the country. Rather than working through local housing authorities, as required of the USHA, the DDH often built complexes without local involvement, a source of tension within and without the government bureaucracy.[10]

The DDH made a bold declaration of its spiritual roots when it hired Walter Gropius and Marcel Breuer to design Aluminum City Terrace in New Kensington, Pennsylvania, outside Pittsburgh, to house workers at an Alcoa aluminum plant. Both architects had fled Nazi Germany after having been associated with the Bauhaus, in Gropius's case as its director and the designer of its famed headquarters. They brought to the Pennsylvania project their previous experience designing social housing for European workers, including Gropius's Dessau-Törten Housing Estate, built between 1926 and 1928.

In just thirty days, they completed plans for a 250-unit complex of one- and two-story buildings strewn about a difficult, hilltop site. Elements of modernist design—highly unusual in American public housing—characterized the long narrow buildings, including a combination of recessed picture windows and ribbon windows to bring in light, louvered wooden sunshades, and open floor plans, with half walls separating the kitchens from the living rooms. Though each of the Aluminum City Terrace buildings housed more units than had become typical in garden apartments (making them more like German *Siedlungen* buildings), the project adhered to many of the basic design elements of the low-cost garden apartment as it had developed over the previous decade. (Unlike prewar garden apartments, however, Aluminum City Terrace and other wartime projects did not have garages.)[11]

To design the 477-unit Centerline Defense Housing Project outside of Detroit for workers at the nearby Warren tank plant and a naval armory, the DDH hired Eliel and Eero Saarinen and their partner Robert Swanson. The Saarinen team laid out a mixture of one- and two-story buildings, each containing two to eight apartments, along garden apartment/garden suburb lines, with roads on the periphery, a large central green area, and pedestrian walkways threading the project. As in many wartime projects, individual units at Centerline were small, with a three-bedroom apartment taking up just 925 square feet. To speed construction, the architects

Figure 4.4. Aluminum City Terrace, New Kensington, Pennsylvania, 1994.

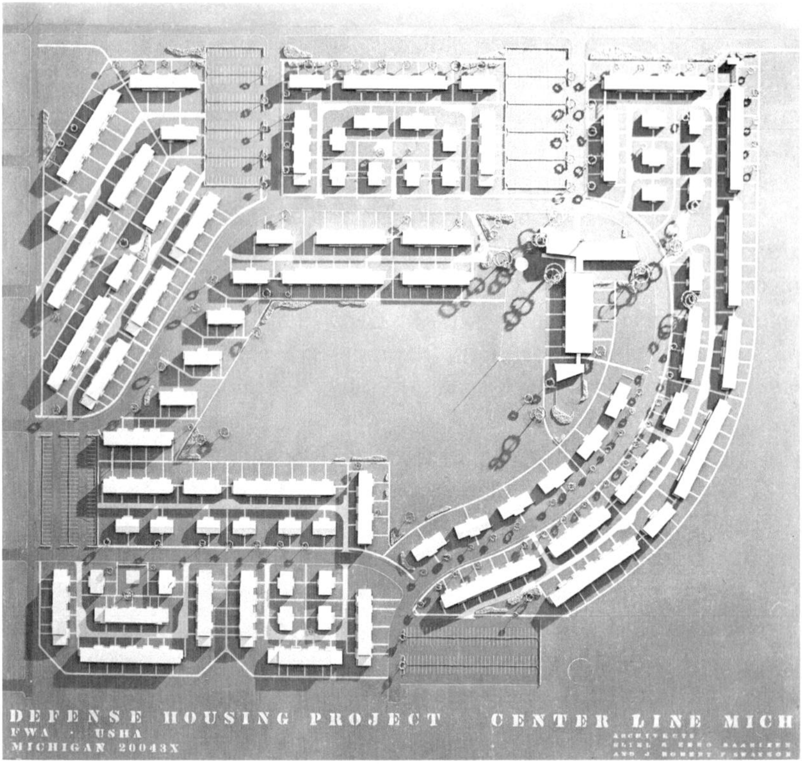

Figures 4.5a and 4.5b. Centerline Defense Housing, model (ca. 1941) and photograph (ca. 1942).

utilized modular prefabrication. To work around wartime restrictions on steel, they used redwood for columns, girders, and external cladding, staining visible surfaces red, yellow, or green. Asbestos floor tiles were laid directly on concrete slabs.

After the war ended, tenants of Centerline, 90 percent of whom belonged to the United Automobile Workers (UAW), formed a cooperative that bought the project from the federal government, renaming it Kramer Homes Co-Operative. In 2023, to buy into the cooperative cost between $5,500 and $8,500, depending on the size of the unit, with monthly carrying charges ranging from $412 to $460.[12] Eighty years after its hasty construction, the project still provided remarkably inexpensive housing for working people.

Louis Kahn was one of the most prolific defense-worker public housing architects. In partnership with George Howe and Oscar Stonorov, in 1941 and 1942 he designed seven projects, five of which were constructed. The most architecturally significant was Carver Court, built in Coatesville, Pennsylvania, for black workers at a nearby steel mill, the result of lobbying by the United Steelworkers of America.

The union involvement was not unusual. From the start of the defense buildup, individual unions and the two major national union federations, the American Federation of Labor (AFL) and the Congress of Industrial Unions (CIO), pushed hard for the construction of accommodations for war workers. The federations disagreed about prefabrication, which the AFL saw as a threat to the craft-based building trades unions affiliated with it, while the CIO, which had its main base in factories, generally supported innovative construction techniques. But for both organizations, defense housing—and public housing more generally—meant decent housing for workers and decent jobs for material producers and construction workers.[13]

Kahn's one-hundred-unit Carver Court project had a variety of multifamily one- and two-story buildings arranged in a large oval, with open space preserved in the center of the site. Most striking were the "Plan C" buildings, which rested second-story living space on vertical slabs, a design probably influenced by Le Corbusier's work. Kahn repeated this device at Stanton Road, a defense-worker housing project in Washington, DC, and used variations of it in some of his better-known postwar structures. Lifting the main rooms off the ground left the first story free for mechanical and storage spaces, porches, and open carports, the latter designed not only for parking but also as work and play areas and for possible later enclosure to add more living space. Eliminating basements reduced costs and sped up construction. With wood siding and flat roofs that overhung the front facade to provide shade, these modest but extremely handsome structures were of sufficient distinction to appear in a 1944 exhibition

Figure 4.6. Carver Court, Coatesville, Pennsylvania.

at the Museum of Modern Art. Just as its architects hoped, the design of Carver Court, which included a community center with a nursery school and an event room, promoted a strong sense of community. In oral histories, longtime residents recalled doors and windows left unlocked and myriad cooperative endeavors, including flower and vegetable gardening, endless baseball games, winter sledding, Friday-night dances, and a semiannual pig roast.[14]

The Wartime Politics of Race

Carver Court was part of the wartime continuation of the New Deal policy of building affordable housing for African American families, as well as white, Mexican American, and Puerto Rican families, but in most cases, doing so on a segregated basis. In the racially charged atmosphere of overcrowded centers of defense production, teeming with new arrivals competing for housing and services, even that could be explosive. In Detroit it resulted in racial violence that previewed more serious rioting to come.

In mid-1941, the federal government authorized a thousand units of defense housing in Detroit, a key center of military production, with two hundred units reserved for African Americans. The DDH picked a site for a housing development for African Americans in a sparsely populated industrial area not far from both white and black communities. The Detroit Housing Commission, with which the DDH worked, suggested naming the project after abolitionist Sojourner Truth.

Very quickly opposition arose to the project. At first, it included concerns from residents of a nearby middle-class black neighborhood, who were worried that the project might reduce their house values and make mortgage borrowing impossible. Their opposition faded as it became clear that the project was not to be temporary war housing but a permanent project that would be for civilians after the war. But opposition from residents of an adjacent white neighborhood proved fierce and long lasting. By January 1942, with the support of a local white congressman, it became so great that federal housing officials—by then both John Carmody and Clark Foreman had left the FWA—reassigned the project for white tenancy, promising to build housing for African Americans elsewhere. That decision created a new uproar, this time in the black community and from municipal officials, leading the federal government to reverse itself again and redesignate the project for African Americans.

On February 28, 1942, when the first black families were scheduled to move into Sojourner Truth—a collection of nondescript one- and two-story brick-and-wood garden apartments—a massive crowd of white people, recruited on an openly racist basis, gathered to try to stop the occupancy, while a large crowd of black locals gathered to support the move-in. Fighting soon broke out, leaving forty injured and 230 arrested.

In the aftermath, the Detroit Housing Commission established a formal policy not to site public housing in such a way as to change the racial makeup of a neighborhood. The next year, Detroit had one of the worst race riots in US history.[15]

The federal endorsement of housing segregation was sometimes justified as a way of avoiding racial conflict, though it clearly could cause

Figure 4.7. Flyer for demonstrations to keep African Americans out of the Sojourner Truth housing project in Detroit.

conflict as well. Conversely, some racially integrated, federally funded projects demonstrated that relatively harmonious race relations could be maintained even when open racial conflict erupted in nearby communities. Channel Heights, one of the Los Angeles garden apartment projects designed by Richard Neutra, was a case in point.

Like Kahn, Neutra—who already had done some consulting and design work for New Deal projects—became a prolific architect of defense housing, much of it innovative and modernist in design. One project, Avion Village, he undertook under the auspices of the Mutual Ownership Defense Housing Division of the FWA. The division, the brainchild of Lawrence Westbrook, a left-wing New Dealer and veteran of the FSA, constructed defense housing projects with the intention of selling them after the war to cooperative associations formed by their tenants. The mutual ownership model had been developed by Westbrook and John Green, the president of the Industrial Union of Marine and Shipbuilding Workers of America (CIO), for Audubon Village, a housing project for shipyard workers near Camden, New Jersey. Designed by Oscar Stonorov and Joseph Hettel, Audubon Village consisted largely of two-family homes, with some larger structures as well, constructed with factory-prefabricated wall and roof sections. Green, a lifelong socialist, was familiar with the Carl Mackley Houses in nearby Philadelphia. Perhaps he also knew about the earlier Milwaukee government effort at cooperative housing, which the mutual ownership plan closely resembled.[16]

Many of the Mutual Ownership projects consisted of small semi-detached homes, but Avion Village, in Grand Prairie, Texas, built to house workers at a nearby aircraft plant, incorporated many garden apartment

Figure 4.8. First family moving into Sojourner Truth Homes.

Figure 4.9. Avion Village, Grand Prairie, Texas.

features. Neutra, working in collaboration with federal staff architect David Williams and local architect Roscoe DeWitt, designed a mixture of one-story duplexes and two-story garden apartment–type units, with porches and expansive windows, which were arrayed along cul-de-sacs running toward a central green space from an oval perimeter road. The community center Neutra designed—low, attractive, and modern in appearance—included administrative offices, meeting rooms, a library, a nursery school, an assembly hall, and a kitchen. Like Audubon Village, Avion Village used prefabrication techniques, allowing the project to be completed with remarkable speed; its three hundred units were built in just one hundred days. In a stunt that attracted national attention, two teams of fifty workers apiece competed to erect a house out of premade elements in less than an hour.[17]

In Southern California, Neutra, with partners, designed four defense housing projects. Two, Pueblo del Rio and Channel Heights, were built and managed by the Housing Authority of the City of Los Angeles (HACLA), which served as an agent for the federal government for defense housing. Pueblo del Rio was a 390-unit garden apartment complex. Channel Heights, built for shipyard workers in nearby San Pedro harbor, used a mixture of one-story duplexes and two-story, four-unit buildings to house a total of six hundred families. In the neighborhood unit spirit, it included a store and market building and a building that housed a nursery school and a community center. Like several other Los Angeles public housing projects, it even included an on-site medical clinic, which residents had access to if they subscribed to a prepaid medical plan (though opposition from the local medical establishment ultimately led to its demise). Using bolder, more modernist forms than Avion Village, Channel Heights reflected Neutra's European roots, reminiscent of interwar German social housing and the style of Bauhaus, where he had briefly worked. It was for Channel Heights that Neutra designed the Boomerang Chair and other inexpensive modernist furniture.

From the start, Channel Heights had African American and Mexican American families living among the white families who made up a majority of the tenants. This was in accord with the HACLA policy, instituted in 1940, against racial discrimination in its projects, at least in areas that were not already segregated. With families arriving from all over the country—many of them from the South—to take jobs in the nearby ports of San Pedro and Long Beach and at local defense plants, what was for many a novel living situation provoked plenty of grumbles and unpleasant comments. But race relations improved over time, in part through the

Figure 4.10. Pueblo Del Rio, Los Angeles.

Figure 4.11. Channel Heights, Los Angeles.

Figure 4.12. Interior of a Channel Heights apartment, with custom furniture designed by Richard Neutra, including a Boomerang Chair.

very active efforts of a residents' council. Even during the venomous LA Zoot Suit Riots, things remained calm at Channel Heights. The project was later sold to commercial developers and torn down.[18]

While public housing had a mixed wartime record in serving Americans equally, private housing built for war workers and the military did far worse. At the end of 1944, African Americans had received 10.2 percent of all "priority" housing built for those serving war needs. But only 1.6 percent of privately financed housing went to African Americans. Robert Weaver, testifying at a postwar Senate hearing, argued that while in part this reflected "the delayed migration of colored labor to war centers," more important was the "traditional hesitancy of private enterprise to build for Negro occupancy and the difficulty of finding vacant sites for such construction." Private construction of racially integrated housing apparently was so rare that Weaver did not even bother discussing it. At Parkfairfax, Metropolitan Life not only banned African American residency, but it kept out Jews, too, in a project largely inhabited by civilian professionals engaged in the war effort and members of the military.[19]

Pushback

The period of defense buildup constituted an extraordinary moment when housing reformers, left-wing New Dealers, labor leaders, and progressive architects came together, hoping to use the defense housing emergency to launch a postwar program to house working people in modern dwellings that were situated so as to not only provide safe green space but also to promote the growth of democratic ideas and institutions, including public and cooperative ownership of homes. At a time when many of the boldest New Deal experiments in art and culture had already ended, some of the most imaginative architects in the country developed variations on the garden apartment that combined sophisticated site planning with aesthetically attractive, highly functional, and inexpensive buildings.

For a while, it looked like housing reform dreams might be realized. Some 167,700 units of federally funded housing designed to be permanent went up during the defense buildup and the war, most between 1940 and 1942. Some modernist architects saw such projects as key to the future of their profession. At the end of the war, Richard Neutra worried that "unless Canada and the United States take the lead in the development of contemporary architecture, with particular emphasis on housing for low income groups, they will be outpaced by the war-torn nations of Europe."[20]

But the window for experimentation proved narrow. The accomplishments of the liberal-labor-modernist alliance that emerged during the defense buildup did not reflect a fundamental change in the balance of forces that had severely constrained the prospects for social housing in the Housing Act of 1937. Rather, they grew out of short-term opportunities created by the 1939 reorganization of federal housing agencies; the impact of the appointment of a few key progressive housing officials, including Carmody, Foreman, and Westbrook; and the chaotic dash to get defense housing up as quickly as possible. By the time the United States entered combat after Pearl Harbor, a strong pushback already was underway that would shut down the possibilities for using defense housing to set the standards and agenda for postwar construction.

The usual opponents of public housing—principally real estate interests and congressional conservatives—found an opening to take on the defense housing program in the scale of need for dwellings for war industry workers. Though by prewar standards the FWA had moved quickly to put up new structures, it fell far short of the urgent necessity for living space for hundreds of thousands of defense workers. Rather than building permanent housing, which would be repurposed for low-income families and the general public after the war, critics of the defense housing program called for the construction of strictly temporary quarters that could be quickly and cheaply erected without worrying about durability or threatening established real estate interests. Another source of opposition to the defense housing program, Carmody believed, came from local politicians who did not want new voters, who might not support them, moving into their districts.

Every time Congress debated additional appropriations under the Lanham Act, critics of the defense housing program managed to chip away at it, limiting the discretion of housing officials and pushing back at the notion that public housing should provide anything above the most rudimentary shelter. The opposition mindset was captured in April 1941, when members of Congress, upset that some defense housing projects had provided residents with electric refrigerators and ranges, added an amendment to the Lanham Act forbidding the inclusion of "moveable equipment" in defense houses unless it was specifically deemed in the "public interest." That fall, a special Senate committee led by Harry Truman, investigating defense spending, held hearings on the housing program, piling on criticism.[21]

Local architects joined the attack, taking aim at the hiring of architects from outside their regions for defense housing projects, especially modernists with sensibilities different from the mainstream of the profession. The issue came to a head in a controversy over a proposed one-hundred-unit DDH project for Pittsfield, Massachusetts, an important industrial center, designed by Frank Lloyd Wright. DDH head Foreman, committed to involving cutting-edge architects in the defense housing program, personally offered Wright a contract for the Pittsfield project in mid-1941. Foreman's own office then took charge of it, rather than leaving it to the agency's New England unit.

Wright came up with a design for what he called "Cloverleaf" buildings, four-apartment structures so arranged that the residents of each unit had virtually complete privacy, with their own entrance and private yard, a sophisticated take on the garden apartment idea. (See plate 13.) Wright's innovative plan soon ran into objections from Massachusetts architects, miffed that government work had gone to an outsider. Massachusetts Congressman John McCormack took up their cause with Foreman, who tried to blow off his objections with talk about architectural excellence and developing models for future low-income housing. But McCormack, not Foreman, was in tune with the times.

The issue was not just local architects but also local aesthetic and cultural norms. In congressional debates going on about amending the Lanham Act, even as the fate of the Wright project was up in the air, Texas Congressman Fritz Lanham, who gave the act its name, proposed that housing under it should be required to conform to "local city planning and city traditions" and involve a local architect. Lanham complained, "I have seen pictures of some housing done under this act . . . which I do not believe would be decent housing in any community." Truman agreed, reporting that the committee he chaired "found that most defense housing under the original Lanham Act has been built without sufficient consideration for local conditions and problems." "In many instances," he added, "the architectural design of the housing units is foreign to anything ever erected in that community."[22]

The debate over the defense housing program ended in an across-the-board conservative victory. In November 1941, Carmody left his post heading the FWA, claiming ill health, and transferred to a less taxing position as a member of the Maritime Commission. USHA administrator Nathan Straus, who bitterly complained that Carmody had shut him out of the defense housing program, while at the same time coming under heavy congressional criticism as a leading proponent of public housing, was the next to go, in early January 1942. Straus claimed that he was told that, unless he resigned, the Senate would agree to a Lanham Act amendment proposed in the House, which would forbid the postwar sale of defense housing projects to local public housing authorities, requiring instead their sale to private buyers. In any case, by then Straus had thoroughly alienated Roosevelt's key advisors with his attacks on other agencies. Foreman was forced out, too, in his case as a result of pushback against the Sojourner Truth housing project, with Carmody no longer there to protect him.[23]

With the exit of the reformers who so irritated Congress and the expectation of changed policies, in January Congress appropriated more money under an amended Lanham Act. In late February 1942, Roosevelt, hoping to further placate Congress, followed the call of his longtime advisor, Samuel I. Rosenman, for a "a complete reorganization—ruthless in nature" of federal housing efforts. Giving critics of the defense housing program (and of public housing more generally) most of what they wanted, the president consolidated sixteen federal agencies in a new National Housing Agency headed by John B. Blandford Jr., a former general manager of the Tennessee Valley Authority. Blandford committed to using 90 percent of new defense housing funding for temporary structures. Building them became primarily the responsibility of the Federal Public Housing Authority, which took over the responsibilities and programs of the USHA and the FWA (whose Defense Housing and Mutual Ownership divisions disappeared as separate entities). The new agency paid greater deference to private housing interests and had less taste for modernist architecture and cooperative ownership than either of its predecessors. While Roosevelt professed to strongly support social housing, he was unwilling to use political capital to defend it. Going from "Dr. New Deal" to "Dr. Win-the-War," as he later put it, he abandoned the use of wartime housing to set a postwar trajectory. Instead, the government focused only on meeting defense needs. With the changes, "for the first time since the construction program started," *Architectural Record* noted, "the Administration has divorced the social aspects of the housing campaign from the immediate exigencies of the critically short housing situation."[24]

Even as Congress forced the administration to curtail its program of publicly built permanent housing, it took steps to encourage the construction of privately owned rental housing for war workers. In March 1941, Congress added a new Title VI to the National Housing Act to insure mortgages for war-worker housing. In a departure from past practice, it allowed insurance on 90 percent mortgages for one- to four-family homes to be issued to builders and investors, not just owner-occupiers. This proved to be a highly popular program, with 329,618 mortgages insured as of September 30, 1945. In May 1942, section 608 was added to the title, authorizing insurance for mortgages and construction loans for large-scale rental projects for war workers. Though only 473 mortgages were insured under section 608 as of September 30, 1945, after the war it would, in revised form, become enormously important in the proliferation of privately owned garden apartments.[25]

Ultimately, roughly the same number of dwellings for war workers were constructed by the private sector as by the government, each contributing about three-quarters of a million units. The vast majority of privately owned dwellings were one- to four-family homes. By contrast, public housing mostly consisted of larger rental projects, though it also included a substantial number of dormitories, trailers, and other kinds of "stop gap shelter."[26]

Limits and Achievements

The political and organizational reconfiguration of the defense housing effort, just months after Pearl Harbor, meant that some of the most ambitious wartime projects were never built. The ten-thousand-unit "Defense City" the UAW proposed for workers at the massive Willow Run aircraft plant outside of Detroit illustrated the limits on wartime social housing. The union went as far as commissioning Stonorov and Kahn to develop plans for the community, to be built with prefabrication methods. Their proposal included structures with a strong resemblance to the "Plan C" buildings at Carver Court and incorporated extensive communal facilities. Some of the most prominent figures in the labor-liberal alliance that animated the New Deal pressed for its authorization, including Eleanor Roosevelt, UAW president R. J. Thomas, and Sidney Hillman, the president of the Amalgamated Clothing Workers and associate director of the federal Office of Production Management. But amid shifting wartime politics, the project faced strong opposition from local real estate interests; the Ford Motor Company, which ran the aircraft factory; and some members of the UAW, who preferred single-family homes to the multiunit housing proposed by the union. With a hot potato in his hands, FDR asked his uncle, Frederic A. Delano, chairman of the National Resources Planning Board, to study the issue. In the end, Delano killed the project, arguing that it could not be built quickly enough to meet immediate needs, suggesting instead various short-term measures.[27]

The defense housing that did get completed provided a powerful demonstration that well-designed garden apartment complexes, some with modernist touches still rare in the country, could be quickly built at affordable prices. The wartime housing effort suffered from organizational chaos, competing demands for material, and extreme haste. Nonetheless, it demonstrated how much could be accomplished if government resources were mobilized on a large-scale, expedited basis.

The early successes of the defense housing program made clear what a threat public housing posed, ideologically and economically, to the private real estate industry. The backlash, supported by congressional forces hostile to both public housing and aesthetic modernism, proved unstoppable at a time when the political power of New Deal liberalism was in steep decline.

The degree of innovation in the design and construction of garden apartments during the war would not be matched after it. But the retreat from wartime innovations did not mean an end to garden apartment development. While the most forward-looking and expansive versions of the garden apartment never reached full realization, humbler and more utilitarian versions would, on a scale previously unimagined. Most of the history of that plebian utopia, the garden apartment, still lay ahead.

5 *Garden Apartments Everywhere*

When infantry private first class Harold Freeman, my father, came back to Brooklyn after fighting his way across Europe, he was among the fortunate ones to have a home to return to. Older than most soldiers, before the war he and my mother, Beatrice, had rented an apartment in a new, six-story apartment building, where she remained during his absence. When he took a job in Philadelphia a few weeks after his discharge, his luck held out, as he found an apartment near Fairmount Park, big enough for the two of them and then for their baby daughter, too. But when Beatrice became pregnant again, they needed more space, which proved very difficult to find amid the worst housing crisis in the history of the country. Finally, they reserved an apartment in a garden apartment development under construction in Haddonfield, New Jersey, across the Delaware River from Philadelphia. A couple of years later, when my father took a job back in New York, the story repeated. For five months my mother, sister, and I stayed in Haddonfield while my father slept at his parents' apartment in Brooklyn and searched for a new home. Finally, he again managed to rent a garden apartment in a complex not yet completed, this time in Queens.[1]

Millions of veterans had it far worse. When the fighting stopped in 1945, the United States faced a massive housing shortage. Housing construction had dropped precipitously during the early years of the Great Depression, rising only modestly with the implementation of New Deal housing programs. The wartime ban on residential construction, except for defense workers, exacerbated the situation. When GIs returned home hoping to start new households, they found it nearly impossible to do so. Many went back to living with their parents, doubled up with friends or relatives, or moved into army barracks, Quonset huts, or abandoned schools designated for temporary veteran housing. In early 1946, one federal housing official declared that it would take 2.7 million new units of housing over the next two years "only to take the edge off the demand and be a beginning upon the need." As late as 1951, New York City veterans and their families were living in barracks at military posts around the city

Figure 5.1. The Freemans at Wallworth Park Apartments, Haddonfield, New Jersey.

and in schools and tenements converted to emergency housing. Nationally, in the mid-1950s, some two million married couples or single-parent families still lived with relatives, unable to find homes of their own.[2]

There was nothing unanticipated about the shortage. During the war, economists, housing reformers, real estate operators, unionists, and public officials wrote extensively about the need for postwar housing, proposing various schemes to address the predicted crisis.[3] The federal government took some steps to promote postwar housing construction, including a provision in the 1944 GI Bill offering mortgages to veterans on very favorable terms. But the main effort to develop an omnibus postwar housing program, the bipartisan Taft-Ellender-Wagner bill, failed to win passage. The legislation included provisions to increase available credit for private home construction, facilitate privately built rental projects, encourage slum clearance, fund public housing, provide mortgages for cooperative housing, and support research into innovative building methods. It won backing from some veterans' organizations, the labor movement, the Catholic Church, and public housing officials. But opposition from builders, material producers, lenders, and the American Legion, all of whom hoped to check the trend that had begun during the New Deal toward ever-greater state involvement in the housing market, helped kill the measure.

Even if it had passed, the bill would have provided very limited immediate help to veterans looking for a place to live. For one thing, many of its provisions would have facilitated construction of dwellings too expensive for most veterans to afford. For another, it did nothing—and really could do nothing—to address the most immediate obstacle to providing new housing, the acute shortage of building materials in the face of the wartime diversion of inputs to military needs. When on October 15, 1945, the federal government lifted wartime restrictions on home construction, nothing happened; it would still be a long wait until building materials became available.[4]

The dire situation made housing a more prominent issue than at any other time in United States history. In Washington, state capitals, and city halls, politicians debated plans to meet the housing needs of veterans and the general public. Veterans' groups, unions, political parties, and housing reform organizations pressed for action. Discharged soldiers and sailors took to the streets. In St. Louis, in December 1945, ex-GIs formed a "Veterans Committee on Housing and Jobs" and, with their wives, picketed city hall, demanding that homeowners be allowed to rent rooms to boarders (banned under zoning laws at the time) until better housing became available. In New York, veterans and their allies fought for the continuation of rent control; picketed office construction sites, insisting that building materials be redirected toward apartment construction; and, in October 1946, occupied the New York State senate chamber for nearly a day, demanding that the governor call a special session of the legislature to deal with the housing crisis. In Los Angeles, to house veterans the housing authority converted army and WAC barracks into "light housekeeping apartments" and a defense-worker dormitory into "kitchenette-type units." It also placed hundreds of trailers and Quonset huts into city parks. But it was not enough. In 1947, with the housing shortage still acute, 1,500 veterans, some with their families, camped in a Los Angeles park to protest.[5]

The housing shortage and veterans' protests placed intense pressure on the federal government to do something to alleviate the crisis. As Congress continued to debate a possible omnibus housing act, most federal officials saw individually owned, single-family dwellings as the ideal form of housing for veterans and everyone else. The New Deal, if anything, had

Figure 5.2. Quonset hut residences in Rodger Young Village, a temporary Los Angeles housing project, built in Griffith Park.

reinforced that long-standing American faith. FHA commissioner Raymond M. Foley wrote that "real home ownership is to be encouraged as typically American—and essential to America." But even such officials realized that in the short term there was no way to adequately house the nation by relying only on owner-occupied dwellings. Given the massive need for housing and the difficulty, for many, of affording to buy a home, even with a GI Bill loan or FHA mortgage insurance, government leaders encouraged the construction of rental housing as well. In late 1946, President Harry S. Truman declared, "The main point of emphasis for 1947 is rental housing. . . . More family units must be made available for rent to veterans. They should not be compelled to buy in order to get shelter."[6]

Section 608

The main vehicle for promoting postwar rental housing was what had been an obscure provision of the National Housing Act, section 608, added by Congress in 1942. In its original form it promoted private-sector construction of rental housing for war workers by offering mortgage insurance that made lending for such projects essentially risk free. In May

1946, as part of a law establishing a federal Housing Expediter to speed up housing construction and hold down home prices, Congress amended section 608 to give priority to projects for "veterans of World War II and their immediate families." Garden apartments made up the bulk of dwellings produced under section 608, though it provided support for other forms of rental housing as well. More garden apartments were built under this long-forgotten FHA provision than as a result of any other government effort.

To attract builders and investors to section 608 projects, terms for insured mortgages were liberalized. Working capital requirements were reduced and longer loan amortization allowed, reducing developers' monthly obligations. Rent caps were set to yield 6.5 percent after-tax returns, a slightly higher profit rate than historically allowed for government-aided philanthropic and limited-dividend housing. Also, the Bureau of Internal Revenue allowed more rapid depreciation of rental housing, which, as a government brochure promoting section 608 housing informed potential investors, "reduces tax requirements, and permits a larger net return from earnings." Application and approval procedures were streamlined. FHA personnel, the government announced, were "available to help private sponsors plan rental projects and expedite processing of applications."[7]

These measures contributed to the success of section 608. But an unpublicized aspect of the program contributed to its achievements as well. The FHA, without ever explicitly saying so, administered section 608 in such a way that developers could make substantial profits before any tenants moved into the apartments they constructed. This was important because during the postwar period the prospects for making money from ongoing operations were uncertain, ironically due to another federal program meant to aid people of modest means—rent control. Instituted as part of the general price controls put into place during World War II, federal rent control continued in some parts of the country until 1950 to prevent landlords from taking advantage of the severe housing crunch by jacking up rents. Thereafter, some states picked up the program. So in addition to rent limits the FHA could impose on section 608–insured projects, other controls on rent might apply as well. Rent control presented a problem for developers not only because it limited revenue from their own projects but also because it meant that they had to compete with older buildings with rents capped at lower levels. In an inflationary period, when labor, tenant, and consumer groups backing rent control had considerable political clout, the economic calculus for building rental housing looked very uncertain.[8]

But shrewd investors had no reason to worry. Their main tool for making money was to take out a mortgage, insured by the FHA, for an amount greater than the cost of construction. Section 608 allowed mortgages for up to 90 percent of the estimated "necessary current cost" of a project. Builders, sometimes with the connivance of FHA officials, routinely submitted applications with estimated costs considerably higher than what they anticipated they actually would spend. The excess mortgage money was then distributed to the owners of the projects as profits, what was known as "mortgaging out." The completed projects bore the burden of unnecessarily large mortgages, but the mortgage providers, often local banks, faced no risk since the FHA insured the loans. The excessive carrying costs of the mortgages could be used to justify higher rents. Tenants, in effect, were forced to pay for the developers' upfront profits. Some developers also profited by leasing land they owned at inflated prices to projects they were developing or by charging their own projects excessive fees.[9]

Such shenanigans could be quite profitable. The owners of the Gross-Morton Co., which built Glen Oaks Village, a 2,904-unit garden apartment complex on the eastern edge of Queens, put up only $90,000 in capital stock, then borrowed $26,759,000. The project ended up costing only $21,740,367. Out of what a Senate investigating committee deemed a "windfall" of $5,018,633, the owners of the company paid themselves dividends of approximately $4.6 million, their profit prior to any revenue from renting the apartments they built. They also received $108,794 annually for leasing to the project the land on which it was constructed.[10] Other profiteers from 608 mortgaging out included members of the Tishman family, then and now a major force in New York City real estate; several du Ponts; and Fred Trump (Donald's father). Trump used loans guaranteed through section 608 to build six-story apartment buildings in Brooklyn and garden apartments in Staten Island.[11]

Rather than criticizing developers who mortgaged out, the federal government extolled their success in quickly erecting garden apartments for veterans. Gross-Morton made a twenty-two-minute film, *Story of Glen Oaks Village*, celebrating the rapidity of its construction using mass production techniques; the cooperation of the FHA, which had an on-site office to approve construction details; and the quality of the resulting community. The United States Information Service bought rights to the film for its overseas public diplomacy effort. To spread the story of garden apartment America, it translated the movie into fourteen languages, including Bengali, Gujarati, Hindi, Urdu, Tamil, Turkish, Serbo-Croatian, Swedish, Spanish, and French. Viewers on the Indian subcontinent could learn, "Here is apartment living without the confinement of the usual city apartment house. . . . Here is suburban living without the trouble of keeping up a home."[12]

In spite of, or because of, the corrupt practices associated with it, the

Figure 5.3. Glen Oaks Village under construction, 1947.

FHA 608 Veterans' Emergency Housing Program succeeded in what it was intended to do: produce a lot of affordable housing, and quickly. Between May 1946, when Congress amended section 608 and section 603 (which insured one- to four-family dwellings) to serve veterans, and September 1947, developers completed 551 projects containing 27,500 units that utilized loan guarantees under the programs, with another 32,000 units under construction. The large majority of these units were garden apartments. Most were not in sprawling developments like Glen Oaks Village but in small clusters. The typical 608 project had roughly twenty apartments. By the end of March 1948, over 66,000 units had been completed. By the time the program wound down in 1953, 469,644 units of 608 housing (wartime and postwar) had been built. That is roughly the same ratio of housing units to population as for current public housing of all kinds; in 2020 there were 907,550 units of public housing in the United States, for a population twice as large as in 1953. The average household in 1950 consisted of 3.51 people, so in the early 1950s it is likely that close to 1.4 million people lived in section 608 dwellings, mostly garden apartments. Section 608 is the largest housing program no one has ever heard of.[13]

The proliferation of 608 rental housing was an example of government assistance and sharp financial practices together resulting in both windfall profits and genuine social advances. Making money through overcapitalization and self-dealing, rather than ongoing operations, was nothing new. Many nineteenth-century railroad and streetcar fortunes, for example, were made this way. But the section 608 projects were unusual in their link between nonoperating profits and affordable housing. In effect, the FHA promoted, or at least looked away from, abuse of its insurance program to fulfill the Truman administration's desire to quickly provide rental housing for veterans.

The windfall profits of section 608 developers were sometimes publicly justified because they led to a social good, much like the rationalizations for questionable railroad profits in the nineteenth century and for oligarch fortunes made from the privatization of state industry after the collapse of communism in the Soviet Union and Eastern Europe. *The Architectural Forum*, though generally critical of the 608 program, opined in 1950 that the "combination of public risk and private profit is perhaps the only way an apartment building boom could have got started under rent control, which suspends the normal action of supply and demand on all postwar housing." In testimony to the Senate Committee on Banking and Currency four years later, William J. Levitt, then America's most famous builder for his development of the Levittowns on Long Island and in Pennsylvania, declared:

> The title VI program, both sections 608 and 603, was a program of desperation. You had no building for 5 solid years and you had a tremendous amount of people who needed to be housed. In all commonsense you would never have gotten any builder over the age of 16 to go in and venture either time, trouble, money, or anything else and get the volume of housing that had to be gotten. Certain evils had to be experienced. . . . I think it should be borne out that while sections 603 and 608 were moneymakers, the housing was produced.[14]

Cooperative Housing

In addition to for-profit rental garden apartments, the FHA insured mortgages for cooperatively owned garden apartments, facilitating their production as well. Within the New Deal, there always had been some interest in cooperative housing, evident in the original plans for the Resettlement Administration garden cities. The National Housing Act of 1934, which created the FHA, included a provision, section 207, that allowed mortgage guarantees for limited-dividend cooperatives. During and immediately after the war, interest in what at the time was often called "mutual housing" grew, reflected in and stimulated by the federal program of cooperative housing construction for war workers. The wartime interest of organized labor in cooperative housing continued after the war. Some unions set up housing entities, hoping to sponsor cooperative developments for their members, with federal support.[15]

Ironically, one of the first large-scale postwar cooperative garden apartment complexes, Bell Park Gardens in Bayside, a neighborhood in Queens, was created not by New Dealers or leftists but by a Republican state administration and traditionally conservative veterans' groups. Herman T. Strichman, who headed the New York State Division of Housing from 1944 to 1955, serving under Republican governor and two-time presidential candidate Thomas Dewey, revived the use of the 1926 New York State Limited Dividend Housing Companies Act to promote housing for families in "no man's land." These were families "with incomes too large to be eligible for low rent public housing and not large enough to afford the prices charged for new speculative private construction." The state law offered housing developers, including cooperatives, an exemption from state taxes and, if a municipality agreed, reduced local taxes in return for limiting annual profits to 6 percent or less.

To build Bell Park Gardens, Strichman put together a sponsoring entity, the United Veterans Mutual Housing Company, backed by the union of New York City firemen, the Brooklyn and Queens chapters of the American Legion (including the chairs of their "Americanism" committees), and the Veterans of Foreign Wars of Queens. The participation of the American Legion, a notoriously conservative group, in nonprofit, government-backed cooperative housing was a measure of how broad the coalition was for using public resources to house veterans and how relatively uncontroversial cooperative housing was at the time. Residents provided capital in the form of down payments of about $240 per room ($3,244 in 2025 dollars), while the FHA provided mortgage insurance under section 207. With the eight hundred Bell Park Gardens units fully occupied from their completion in 1950, the sponsoring group and the state rapidly moved to build two similar complexes nearby.[16]

Strichman also arranged for the use of the 1926 law to facilitate a large, union-sponsored cooperative housing project, Electchester, a few miles away. In lauding that effort, Governor Dewey laid out the conservative case for co-ops: "We just simply cannot tax the people to the extent that would be necessary to give government housing, with its free services, to all. Furthermore, American citizens who are not in the lowest wage-earning groups do not want to live in housing that is being paid for by somebody else; they want to pay their own way as much as possible."[17]

To further facilitate nonprofit cooperative housing, Congress added a new provision to federal housing law in 1950, section 213, that allowed

Figure 5.4. Bell Park Gardens brochure. Note the World War II "ruptured duck" honorable service lapel pin.

the FHA to insure mortgages for such projects with enhanced terms if they largely served World War II veterans. As of September 1953, 29,728 apartments had been built with section 213 insurance. Many, though not all, were garden apartments.[18]

Epicenter Queens

The roughly 400,000 postwar FHA-insured garden apartments, privately or cooperatively owned, were scattered all over the country, though not evenly. Every state in the union had section 608 projects (as did Washington, DC, Alaska, Hawaii, and Puerto Rico), ranging from 736 projects with 85,807 units in New York State to 3 projects with 43 units in North

Dakota. The heaviest concentrations were in and around New York City, Washington, DC, Baltimore, Chicago, and Los Angeles.

Many big-city complexes had hundreds or even thousands of units. Smaller cities, suburbs, and towns housed projects that were generally more modest in scale. While Glen Oaks Village, with 2,904 apartments and an associated shopping center, built by a large, experienced development company, represented one end of the spectrum, Saratoga Apartments, 160 miles north in Saratoga Springs, New York, was more typical. Taking up one square block, with forty-four apartments in two-story, red-brick buildings, the project was developed by three local lawyers, using an FHA-insured mortgage issued by a local bank.[19]

Queens, New York, was the epicenter for postwar garden apartments, much like Arlington County, Virginia, was the prewar and wartime epicenter. In the dozen years following V-J Day, at least thirty garden apartment complexes were built in the borough, together providing more than 23,048 living units. At least 16,425 of these were in section 608 projects. Another 5,954 were part of FHA-insured cooperatives.[20]

Flying into one of the two Queens airports during the postwar decades, garden apartments would have been impossible to miss. Their superblock layouts interrupted the street grid, and their still raw landscaping left highly visible the recurring modules of two- or three-story buildings, situated around grass courtyards, with garages and parking areas lining

Figure 5.5. Rendering of Saratoga Apartments, Saratoga Springs, New York.

their perimeters. Near the middle of the borough, an airplane passenger might have spotted Parkway Village, the 675-unit development where Betty Friedan lived. Nearby were several other large complexes, including Grand Central Parkway Gardens (386 units), Arrowbrook Gardens (326 units), Campus Hall Apartments (930 units), and Kew Gardens Hills (1,269 units), all 608 projects. Farther east lay the Bell Park Gardens (800 units) and Bell Park Manor and Terrace (847 units) cooperatives. And still further east, approaching the Nassau County border, lay more large projects, including Glen Oaks Village and three cooperatives built for veterans, Clearview Gardens (1,788 units), Beech Hills (816 units), and Deepdale Gardens (1,396 units).[21]

Queens became a center for garden apartments because of several characteristics particular to the borough. Probably most important was simply that it had a lot of available in-city open space. Much like the parts of Frankfurt and Berlin where pioneering social housing was built after World War I, undeveloped land in Queens, not very far from the city center, presented an unusual opportunity for commercial developers and housing reformers alike. Glen Oaks Village, the most distant of the Queens garden apartments, lay just fourteen miles from Times Square.

Some Queens garden apartments were built on what had been farmland. Others covered sites of former golf clubs (a few of which moved farther east on Long Island). Glen Oaks Village occupied part of what had once been the William Vanderbilt estate. The land for Bell Park Manor and Terrace had been a nursery. Other complexes were built on vacant land.

This fit the national pattern. Generally speaking, garden apartments, at least those that were privately built, were not part of urban redevelopment or slum clearance, in which older buildings were torn down to make room for new ones. Rather, they were constructed on undeveloped urban outskirts or land elsewhere with few or no existing structures. This kept land acquisition and construction costs down. In Los Angeles, at least a dozen garden apartment complexes were built in 1949–50 alone, almost all in suburban areas close to freeways, then being threaded through the city. Garden apartments arose in inner suburbs and small towns as well.[22]

Almost certainly, the vast majority of Queens garden apartment dwellers moved to their new homes from a rental apartment. New York was a city of renters. Nationally, in 1950, in cities with 100,000 people or more, 59 percent of households rented their dwellings. In New York City, 81 percent did, more than four out of every five families. The rich, the poor, and everyone in between found nothing unusual or degrading about not owning a home, with upward mobility often conceived of as moving to a bigger or better rental apartment rather than as homeownership. Just as renting a garden apartment fell into a well-established New York pattern, so did cooperative garden apartment living. Both high-end and working-class cooperatives had strong footholds in New York even before the war. Furthermore, there was an institutional structure to support cooperatives in New York. Not surprisingly, New York had by far the largest concentration of section 213 cooperatives in the country.[23]

Garden apartments were not restricted to New York City proper; plenty were erected in surrounding suburbs, too. In Great Neck, just over the city line from Queens and generally thought of as a wealthy community, Great Neck Terrace and Village Garden had, between them, more than seven hundred garden apartments.[24] Westchester County, just north of New York City and home to many upper-class families, had garden apartment complexes in several of its cities and towns.[25] In northern New Jersey, wrote one reporter, "garden apartment buildings are a little like pizzerias—there's at least one in every town."[26]

Embracing Banality

Looking at postwar garden apartments, it is often hard to tell where you are. Most postwar garden apartments look strikingly similar to one another and are often virtually impossible to distinguish from nearby complexes or, for that matter, from complexes hundreds of miles away. Nor are they easy to distinguish from the very first FHA-insured garden apartment developments, like Colonial Village and Buckingham Community, built in Arlington, Virginia, well before World War II. In effect, postwar garden apartment design stepped back from the technical and architectural innovations during World War II to return to prewar norms. Once again, garden apartments—except those in the West—typically had the red-brick, quasi–colonial revival, courtyard designs that had been perfected during the New Deal years.

The primary reason for the postwar spurning of wartime modernism and the embrace of a functional but banal design norm lay in the increasing conservatism of the FHA. Through its review of plans for projects seeking insurance, it effectively had a veto on all architectural, construction, and landscaping issues. As it had before the war, rather than simply responding to the proposals of architects and developers, the FHA proactively issued design guidelines, published suggested apartment configurations, and publicized completed projects as models for new ones. For the most part, these mimicked prewar designs. The more daring wartime projects, carried out by other federal agencies, had little impact on the FHA.[27]

The FHA balanced financial considerations with concern for the quality

Figures 5.6a and 5.6b. The prewar Buckingham Community, Arlington, Virginia (left), and the postwar Ridgefield Apartments, Poughkeepsie, New York (right).

of life of tenants. For section 608 projects, it initially had a loan limit of $1,800 per room; in 1948, the limit was raised to $8,100 per apartment. (The switch from a room to an apartment cap had the unintended consequence of leading many developers to pack their buildings with small "efficiency" units, which allowed them to borrow more for a given amount of floorspace than would be possible with larger apartments.) FHA guidelines promoted the use of durable, low-maintenance materials and cost containment, in part to make sure that insured mortgages would be paid off. "Elements of elaboration of decorative effect and special equipment constitute *luxury* quality," declared a 1947 FHA guide, *Planning Rental Housing Projects*. "Sound investment demands that essential quality be . . . not sacrificed to accommodate elements of luxury."

FHA guidelines did seek to maintain good standards for apartment design from a tenant point of view. Minimum "desirable" dimensions for different types of rooms were specified, though at rather small sizes. A two-bedroom apartment at Arrowbrook Gardens (section 608) in Queens measured only 597 square feet. At Beech Hills (section 213), also in Queens, two-bedroom apartments were a touch larger at 603 square feet. But with no hallways, all the square footage went to living space.

Detailed FHA guides for room layout promoted privacy, light, and good ventilation. Kitchens and bathrooms at Arrowbrook Gardens and Beech Hills had windows (in later years this was not always the case, even in luxury apartments), and at Beech Hills bedroom windows faced two directions. The FHA strongly advocated for a key feature of garden apartments, a low percentage of land coverage, leaving substantial space for landscaping and

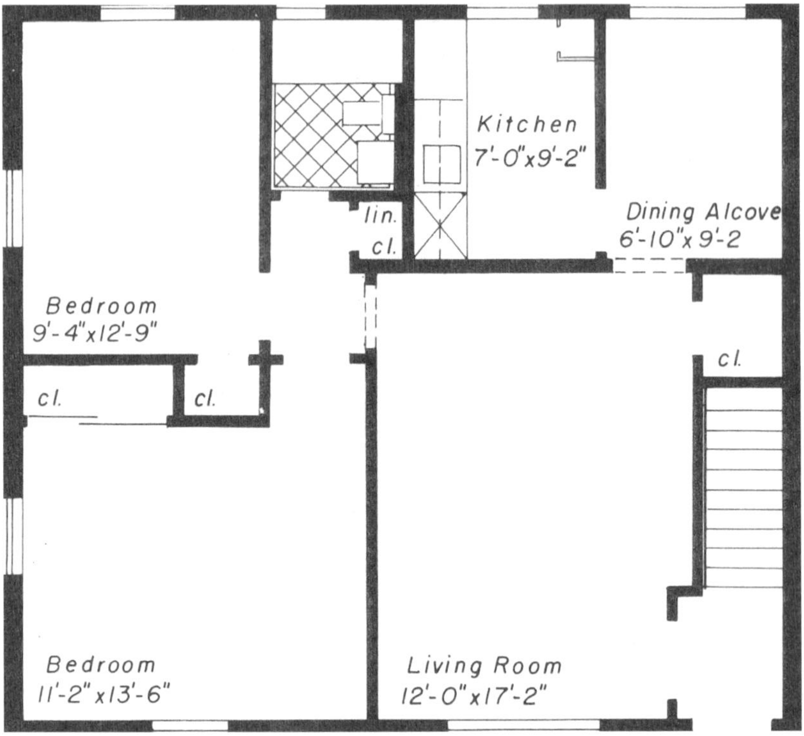

Figure 5.7. Floor plan for two-bedroom apartment, Beech Hills, Queens, New York.

play areas and providing green views from most rooms. No detail was too small to overlook; federal officials even specified how many towel bars there should be in a bathroom and their recommended length.[28]

The FHA had a distinct design aesthetic. While claiming that it did "not set up standards of architectural styles," it nonetheless declared "simple, direct designs which rely for their effect upon mass, scale, and proportion are more attractive to tenants, and the resultant structures are sounder investments, than those which strive for picturesque or unusual effect by means of over-ornamentation or bizarre use of materials. . . . The design should be appropriate to the section of the country in which the property is located, to climate and topography, and to the mode of living common to the area." In practice, this meant that the FHA generally spurned extremes of modernism or elaborate decoration for simple, stripped-down, if sometimes handsome, buildings. What minimal decoration it approved often consisted of simplistic attempts at regionalism, like the neo-colonial touches commonly used in the Northeast or the California ranch style embraced in Los Angeles. Rather like the contemporaneous socialist realism that shaped residential construction in Eastern Europe, the FHA promoted clichéd, backward-looking elements of regional style, even as it embarked on a radical experiment in mass, state-assisted, affordable housing.[29]

The architecture profession recognized the deficiencies in section 608 project design. In 1950, the New York chapter of the American Institute of Architects (AIA) issued a report calling the housing produced under the program "mediocre" and "substandard." It criticized in particular "excessive standardization" and "glorification of the minimum standard," echoing the concerns Oscar Stonorov had raised years earlier in regard to public housing. The report bemoaned too-small rooms, insufficient privacy, and the lack of fire-resistant construction. The FHA, it argued, lacked personnel with the training, experience, and competence to provide sympathetic evaluations of high-quality architectural submissions, resulting in the encouragement of quick, cheap, undistinguished design. The AIA report did acknowledge that many architects had a "disdainful" attitude toward the section 608 program, which it recognized had made an "unprecedented contribution" to relieving the postwar housing crisis. In any case, the report did not seem to have any effect; New York–area garden apartments built after its release differed little from earlier projects.[30]

Some garden apartments built with FHA insurance did have more distinctive architecture, departing from what became standard templates for site layout, material choice, and unit design. But it took a determined effort to do so, as FHA officials looked down on deviations from established norms. As *The Architectural Forum* put it, "as the agency and its standards aged, its initial crusading fervor was buried under an impregnable conservatism." Courtyard layouts, for example, proved highly successful for creating safe environments for families, with plenty of light and air, but FHA officials tended to insist on the mechanical application of this device even on topographically ill-suited sites.[31]

The financial structure for 608 projects also mitigated against innovative design. Under FHA guidelines, developers were allowed to include in their cost estimate 5 percent of the total project cost for architectural fees, but many developers spent much less than that to hire an architect. The difference between 5 percent and the real cost could be taken as profit through mortgaging out. The AIA report complained about the small fees and little authority developers gave to architects. It recommended that sponsors be required to prove that stipulated fees for engineers and architects were actually paid. Low fees, along with the rigidity of the FHA, made cookie-cutter design an attractive path.[32]

Garden apartment developers, not looking for originality, often hired journeymen architects without much of a profile in the profession. Some had experience working for the government. Benjamin Braunstein, who designed Glen Oaks, Beech Hills, Clearview Gardens, Deepdale Gardens, and Hollis Court Gardens, among other projects in New York—a total of over 9,000 units—previously worked for the federal Home Owners' Loan Corporation. William Dowling, who designed four Queens projects with nearly 4,000 apartments, had been the senior designer for the New York State Housing Division. Erwin Gerber, a prolific designer of garden apartments in New Jersey and Queens, had been a deputy chief architect at the FHA.[33] Unlike during the Depression and World War II, well-known architectural innovators, finding lots of other work available, rarely took on garden apartment assignments. The modernist designers of defense-worker housing, who became postwar architectural stars, moved on to other types of projects.[34]

There were exceptions. Ralph Vaughn, the lead architect for Lincoln Place Apartments, a 795-unit complex in Venice, California, near a giant Douglas Aircraft Co. factory, was among the most successful African American architects of his generation. He worked in a rare interracial partnership with Heth Wharton. Lincoln Place had a strikingly stylish design—a mixture of one-story "cottages" and two-story buildings, with unusual, varied fenestration, indented balconies, and large roof overhangs. (See plate 14.) Vaughn and Wharton designed two other Los Angeles garden apartment projects as well. Stanley H. Klein, the architect for Grand Central Apartments in Queens, later achieved a moment of fame when a single-family home he designed was replicated for the 1959 United States exhibition in Moscow. It was in that building that the "kitchen debate" between Vice President Richard M. Nixon and Soviet leader Nikita S. Khrushchev took place. Leading Houston architect S. I. Morris and his partners, who together went on to design the Astrodome, built a sixteen-unit cooperatively owned garden apartment development, with section 608 insurance, for themselves and their associates to live in. Among its unusual features were breezeways between apartments (to which the FHA initially "objected strenuously") and wide overhanging eaves. But more usually, the overwhelming characteristic of garden apartments was their lack of character, their anonymity, their dissolution into the background rather than standing out as a symbol of an important social initiative.[35]

The templates and guidelines from the FHA allowed what one architectural magazine dubbed "amateurs" to build 608 projects. At least two dentists found fortune by becoming developers through the federal program. One ended up with "a string of racehorses and a cruiser on which to entertain jockeys." The other boosted his net worth from $50,000 to $2 million in just six years. Other developers were more experienced. Ray A. Myers, one of the owners of Lincoln Place, cut his eye teeth building gas stations, sounds stages, and single-family homes before erecting thousands of units of wartime housing. Gross-Morton Company, before developing Glen Oaks, constructed thousands of single-family homes and some multiunit dwellings.[36]

Postwar Racial Practices

Critics of FHA racism have sometimes overstated their case, as when Arnold Hirsch wrote that "the FHA's adherence to good 'business' practice virtually excluded non-whites from the enjoyment of the agency's benefits."[37] Though most 608 sponsors were white, African American builders also put up FHA-insured projects, almost always specifically for African American residents. W. H. Aiken, for instance, built hundreds of rental houses during World War II before developing West Lake Apartments, an eighty-unit FHA-insured garden apartment complex in Atlanta. But if the FHA facilitated the construction of some rental housing for African Americans, it did its best to keep government-backed developments from becoming racially integrated.

As before the war, most postwar garden apartment developments, at least at first, served residents of only one race. The FHA supported segregation in its multiunit rental programs, just as it did for single-family homes. Though the 1947 *FHA Underwriting Manual* no longer referred to "racial groups," it euphemistically warned about the dangers of incompatible "user groups" living together or in proximity. "Compatibility among neighborhood occupants," according to the manual, had to be factored in when rating lending risks. The FHA continued to insure mortgages for properties with racial covenants until 1950, two years after the US Supreme Court ruled them legally unenforceable in *Shelley v. Kraemer*. Even when no formal bars prevented black families from moving into white garden apartment complexes, siting or informal practices often kept them out.[38]

That was not always the case. Racial integration was the very reason

Figure 5.8. West Lake Apartments, Atlanta.

Figure 5.9. Gladys Weaver and her son Lester at Merrick Park Gardens as it was being built. She and her family moved into the co-op as soon as it was completed.

for the existence of Parkway Village. The New York City government, as part of its effort to attract the headquarters for the newly created United Nations, pledged to find housing for its staff and the diplomatic corps. But an arrangement to lease apartments at Peter Cooper Village in Manhattan and Fresh Meadows in Queens collapsed when their owners, Metropolitan Life Insurance Company and New York Life Insurance Company, refused to agree to rent apartments on a nondiscriminatory basis to non-white UN delegates and employees. As an alternative, the city arranged for the construction, by a private developer, of Parkway Village, just off Grand Central Parkway in Jamaica, Queens. The UN rented the entire complex for five years, subletting to outsiders the apartments its own affiliates did not fill. Civil rights leader Roy Wilkins lived in the complex, as did diplomat and Nobel Peace Prize–winner Ralph Bunche.[39] Another, much smaller, garden apartment complex in Queens, Merrick Park Gardens, announced that it, too, would accept tenants "without regard to race, color or religion." Developed as a cooperative by a white lawyer, William Brafman, Merrick Park Gardens received FHA mortgage insurance under section 213.[40]

As notable as Parkway Village and Merrick Park Gardens may have been, they were islands of integration in a sea of all-white or nearly all-white garden apartments that sprang up in Queens after the war. One census tract in northeastern Queens, composed primarily, but not exclusively, of Glen Oaks Village, in 1950 had only seven "Negro" residents among its population of 8,398. Ten years later, with the completion of the smaller, adjacent Grand Central Apartments, the population in the tract had grown to 11,059, but the "Negro" population had risen to only eighteen, less than two-tenths of a percent of the total in a city that was more than 13 percent African American.[41]

Racially exclusive residential patterns in New York largely resulted from informal practices, cultural codes, and siting rather than explicit regulations enforcing segregation (though some building owners, like Metropolitan Life, did have such rules). What is remarkable is not the extension of segregation as New York expanded outward—that was happening all over the country—but that it took place in a city and state that had strong nominal commitments to ending racial inequality. During the postwar decades, New York City had a very active, multifaceted movement against racial discrimination. In 1945 the New York State legislature passed the first state law in the country against discrimination in employment and set up a State Commission Against Discrimination. A prolonged fight ultimately forced Metropolitan Life to end its ban on African Americans in its massive Stuyvesant Town development in Manhattan and contributed to the passage of laws in 1950 and 1951 that effectively banned discrimination in state- and city-aided housing projects. Nonetheless, for decades Queens garden apartment complexes—including those filled with tenants committed, at least in the abstract, to brotherhood and integration—remained for the most part racially homogeneous.[42]

The mass construction of garden apartments contributed to a deepening of residential apartheid. No data exists to allow for a precise calculation of the national extent of racial segregation in garden apartments, but all indications from individual projects suggest that it was the norm in the immediate postwar years, in some places as a result of formal bars on race mixing and in other cases even in their absence. Government and private policies related to single-family homes probably had more impact than those related to garden apartments because they imposed patterns of segregation and discrimination over vast swaths of newly built suburbia as the United States transitioned from a predominantly urban country to one in which suburban living became dominant. But, in a more limited way, garden apartments helped segregate and resegregate America. As massive interregional and intraregional population shifts occurred after World War II, the development of housing on a segregated basis played a major role in the reproduction of racial inequality.[43]

Public Housing

FHA-insured private and cooperative projects accounted for most of the garden apartments built after World War II, but public housing construction contributed to their spread as well. In 1949, after four years of maneuvering, a bipartisan coalition in Congress won passage of a revised version of the Taft-Ellender-Wagner bill. In a last-ditch effort to block the bill, Senate conservatives introduced an amendment banning racial and ethnic discrimination in public housing, hoping to split the Southern Democrats and liberal Northerners supporting the bill, but the Northern senators accepted segregation as a price they were willing to pay for public housing; they joined with Southern Democrats to kill the amendment and then pass the bill. Among other things, the Housing Act of 1949 authorized the construction of 135,000 units of public housing per year for the next six years. Rents in the funded projects had to be 20 percent below the lowest rent for comparable units in their area and priority had to be given to World War I and II veterans and residents displaced by slum clearance projects.

In practice, nothing like the authorized number of dwellings were constructed by the mid-1950s. For one thing, the Korean War and then Republican control of Congress limited spending. Also, during the Korean War, the government again restricted access to building materials. For another thing, many housing authorities found it difficult to design projects that met the $1,750-per-room cap written into the law (24 percent less, adjusted for inflation, than the cap Congress instituted for section 608 housing). But perhaps even more important was a massive campaign against public housing led by the real estate industry. Among its most effective tactics was to force localities to hold referenda on the construction of specific projects, in most cases leading to their defeat.[44]

Still, public housing did get built in cities large and towns small. Many big cities in the Northeast and Midwest moved entirely to high-rise structures. New York City, with far more public housing than any other metropolis, constructed only one more garden apartment–style public housing project after completion of Clason Point in 1941, the Edwin Markham Houses, built on Staten Island during World War II. Thereafter, it erected only larger-scale apartment buildings.[45] But some major metropolitan housing authorities continued to build garden apartments. The Chicago Housing Authority, even as it put up many high-rise projects, built three postwar garden apartment complexes: LeClaire Courts, Racine Courts, and Lowden Homes, together containing well over five hundred units.[46]

The Housing Authority of the City of Los Angeles, which already operated multiple garden apartment developments built before and during

Figure 5.10. Racine Courts, Chicago.

World War II, constructed three garden apartment complexes during the 1950s and added units to several existing projects.[47] Mar Vista Gardens, in the Del Rey neighborhood on the west side of Los Angeles, with 601 apartments in sixty-two two-story buildings, opened in 1954 as the first public housing project in the city built using funds from the Housing Act of 1949. Because of funding limits and the desire to maximize the number of apartments available at a time of continuing housing shortages, the Los Angeles housing authority designed it with greater density, less green space, and lower standards than characteristic of earlier city projects. With an average of nine units per building, the Mar Vista structures were unusually large for garden apartments. Architect Albert Criz positioned the buildings parallel to one another, perpendicular to surrounding streets, with one central green space, rather than placing them around courtyards. A history of the project described the building interiors as "utilitarian in design and layout," while the exterior design, also "utilitarian," had "International Style influences, seen in the low-pitched roofs, common prefabricated materials, horizontal bands of windows, and minimal ornamentation."[48]

One year later and ten miles away, in Watts, the Los Angeles housing authority opened an even larger garden apartment development, Nickerson Gardens. With 1,064 apartments, it was the largest public housing project

Figure 5.11. Mar Vista Gardens, Los Angeles.

in the western half of the United States. Designed by prominent African American Los Angeles architect Paul R. Williams, it consisted of two-story buildings similar to those at Mar Vista, but with a more sophisticated site layout featuring courtyards and varied placements. (See plate 15.) The project included a community center with a large auditorium, meeting rooms, a communal kitchen, and a snack bar. Like other Los Angeles public housing, it was racially integrated.[49]

The Housing Authority of New Orleans, also using funds from the Housing Act of 1949, topped the Los Angeles developments with its Desire Street garden apartment complex, 1,860 apartments crammed onto a site of less than one hundred acres. It exemplified low-rise public housing at its worst. Built to accommodate the growing postwar African American population in the city (and strictly segregated), the housing authority sited the Desire development on soggy land that had been a dump, largely cut off from the rest of the city. Over seven hundred black families and twenty black-owned businesses were evicted to make way for the project. Opened in 1956, within two years it had 13,450 residents, making it the most densely populated area of the city. The thousands of children living in the project had access to only a single playground. While prewar New Orleans public housing projects had been built to high standards, the city constructed Desire cheaply and shoddily. Instead of concrete foundations and solid masonry or brick walls, the buildings had wooden foundations and wooden outside walls, covered with brick veneer. Almost immediately, settling on the wet ground led to problems, including water and gas leaks, separating stairs, and dampness inside. Even so, some residents remembered it as "a 100 percent improvement" from their previous dwellings, a testament to how poorly Louisiana African Americans were housed.[50]

Far more numerous than the big-city projects were modest public housing developments in smaller cities and towns. Southern white leaders embraced public housing and the federal funds it brought with exceptional enthusiasm, as long as segregation reigned. One hundred and eighteen Georgia communities set up local housing authorities, along with 111 in Texas and 84 in Alabama.

Though it is hard to identify a typical small project, Hollinsworth Grove, in Little Rock, Arkansas, with 180 units, might fit the bill. Opened in 1952 and funded by the 1949 housing law, the one- and two-story garden apartment buildings came about as part of an urban redevelopment scheme meant to preserve and deepen racial segregation. As the local housing authority cleared black neighborhoods downtown, it built public housing on the urban periphery, far from white neighborhoods, to house the displaced residents. This fit a common Southern pattern of using urban renewal and public housing to push African Americans out of center city areas into new, highly segregated communities.[51] Or one could choose the forty-six-unit, single-story garden apartment complex belonging to the Midland City Housing Authority in southeast Georgia, a modest, small-town project outside of the small city of Dothan. Like privately

Figure 5.12. Desire public housing, New Orleans.

owned garden apartments, publicly owned garden apartments popped up just about everywhere.[52]

"The Right of Every Family to a Decent Home"

The huge wave of garden apartment construction after World War II directly stemmed from government action, most importantly the addition of section 608 to existing federal housing law and the Housing Act of 1949. Both represented, in very compromised form, expressions of the New Deal vision of state responsibility for fulfilling what Franklin Roosevelt, in his 1944 "Economic Bill of Rights," called "the right of every family to a decent home."

By the time World War II ended, a national shift away from the political left stripped the ability of the New Deal coalition to pass its most ambitious measures, including not only the original Taft-Ellender-Wagner housing bill but also a proposal for a system of national health insurance, the creation of additional Tennessee Valley Authority–type regional development agencies, and a full employment bill that would have committed the government to ensuring a job for every person who wanted one.[53] But the national housing crisis and the moral and political claims of veterans made housing one of the few areas to see a postwar extension of the New Deal. The result was a limited program that used government resources to facilitate for-profit, private-sector garden apartment development and to build public housing for the poor.

Postwar federal housing efforts built on principles established by the New Deal, but compared to undertakings before and during the war, they proved diminished in imagination and standards. The kind of architectural innovation in PWA-funded projects like the Carl Mackley Houses or defense-worker housing like Carver Court was almost entirely absent in postwar projects. Communal amenities in postwar projects paled in comparison to those in some earlier efforts. And in public housing, basic standards for construction quality, density, recreational facilities, and the like were generally below those in projects built a decade or two earlier, as was painfully evident in the differences between the Lafitte and Desire housing projects in New Orleans.

But lots of decent garden apartments were built as a result of government action, and at a very low cost to taxpayers. The FHA charged builders who received 608 mortgage insurance an annual premium of one-half of 1 percent of the value of their mortgage. These premiums and various fees more than covered government costs, including liabilities associated with defaults. In 1941 Congress allocated $5 million ($112 million in 2025 dollars) to establish the War Housing Insurance Fund, which was used to guarantee mortgages under sections 603 and 608, as well as several small, related programs. By June 1954, the fund had not only repaid the original allocation with interest but had a cumulative net income of $119 million. The government had invested less than a dollar (in current currency) per person in the United States and had gotten all its money back, accumulating a profit on the operation.[54]

The cumulative cost of garden apartment–style public housing is impossible to calculate because the relevant data is not disaggregated by building type. But the cost of public housing of all types to federal, state, and local governments was remarkably small. During the decade following the passage of the Housing Act of 1949, construction was started on 588,000 units of public housing. In those years, federal, state, and local government agencies together spent $816 million on public housing and some additional housing subsidy programs. With a US population of 161 million in 1955, that meant that public housing was costing on average about fifty cents per person per year. Even calculating in inflation (fifty cents in 1955 was the equivalent of $5.95 in 2025), this was a very cheap program.[55]

For all their deficiencies and for all the missed opportunities, postwar garden apartments made a significant dent in the desperate need for housing after the Second World War. For my family, it meant—twice—getting a comfortable, modest-cost apartment in the middle of a national housing crisis. Garden apartments, for families who could not afford to or did not want to buy single-family homes, provided an attractive alternative. In doing so, they helped sustain urban life as the great rush to the suburbs began, while also making suburban living possible for some families who otherwise might not have been able to move.

Section 608 proved to be one of the most successful public-private social provision programs in the history of the United States. For millions of Americans, moving into a garden apartment after World War II brought a great improvement in their daily lives. Even as the country grew reluctant to endorse a further expansion of state action for social welfare, garden apartments proved how beneficial such action could be.

6 *The Experience of Community*

What was it like to live in a garden apartment? The great variety of projects and the diversity of their residents make generalizations difficult. But in contemporary accounts and later recollections, certain themes appear over and over.

A Child's World

For children, garden apartments meant the freedom to roam. Marina Budhos, remembering Parkway Village: "a summer evening . . . I am twelve, still nestled in half-childhood. . . . Now is the time when doors open, voices call out, teenagers start to rove the Green and the playgrounds like summer phantoms." With the warm nostalgic glow, characteristic of such accounts, she recalled, "Tribes of children rove up and down these private roads, coalescing, regrouping, surprised by the discovery of yet another group, one courtyard over." Not far away, in Bell Park Gardens, it was the same. Jan Oxenberg remembered it as "like a paradise for kids . . . It was like you never had to be home. . . . We were running in packs." So many children were out that they could play games like ring-a-levio that required huge groups.[1]

Publicly owned garden apartments were no different. Randall DeGroat, a former resident of LeClaire Courts, a racially integrated project near Chicago's Midway Airport, recalled, "As kids growing up there we never had boring days." Dan Perkins grew up in the Desire Street Housing Project in New Orleans, which lacked many of the amenities other developments had. But he, too, had fond memories, especially of children everywhere. Play facilities were woefully inadequate: "we had to wait our turn to get on the swing, some time we had to wait two days to get on a swing!" So the Desire children took things into their own hands. "We made fun. We found pleasure. . . . We had no other choice. . . . They always say no good thing came outta this project, but they were wrong."[2]

Figure 6.1. Grand Central Apartments, Queens, New York, January 1954.

Community

Among adults who lived in garden apartments, a sense of community comes to the fore in their recollections. Sandra Walton remembered of LeClaire Courts, "The camaraderie was absolutely wonderful. . . . We all took care of each other like a village." When a family had a financial setback, sometimes neighbors would hold a rent party to help them get through.[3] Linda Allen said of Fairlington, in Arlington, Virginia, "We have a standing joke here. This is the best place to go through a crisis: the death of a spouse, the death of a child, divorces, cancer, whatever. People seem to know when there is trouble and they just show up and take over the children or the cooking or the shopping. There is always someone to organize." Blanche Smith recalled Carver Court in the post–World War II years as "a village of love and togetherness." For Betty Friedan, much of

Figure 6.2. Children at the Pueblo del Rio housing project, Los Angeles.

her attraction to Parkway Village lay in the strong sense of community she felt there. Claudette Warren said of the Calliope Housing Project in New Orleans, "Even though it was public housing, it was like a big family."[4]

The familial atmosphere at garden apartments sometimes reflected literal family ties. Jesús Hermosillo recounted how at Wyvernwood, in Los Angeles, children who grew up in the project married one another, moved into apartments of their own in the complex, and started families. Commonly, residents had cousins, aunts, and uncles living in the development. Adrian Woods, who grew up in the Desire project, remembered being surrounded by family: "My oldest sister lived on the second porch. And then the second oldest sister lived in the porch behind us, and my grandmother lived downstairs from us. . . . it was very family oriented. Whether they were related to you or not, you know, everybody was your cousin."[5]

With community came a sense of security. Budhos, who grew up in Parkway Village a generation after Friedan moved out, recalled "a sense of safety too—at each end of the complex stands concrete pillars, demarcating that you are entering a different, protected space. Inside we are safe, reassured by the pattern of interlocking brick buildings, a sameness that has gathered us all together." Tina Lincer, raised in Bell Park Gardens, looked back

Plate 1. Kerry James Marshall, *Watts 1963*, acrylic and collage on canvas, $115\frac{3}{8} \times 137\frac{7}{8}$ inches, 1995.

Plate 2. Corlies Manor Apartments, Poughkeepsie, New York.

Plate 3. Bell Park Gardens, Queens, New York.

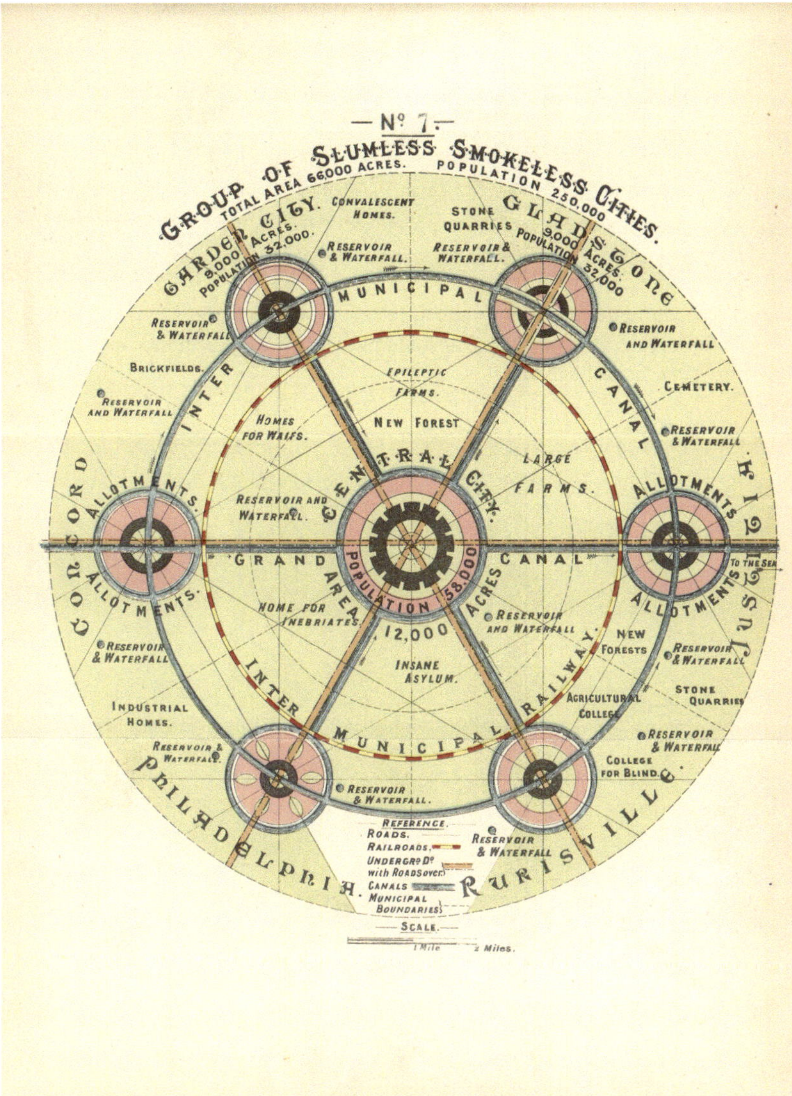

Plate 4. This diagram, from Ebenezer Howard, *To-Morrow: A Peaceful Path to Real Reform*, illustrates how clusters of garden cities might be laid out to house a population of a quarter million.

Plate 5. Worker housing in Port Sunlight, the company town near Liverpool, built by William Lever starting in 1888. The buildings bear a striking resemblance to later American garden apartments.

Plate 6. Karl-Marx-Hof, Vienna.

Plate 7. Gartenstadt Falkenberg (Falkenberg Garden City), Berlin.

Plate 8. Siedlung Schillerpark, Berlin.

Plate 9. Großsiedlung Britz, Berlin, also known as the *Hufeisensiedlung* (horseshoe settlement).

Plate 10. Clason Point Gardens, Bronx, New York.

Plate 11. Tindall Heights, Macon, Georgia.

Plate 12. The Village Green, originally Baldwin Hills Village. The pictured landscaping replaced the original design following a 1963 flood.

Plate 13. Frank Lloyd Wright's design for an unbuilt Pittsfield, Massachusetts, defense worker housing project.

Plate 14. Lincoln Place Apartments, Venice, California.

Plate 15. Nickerson Gardens, Los Angeles, 2024.

Plate 16. WPA poster, ca. 1940.

Plate 17. Chase Knolls Garden Apartments, Los Angeles.

Plate 18. Wyvernwood, Los Angeles, 2023.

Plate 19. Racine Courts Co-operative, Chicago.

Plate 20. The new Valencia Gardens, San Francisco.

Plate 21. Centennial Place, Atlanta.

Plate 22. Faubourg Lafitte, New Orleans.

"with an appreciation of not only the physical shelter it provided but the emotional harbor it was, too. . . . We were safe, surrounded by family and neighbors who watched over us, and legions of kids. We made friends for life." Neighbors kept children in line; in LeClaire Courts, Sylvester White recalled, "everyone's father could act as your father, everyone's mother would be yours, especially if you got out of line."[6]

Strong community feelings developed in other types of housing during the postwar decades. But garden apartments, unlike most dwellings, were designed specifically to promote community and keep children safe from cars and the outside world. (See plate 16.) Whether conscious of it or not, garden apartment developers operated within a set of rules and assumptions derived from the prewar idea of the "neighborhood unit" and experiments with creating safe green space in new towns and settlements. Budhos wrote of her childhood home, "Parkway was a concept born out of the belief that a community could be molded, created from scratch with just the balance of privacy and shared space. It has worked: they have sealed us into a new kind of identity, a local village out of world origins."[7]

Spatial arrangements spawned social ties. Lewis Mumford recalled from his experience in the 1920s and '30s living in Sunnyside Gardens that "when Sunnyside began to grow, no one had anticipated that in a few years its layout would help to generate a more active social life once people of different vocations, interests, and appetites were drawn so conveniently together." Group interactions were facilitated when the development set up ad hoc community rooms in building basements and then built a freestanding community center.[8]

In a 1960 article reviewing sociological studies of wartime housing projects and postwar suburbs, Herbert Gans, a leading scholar of community life, reported that "social relationships appear to be influenced and explained by *propinquity*. As a result, they are affected by the site plans and the architectural design." Courtyards, narrow road loops, and cul-de-sacs were particularly effective in bringing residents into contact with one another.[9]

Garden apartments had those features to bring people together, and much more. As Tina Lincer recalled of Bell Park Gardens, "Nearly everything was shared, including playgrounds, lawns, laundry rooms, drying yards, garbage rooms and stoops." Design devices, pioneered in Radburn and Chatham Village, for separating vehicular and pedestrian traffic meant that, typically, when garden apartment residents stepped out of their homes, they entered protected spaces where casual encounters could take place, lawn chairs be planted, and children let loose. "Court parties" were a regular feature of life at garden apartment developments to celebrate birthdays and holidays like New Year's Eve and the Fourth of July. At the Lafitte project in New Orleans, shared porches and balconies, as well as courtyards, “encouraged neighbors [to] get to know each other, and many residents helped each other with childcare.”[10]

An extreme example of garden apartment community occurred at Wyvernwood following a 1987 earthquake that badly shook the Los Angeles region. By then, the project’s population had become overwhelmingly Hispanic. Much less information about the quake, ongoing risks, and government action was available in Spanish than in English, leaving Wyvernwood residents with the sense that they had to fend for themselves. Fearing aftershocks and building collapses, residents of the development, many of whom had lived through earthquakes in Mexico or Central America, decided to sleep outdoors in the days that followed. In short order, the residents erected a communal campsite in Wyvernwood’s open spaces. Families with stalls at local markets contributed tarps, others brought tents and blankets, and communal cooking facilities were set up. The ad hoc outdoors community functioned in lieu of normal living arrangements until people were convinced that it was safe to return to their homes.[11]

Sharing had its downsides. “Living in close proximity,” Lincer remembered, “meant you could smell your neighbors’ meatloaf wafting through the screen doors or see their Fruit of the Looms blowing on the clotheslines. It meant that my father, a mild-mannered man and Army private who never made it to the front, was transformed into a citizen warrior when he pounded on the ceiling with a broom handle to quiet the wrestling boys upstairs after their parents went out on a Saturday night.” Maurice Washington found his new apartment in Nickerson Gardens Housing Project spacious and attractive, but he could hear his neighbor’s music through his bedroom wall. Neighborly relations in garden apartment developments, negative as well as positive, tended to be thick.[12]

Garden apartment design could undermine a sense of security as well as promote it, depending on the social circumstances. Washington moved to Nickerson Gardens as a nine-year-old in 1981. “At first sight, the projects were a huge, mind-blowing labyrinth of off-green structures connected to one another that seemed to go on and on . . . and on . . . gated off, isolated and a world all to itself.” But not a safe one, with gangs a pervasive presence. While still a child, a gang murder took place behind his apartment. “My environment was a manufacturer of thugs.”

Gangs and violence stemmed from larger social conditions and could be found in many types of communities. But the typical garden apartment layout facilitated gang domination. Interior spaces set away from the street, behind buildings or between them, were easier for gangs to control than sidewalks or front yards with cars continually passing by. Police were often reluctant to go into internal project areas, which they might have to enter on foot. Courtyards could become zones of danger. Living in a courtyard meant that you could not walk straight from a car into your apartment or get a taxi to pick you up at your front door.[13]

Collective Activity

In many garden apartment complexes, numerous committees, organizations, and activities promoted community life. Cooperatively owned projects, which by their very nature required a certain level of community organization, had especially robust goings-on. The *Long Island Daily Press* wrote in 1957 that while many people who bought co-ops "did not expect to find a new way of life," once there they discovered an unusual degree of community, with art classes, camps for children, weekly mahjong and poker games, block parties, and the like, along with the shared governance of the projects themselves.[14]

At Bell Park Gardens, in addition to the board of directors, which had ultimate authority over the cooperative, there were resident committees dealing with everything from a children's summer play program to civilian defense (a Cold War obsession). *Bell Park News*, sponsored by the residents' Community Council, came out monthly. The complex had an annual blood drive, a choral group, a Boy Scout troop, a dieting club, a literary club, a credit union, and a veterans' affairs group. Trips were organized to museums, for weekend gateways, and to dinner dances.[15]

While these types of activities could be found in many postwar communities, not just garden apartment complexes, their sheer density at Bell Park Gardens made it, by American standards, unusually communal. A few programs fell entirely outside the boundaries of usual national practices. Soon after families began moving into Bell Park Gardens in August 1949, a Community Council committee arranged for health care to be offered to residents through the Health Insurance Plan of Greater New York (HIP), with the premiums collected at the same time as the monthly maintenance fee (the equivalent of rent for the cooperative owners). HIP was an innovative, nonprofit, prepaid medical service plan initiated in 1944 by the New York City government, health reformers, and labor unions. In just a short time, well over half the residents signed up for the program, with Blue Cross hospitalization insurance soon added. At the time, most Americans had no health insurance. What health insurance there was either came through expensive individual plans or through employers, often as a result of union-negotiated arrangements. Offering health care coverage through the home, as part of rent, rather than through the workplace, represented a radically different approach, decoupling social benefits from employment. Such an alternative path might have led to different shapes for both the national welfare system and the labor movement. Though the Bell

Figure 6.3. "Home Counselors inaugurate annual inspection of apartments," Housing Authority of New Orleans.

Park–HIP experiment remained exceptional, it expressed the expansive, democratic social vision of the garden apartment cooperators. So did the decision, when a surcharge was added to the Bell Park Gardens maintenance fee, to scale it to residents' income levels, with zero, twenty-five, and fifty percent brackets.[16]

Rental garden apartment complexes were less likely than co-ops to host collective institutions, but some had a strong communal feel. Parkway Village had a seemingly countless number of community activities. During the 1950s, mothers in the development created a cooperative nursery (as did those at Electchester). Like Bell Park Gardens, it had its own newspaper, *Parkway Villager*, which Betty Friedan edited from 1952 to 1954.[17]

Many public garden apartment complexes also had extensive community activities and institutions. At the Lafitte project, at least in the early years, the Housing Authority of New Orleans offered courses on cooking and nutrition, took children to the local public library, put on fashion shows, and had programs for the elderly. To some residents' dismay, the Housing Authority also had "home counselors," who did household inspections for cleanliness and "good housekeeping." Later the community had its own basketball, swimming, football, and volleyball teams and the Sojourner Truth Community Center, built as a result of tenant organizing.[18]

At the Mar Vista Gardens Housing Project in Los Angeles, the city's Department of Recreation and Parks ran programs for children, taking advantage of the community building constructed as part of the project. Tenants at Mar Vista and other Los Angeles public housing developments (and in other cities, too), elected resident advisory councils, some of which eventually had their own offices within the complexes and took on some managerial responsibilities.[19]

Homogeneity

In his look at postwar communities, Gans argued that while "propinquity brings neighbors into social contact, a certain degree of homogeneity is required to maintain this contact on a positive basis."[20] The dense web of communal life in postwar garden apartments reflected a high level of shared experience. Garden apartments abounded in homogeneity, of many kinds.

Age was one. The first occupants of Bell Park Gardens were typical of postwar garden apartment residents. Most were part of young families,

Figure 6.4. "Mar Vista Gardens Housing Project, Community Activities, Community Building, under Sponsorship of Los Angeles City Department of Recreation and Parks, Ribbon Dance, Ages 10–17."

with the average age of the head of household 31.5 years old. Initially, there were 760 children living in the 800-unit complex, overwhelmingly still below school age. In the census tract that consisted largely of Glen Oaks Village, in 1950 only 9.6 percent of the population was age 45 or older. Ten years later (with Grand Central Apartments then also in the tract), the percentage of the population age 45 or over had only risen to 16.3, with the median ages for male residents at 26.8 and for female residents at 25.4. When Queens garden apartment residents moved in, they left behind not only their parents, other family members, neighbors, and friends but also the broad age distribution of residents in older urban neighborhoods.[21]

For those who fell outside the age norms, life could be difficult. In 1952, Jack Metzgar, then age nine, moved with his family from the Johnstown, Pennsylvania, house his steelworker father had managed to buy to a somewhat isolated public garden apartment development because his mother could no longer climb stairs following a heart attack. While their new home, with its modern appliances and casement windows, impressed them, Jack and his older sister felt bereft. The development, Belmont Homes, Metzgar recalled, "was populated with lots of young couples with very young children or childless couples, some other steelworkers, but also a lot of white-collar men who seemed mostly in sales of some kind. It was pleasant and green, lots of surrounding open space." But without their old friends or the opportunity to make new ones, Jack was "pretty miserable" and his sister "worse." When three years later they moved into a denser urban neighborhood, full of steelworker families, it was a great relief.[22]

The abundance of young parents and children in garden apartments reflected the demographic trend in the country at large. The boom in garden apartment construction coincided with, and was meant to accommodate, the postwar baby boom. But it also reflected the common requirement, at least in private rental and cooperative projects, that all or a high percentage of families include a World War II veteran. FHA sections 608 and 213, under which most garden apartments were built, were designed specifically to meet the housing needs of demobilized soldiers and sailors. In 1957, the typical applicant for a cooperative garden apartment in Queens still was a World War II veteran with preteen children. As late as 1986, Bell Park Manor and Terrace only accepted families with a veteran. In Los Angeles, 2,234 of the 3,339 families accepted for public housing (which mostly consisted of garden apartments) between July 1, 1953, and June 30, 1954, included a veteran.[23]

So many veterans living side by side meant widely shared experiences among garden apartment families: for men, life in the army or navy, often including combat; for women, waiting, worrying, and sometimes war-related jobs; for everyone, leaving behind the old neighborhood and start-

Figure 6.5. Bell Park Gardens, Queens, New York, summer 1959.

ing anew. No wonder such families bonded so tightly. Lincer believed that Bell Park Gardens provided "an emotional harbor" for veterans like her father. "Nearly every stoop had a metal milk box that was perfect for jumping on—if the dads hadn't already claimed them as seats. The dads, all veterans and mostly first-generation Americans, would huddle on those boxes on weekends and evenings, schmoozing and passing the time."[24]

Garden apartment families were overwhelmingly two-generation families, not three. Garden apartments were designed with nuclear families in mind. Most had one or two bedrooms, with three less common. Very few complexes had apartments larger than that. Accommodating grandparents presented a challenge, as reflected in the age profile of the developments.[25]

The paucity of large apartments and economic constraints meant that garden apartment living could be crowded. Jan Oxenberg shared a bedroom with her sister and brother in Bell Park Gardens in the 1950s (though she has only fond memories of the arrangement). Jack Metzgar shared a bedroom with his father (who to his misery snored loudly), while his sister shared with their mother. Jesús Hermosillo's family of seven lived in a one-bedroom apartment in Wyvernwood when he was growing up in the 1980s. Three families shared the neighboring apartment with an identical layout. One girl, Jesús's age, slept under the dining room table. Multiple families living in a single apartment was common in the complex at the time. Eleven children lived in Dan Perkins's three-bedroom apartment in the Desire project.[26]

One disadvantage of garden apartments was that they were difficult or impossible to expand, unlike bungalows, cottages, or small Levittown-style detached homes, where a handy resident could add another room on the side or back, finish a basement or attic, add a dormer or even a whole second floor, convert a garage into a room, or close in a porch to make more space. One family in Deepdale Gardens, a cooperative garden apartment project in Queens, broke into the attic and installed a fold-down staircase to create an additional bedroom upstairs, and used roll-down bamboo curtains at night to section off part of the living room to create another. Evading rules to take over an attic might occasionally have been possible, but generally, garden apartments lacked the flexibility and expandability of freestanding homes.[27]

In addition to a narrow age range, garden apartment developments typically had a high degree of economic homogeneity. In public housing, regulations set limits that ensured that virtually all residents were in low-income families. Private and cooperative developments, even without formal regulations, tended to attract families in particular economic strata based on their rent or maintenance charges; generally, they drew in better-paid working-class families and the bottom half of the middle class.

In the Glen Oaks Village census tract, the median income in 1949 for families and unrelated individuals was $4,997 ($66,142 in 2025 dollars), considerably above the national urban median of $3,100. (New York incomes generally were higher than those nationally.) But only 8.1 percent of families and unrelated individuals made $10,000 or more ($132,363 in 2025 dollars), while 12.7 percent made less than $3,000 dollars. Ten years later, the median had risen by 16.7 percent (after adjusting for inflation), an increase far below the national jump of 73.7 percent. Just 2.5 percent of families had incomes of $15,000 or more ($163,187 in 2025 dollars). In public garden apartments, no families had such high income, which would have exceeded mandated caps and led to eviction. Families entering Los Angeles public housing from mid-1953 to mid-1954 had an average income of just $2,215 ($26,158 in 2025 dollars).[28]

The similarity of incomes in garden apartment developments and the fact that everyone lived in similar apartments imparted a democratic air

Figure 6.6. The first section of Glen Oaks Village to open, fall 1947. Note the uniformity of well-dressed white people of similar age, the many children, and the postwar-model automobiles.

to them. Jan Oxenberg remembered at Bell Park Gardens, "It was like everybody was just the same. The status of people really wasn't an issue." The actor Richard Dreyfuss, who also grew up in the project, described it to her as "a kibbutz without the work."[29]

A narrow income profile did not necessarily reflect occupational homogeneity. To the contrary, garden apartment complexes housed workers in quite varied jobs. In the 1950 Glen Oaks Village census tract, 48.3 percent of male workers were professionals or managers, 31 percent clerical or sales workers, and 19.2 percent craftsmen, operators, or service workers. Nearly a quarter of the women were in the labor force, the bulk as "clerical and kindred workers" or "professional, technical, and kindred workers."[30]

Very commonly, garden apartment developments had a mix of people for whom they were the final stop and people for whom they were a way station on an upward path toward single-family homeownership. David Grayson recalled Parkmerced in San Francisco as "a transitional space. Disparate families lived side by side, some moving up the ladder and others struggling. Before high school, two close friends moved to the outer reaches of the East Bay—one to Danville and the other to Pinole. . . . Our next-door neighbors returned to the Ingleside. . . . My parents, too, moved away—to Santa Rosa, where they could finally afford to buy." One former resident of the Calliope public housing project in New Orleans recalled that many families lived there only for brief periods, before moving into purchased homes. That became easier once the civil rights movement forced the end of discrimination elsewhere in the city. Los Angeles public housing between July 1, 1953, and June 30, 1954, had a turnover rate of 33.2 percent.[31]

Some co-op owners were drawn to suburban homes by the idea of full ownership of a dwelling and a private backyard where their children could play. By contrast, Tina Lincer's family stayed in Bell Park Gardens. "My parents never did pick up and leave for Long Island like so many other families did," she wrote. "They never even made it to another part of Queens where we could have a two-story house ('our own home,' as my father used to say, wistfully). . . . He always wanted to go out into the wider world but my mother wanted to stay where she was."[32]

When the flood of garden apartment complexes opened in the late 1940s and early 1950s, there were few possibilities for purchasing single-family homes even for those who could afford them, given the national housing shortage. But within a few years, large tracts of low-cost homes arose in the suburbs surrounding major cities like New York, Los Angeles, Houston, and Chicago. A house in Levittown, just across the Queens border from New York City (initially, like many garden apartments, only available to veterans), could be rented or bought at a cost affordable to many of the families who had moved into garden apartments, especially if they were moving up a job ladder or getting substantial raises.[33]

The exit of upwardly mobile families may explain the lagging median income in Glen Oaks Village as the country went through an era of broad economic gain. Over the years, the development continued to house blue- and white-collar families with solid incomes, but the relative economic position of its residents slipped. Between 1950 and 1960, the percentage of male workers in the Glen Oaks Village census tract with professional or managerial jobs fell from 48.3 to 36.1 and the percentage with clerical or sales positions from 31 to 24.2, while the percentage with craftsman, operator, or service positions jumped from 19.2 to 35.7. Oakland Gardens, another Queens garden apartment complex with somewhat more professionals and managers and fewer blue-collar workers, followed a similar trajectory.[34]

Racial homogeneity overlay age and income similarities in the typical postwar garden apartment development. In the South, complete racial segregation was the rule in most developments, often enforced by legal mandates. In the North, established practices, formal or informal rules, or sometimes simply location ensured that most garden apartment residents were all or mostly all of the same race. The exceptions included public housing in a few cities, like Chicago and Los Angeles, that actively promoted integration, and a few private developments that did the same.

Beyond racial homogeneity, there was often ethnic and religious homogeneity as well. The local makeup of veterans could lead to this. So could preferences by families for living with people they already knew or who seemed familiar. The first generation of residents at Bell Park Gardens (and many other Queens garden apartments), for instance, was heavily Jewish, with significant Italian American presence as well.[35]

But if racial, ethnic, and religious homogeneity contributed to strong feelings of community in some projects, such feelings sometimes developed in its absence, too. At Parkway Village, unique in its initial connection to the United Nations, heterogeneity apparently presented no obstacle to close bonds. Betty Friedan and her husband created "an extended family" with couples of similar backgrounds who they met at the complex, "but we also made close friends with Mexican and Iranian families, and French and Swiss we met." When Marina Budhos, the daughter of a Jewish mother from Brooklyn and an Indian father from Guyana, moved there in 1964, the development still had a strong interracial, international character: "Accents of all kinds, melodious, off rhythm, clink like an amateur orchestra, twisting into the night air."

It was not always sweetness and light. The Chilean American writer Ariel Dorfman, who lived in Parkway Village as a child while his father worked at the UN, remembered a period of pitched battles between rival groups of children. "The camp I belonged to consisted of French and Latin American lads, with a Liberian and an Egyptian added to the mix, while our opponents came primarily from Scandinavia and England, vaguely replicating a divide between North and South that would be the source of so many toxic combats across the globe in the coming decades." The death during an operation of a child who had tried to be a peacemaker brought the warfare to an end. Not long after, Dorfman became best friends with the Danish boy who had led the rival gang.[36]

On the other side of the country, David Grayson found camaraderie among diversity in Parkmerced. Like the other Metropolitan Life Insurance housing developments, Parkmerced had been strictly segregated, in its case allowing only white residents. In 1970, a group of residents sued the company for racial discrimination under the fair housing provisions of the Civil Rights Act of 1968. The plaintiffs charged that because of discrimination, they lost the social benefits of living in an integrated community, were deprived of the business and professional advantages that would have come from living with members of "minority groups," and suffered stigmatization for living in a "white ghetto." In 1973, after the US Supreme Court unanimously ruled that the plaintiffs had standing to sue, even though they themselves were not the objects of discrimination, Parkmerced settled, agreeing to comply with an affirmative action plan administrated by a federal court.

Grayson's family moved in a year later. "While I was growing up," he recalled, "the families in our courtyard were diverse and on the lower end of middle class. Our next-door neighbors on one side were a Vietnamese immigrant family, the father a former officer in the South Vietnamese Army. The middle daughter was my sister's best friend. . . . Our neighbors on the other side were a multigenerational African American household, headed by the grandfather, who was a longtime Muni driver. Across the courtyard, my friend's father was an Austrian chef who worked at one of the Hyatt hotels. One summer, his family hosted a barbecue in the communal courtyard for his mother's Tongan relatives. As part of the festivities, a live pig ran loose and ended up on a spit for everyone to enjoy."[37]

White residents at LeClaire Courts, racially integrated but over time increasingly African American, had differing memories of what it had been like during its heterogeneous years. One remembered "everyone got along very well." Another fondly recalled his African American best friend and how his brother "learned how to play baseball from guys who had played for the Negro baseball leagues." But a different resident remembered being bullied by both white and black kids, in "the worse living situation I ever had."[38]

Herbert Gans stressed the importance of homogeneity for strong community bonds, but then muddied the issue by admitting "little is known about what characteristics must be shared before people feel themselves to be compatible with others." The sociological evidence, he reported, suggested that "behavior patterns, values, and interests" were more important than demographic similarity.

Perhaps, more than anything, it was the shared adventure of starting on a new life that brought so many postwar garden apartment residents close together: leaving behind old neighborhoods and webs of association and creating new ways of being in new places. For so many, those new lives centered on children. Friedan recalled of Parkway Village, "our friends were the other couples like us, with kids at the nursery school who squealed at each other from the baskets of the grocery carts we wheeled at the supermarket," a recollection that, with variations, comes up over and over again. Given the demography of garden apartments, child raising became perhaps the most important bond among adults, as they babysat for one another, shared joys and complaints, set up nursery schools, and became friends with the parents of their children's friends.[39] Garden apartment projects were designed precisely to serve the demographic that arrived, young couples with young children. They came full of features meant to encourage the everyday communalism that looms so large in the memories of residents.

Communalism in Action

Everyday communalism sometimes spilled over into political activity. In her study of postwar northeastern Queens, Sylvie Murray demonstrated that, counter to the common picture of families that moved to suburban or semisuburban areas as conformist and politically quiescent, new arrivals living in garden apartments plunged into civic and political affairs. Many leaned toward or aligned themselves with the political left, fighting racial segregation, promoting "brotherhood," advocating world peace, supporting civil liberties, opposing Cold War repression, and joining the American Labor Party, the Liberal Party, Americans for Democratic Action, and other left-liberal groups. One man who grew up in Beech Hills, a cooperative project at the far eastern end of Queens, recalled that in his courtyard alone lived three families with members in the Communist Party. Not all Queens garden apartment activists were on the left; there were conservatives and liberal anticommunists as well. Local PTAs became sites for bitter battles between Popular Front leftists and anticommunist liberals.[40]

Sometimes garden apartment residents mobilized over issues closer to home, such as rent increases and poor living conditions. In 1952 and again in 1954, families living in Glen Oaks Village organized to fight rent hikes. At the nearby Grand Central Apartments, half the residents withheld their rent in 1952 to protest incomplete construction and poor maintenance. That same year, Parkway Village residents engaged in a battle with the banks that held the mortgage on the complex, which were pressing for rent increases, a struggle Friedan wrote about in the project newspaper.[41]

Later garden apartment residents also had their share of activists, especially during the 1960s and early 1970s, when dissident political movements swelled. In Parkway Village, as Budhos recalled, "In the basement laundry rooms, next to the churning washing machines, the older kids talk Che, spin out mimeographs, plot revolution. The more liberal parents march for peace, for integration, suck on joints, try a few mod experiments in their marriages." In Parkmerced, Paul and Margaret Trafficante, who later initiated the suit that desegregated the project, alleged they had been denied a lease renewal because of Paul's support for the protesting students at nearby San Francisco State College. (After their complaints, the company did renew their lease.)[42]

There was plenty of political activity in public housing projects, too, often aimed at the authorities that ran them. Residents of public garden apartments remember strong communities and swarms of children, but also life getting worse as a result of a lack of routine maintenance, broken play equipment, and general disinvestment. By the 1970s, in many projects, drugs and crime became serious problems. In the decades that followed, conditions often further deteriorated.[43]

In response, tenants organized to demand basic services, maintenance, security, and amenities. Sometimes they campaigned for seemingly simple requests, like cleaning children's play areas of glass and dirt. Other times, their push to improve deteriorating public housing merged with broader political efforts. In New Orleans, when the Black Panther Party established a headquarters near the Desire project, where it did sickle cell screening, sponsored clean-ups, and pushed drug dealers away from areas where children played, it won widespread support from project residents. After the police raided their office, the Panthers who had not been arrested moved their headquarters into the project itself. When the police subsequently raided that office, Desire tenants surrounded it, forcing the officers to retreat (though yet another raid soon crippled the party). The Black Panthers also had strong support at Jordan Downs, a garden apartment–style project built in Los Angeles during World War II for defense workers and then converted to public housing.[44]

Common Space and Family Space

For all their informal and occasionally formal communalism, what most privately built garden apartment complexes lacked were the extensive physical facilities for communal life that were integral to exemplary labor and left-wing cooperative endeavors and even some public projects. The housing cooperatives built in the Bronx in the 1920s, including the Amalgamated Houses and the Coops, featured libraries, gymnasiums, childcare centers, meeting rooms, recreational facilities, cooperative stores, and communal eating facilities. In this regard, they were in line with European social housing and worker communities built alongside factories in the Soviet Union and Eastern Europe that had extensive community accommodations and amenities. Some federally funded prewar projects, like the Carl Mackley Houses, also included extensive community facilities, such as shared laundry rooms, community centers, recreational facilities, and day care centers. So did some of the federal wartime projects, like Channel Heights, which had its own school, social hall, workshops, play areas, a day care center, and a market.[45]

After the war, in nongovernment projects, such facilities became uncommon. Electchester was an exception that proved the rule. Associated with the complex was a small shopping center and a six-story building that housed the headquarters of International Brotherhood of Electrical

Figure 6.7. Square dancing at the Channel Heights housing project community center.

Workers Local 3, which had created the development. It also housed a public library, a union-sponsored savings bank, a coffee shop, a cocktail lounge, a bowling alley, and a 1,200-seat auditorium—building blocks for a good life. The ability of Local 3 to tap various labor-management funds to construct these facilities distinguished it from most nonprofit or commercial garden apartment developers. For 608 projects, the FHA discouraged the creation of communal facilities. An FHA planning booklet declared, "Public space [inside buildings] . . . is not productive of income and it should be kept to a minimum." Private financing and FHA insurance both facilitated and constrained garden apartment development.[46]

Some large postwar public housing developments had community facilities not found in typical private developments. Nickerson Gardens included a freestanding community center with a gym that could be converted into a large meeting space, a smaller meeting room, a craft room, a communal kitchen, a snack bar, and indoor and outdoor theater spaces. Across the street from the Calliope Housing Project, the Rosenwald Fund built a recreational center and outdoor pool, the only such facility in New Orleans open to African American children (there were ten centers in the city for white families). Nice as these facilities were—one writer said the

Figure 6.8. Summer day camp at the Rosenwald Center, with the Calliope Housing Project in the background.

community center "afforded Nickerson Gardens' residents amenities normally reserved for the wealthy"—they supplemented rather than changed the basic routines of everyday life.[47]

Garden apartment design reinforced rather than challenged family and gender norms, unlike earlier, more radical housing initiatives. In England, Letchworth had its "cooperative quadrangle," with kitchenless homes, a central dining hall, a nursery, and shared recreation space, all designed to make domestic life more communal and at least somewhat lessen its burden on female residents. In the United States, in the nineteenth and early twentieth centuries, there was a feminist reform stream that called for female autonomy through communal provision of domestic services, including laundry and meals. In the Soviet Union, during the 1920s and '30s, there were extensive experiments with communal living arrangements, designed, among other things, to liberate women from the toil of domestic labor, including cooking and childcare. Soviet kindergartens and nurseries within residential buildings allowed parents to leave children for as long as they chose. This was rare in the US, but the Bronx Coops did have some kitchenless living quarters, collective kitchens for their residents, a nearby cooperative restaurant, and a kindergarten and day nursery open from 7 a.m. to 7 p.m.[48]

Garden apartments, by contrast, rather than undoing familial arrangements that burdened women with domestic toil—while men left the home for employment and often recreation, too—bolstered gendered social patterns. Their design assumed and facilitated nuclear families in which women stayed home, cared for children, and took care of washing, cleaning, cooking, and other domestic chores. The tradition from which they emerged in the United States had been so oriented, from the "neighborhood unit" idea, meant specifically to serve nuclear families with children at home, to the refusal to rent FSA greenbelt apartments to families with working women. In a 1934 essay, Raymond Unwin, the preeminent garden city/garden suburb architect, explicitly stated that housing should be designed for single-family units, rejecting the kinds of experiments with domestic and family arrangements Ebenezer Howard and other housing reformers had embraced.

The United States Housing Authority explicitly restricted residence in federally funded projects to families. When the Housing Authority of the City of Los Angeles considered, at the suggestion of the president of the University of Southern California, building a development in which students, among others, could dwell, the regional director of the USHA informed it that the Housing Act of 1937 authorized housing for "families of low income" and, since students were not families, his agency could not finance a project that accepted them. (Ironically, the rules for Aid to Dependent Children, which many public housing residents received, undermined efforts to promote nuclear families, as women could lose eligibility if they cohabited with a man. In the mid-1950s in Los Angeles, more than a quarter of new public housing families received public assistance and nearly a third had only one spouse present.) Even some private developments resisted anyone outside of traditional family arrangements; Electchester had an unofficial policy of not renting apartments to single men. By the post–World War II years, the idea that garden apartments and public housing should be designed for nuclear families had become so normative that most architects, planners, and managers probably gave it little thought.[49]

There were some exceptions, like architect Elizabeth Coit, who worked for the USHA before joining the New York City Housing Authority. She took architects and planners to task for designing apartments that conformed to how they thought low-income families should live, rather than being guided by how such tenants actually used space in their existing dwellings and what they preferred. She urged that low-income developments have a variety of types and sizes of apartments to accommodate individuals and families of various ages and makeups. In her view, a "too purely parent-and-child community" was not particularly healthy for children and adolescents, who might benefit from relationships with adults who were not authority figures of one sort or another. Writing in 1941, at a time when the Great Depression had led to fewer children being born, smaller families, and an aging population, she contended that "housing must avoid establishing a new type of unnecessary segregation in addition to those already effected by school, by religious and political affiliations, by age, by sex, and by national backgrounds, even if the new segregation wear the badge of the disappearing so-called 'normal' family."[50]

If anything, garden apartments—with their units that were rarely big enough to accommodate extended families, where grandparents might help with childcare, cooking, and other chores—desocialized domestic labor compared to earlier forms of working- and middle-class housing, in which multigenerational families, boarders, and other nonnuclear arrangements were common. Some garden apartment features did make women's chores easier, like having kitchens that looked out on courtyards, where children could be watched while cooking and cleaning, or having nearby shared laundry rooms, often in building basements. But the very idea of the kitchen as a separate room (especially a modest-sized one, typical of garden apartments) rather than as part of a large multipurpose living space, as was common in many nineteenth- and early twentieth-century dwellings, isolated the largely female labor of cooking and cleaning up from other family activities. While women were in the kitchen, the living room became a domain for their husbands and children. (The ever-growing size of contemporary kitchens in middle- and upper-class homes, which serve as de facto family rooms, reverses this trend.)

The lack of stores integrated into garden apartment developments also burdened women, who generally did the family shopping. In older urban neighborhoods, it had been the norm to have stores on the ground floor of tenements and to have all kinds of commercial activity interwoven with residential buildings. Stores and street vendors not only provided convenient shopping but also served as nodes for social congregation. Housing reformers and social housing developers, in Europe and the United States, generally looked down upon the hodgepodge of urban life, promoting instead the separation of commercial activity from residential areas.[51]

Very few garden apartment developments had stores on their grounds, though some, like Glen Oaks Village, had adjacent shopping centers. Generally, for garden apartment residents, shopping required more than simply stepping out onto the street; it meant a walk or bus ride or, if lucky, a drive, perhaps with children in tow, to stores some distance away, and a journey back, lugging purchases.

In some respects, garden apartment design spoke to the needs of women. The proximity of garden apartments to one another, along with shared courtyards and play areas, helped overcome the isolation that plagued women who spent their days doing housework and childcare. But it did nothing to change the unequal social roles of the women and men who inhabited them. Rather, it reinforced a particular notion of the family that built on those inequalities.[52]

The Success of the Garden Apartment

Garden apartments, as built in the postwar United States, did not challenge fundamental social structures of gender inequality, family form, racial discrimination, or property relations (except, to a modest degree, in cooperative housing). Still, if garden apartment living constituted only a stripped-down, depoliticized version of the utopian visions of more radical housing experiments, many residents cherished it. Recollections of happy childhoods perhaps are overly bathed in nostalgia, but occupancy rates provide some hard evidence of satisfaction. FHA records show very low vacancy rates for a sample of some two dozen 608 projects in Los Angeles in the years after their completion, dropping from 7.3 percent in 1951 to 1.6 percent the following year and remaining below 3 percent every year through 1956 except one. Samples of projects in the Chicago, Washington, DC, and New York metropolitan areas found vacancy rates generally even lower. Nationwide, in March 1953, only 11,144 out of 397,548 completed section 608 apartments (most but not all garden apartments) were vacant, a rate of 2.8 percent.[53]

Once moving to garden apartments, many residents stayed put for long periods of time. Some thirty-five years after it opened, a significant proportion of Bell Park Gardens residents consisted of the original families that had moved in, with a long waiting list for empty units. At Deepdale Gardens, in Queens, in 2003, fifty years after it opened, two hundred of the original cooperative residents remained. As residents aged, many garden apartment complexes became, as Clearview Gardens, a large Queens co-op, described itself, "a NORC (Naturally Occurring Retirement Community)." A 1991 survey found nearly a fifth of the residents at Lincoln Place age 65 or older, compared to less than half that proportion in the rest of Venice.[54]

Of course, many families did move out of garden apartment complexes. Some fulfilled their desire to own single-family homes. Others moved out when the racial composition of a project changed (as happened at Clason Point Gardens), or if they no longer met the income requirement for public housing (which is what happened to Elvis's family), or when a project deteriorated (the case for Otis Redding), or because they needed more living space (the motivation for Betty Friedan, pregnant with a third child), or for myriad other reasons. But when residents moved out, there usually were plenty of newcomers eager to move in.[55]

Judged by the experience and recollections of those who lived in them, garden apartments proved to be a great success. Not always, but mostly. The big exception were public projects that were shoddily constructed, allowed to deteriorate, or suffered from the social ills of discrimination, poverty, drugs, gangs, and crime.

Garden apartment developments represented one alternative to the dominant postwar model of suburban single-family houses. Garden apartments were more collective than suburban homes and generally more integrated into urban life. Perhaps more important for most residents, they were less expensive. As New Jersey architect William Martin noted, garden apartments helped stabilize urban neighborhoods and smaller towns by providing affordable homes for young people just starting out and places where older people, downsizing from detached homes, might settle without having to move far.[56]

Garden apartments, as enclaves of sorts, often at city edges and sometimes outside them, did not completely escape the ills of suburbia. Some projects were physically isolated, hard to get to and from without a car. For workers that could mean long commutes. For homemakers it could mean isolation. Shopping and obtaining everyday services could involve tiring treks.[57]

Still, more than in most suburban and rural communities, it generally was possible for garden apartment dwellers to get around, even without a car, and partake of the riches of urban life for those who chose to do so. If garden apartments gave younger children freedom on protected lawns and playgrounds, they gave older children the freedom of being able to walk or bicycle to school, stores, parks, and libraries and gave adolescents the freedom of the whole city, even if it meant long trips on public transportation.

Jane Jacobs could see only isolation from urban life in Chatham Village and its likes. Compared to New York's Greenwich Village, where she lived, perhaps so. But compared to so much of the country, garden apartment living held rich possibilities for urban interactions and culture, for those who sought them. People who bother to provide recollections may be a skewed sample, but they very rarely complain about the boredom or insularity of garden apartment life.

Postwar garden apartments—the large majority of all built—came at a moment of great optimism in American life. The United States had triumphed in World War II, a three-decade period of widely shared economic growth had begun, and attacks on racial discrimination were starting to have some effect. The numerous positive reports and recollections of garden apartment living no doubt reflect that social context. But features specific to garden apartments—the large amount of green and recreation space, set off from vehicular traffic; the high level of community interaction; the affordable but generally quite decent apartment accommodations—drew praise not only in the heyday of the golden decades after World War II but long after. For millions of Americans, garden apartments worked, financially and socially, very much as they were meant to do.

7 *Aftermath*

As a story of conception and construction, the history of garden apartments essentially comes to an end in the mid-1950s. The experience of living in garden apartments, though, extended into the decades that followed. So did the challenges of maintaining them. In the last decades of the twentieth century, the history of garden apartments became a story of deterioration, struggle, demolition, preservation, and sometimes rebirth.

The burst of post–World War II garden apartment construction proved short-lived. In the early 1950s, the building of privately owned garden apartments fell sharply. Publicly owned garden apartments continued to be erected for another decade, but in modest numbers. The diminishment of federal support, which had been critical to the proliferation of garden apartments, accounted for most of the falloff. Also, opposition to garden apartment construction intensified in some communities and segments of the real estate industry. Additionally, alternate forms of housing, most importantly single-family suburban homes, began to be constructed in very large numbers, draining away some of the market for garden apartments.

Eventually, a wave of construction of what came to be called "garden-style" apartments began. Ultimately, these dwellings, which shared many characteristics with garden apartments but also significantly differed from them, came to outnumber garden apartments built in earlier years. An approach to housing that began a century earlier in radical European experiments continued to shape the American landscape, but stripped of its remaining social progressivism.

The End of Section 608

The single most important factor in the sharp drop in garden apartment construction was the termination of the FHA section 608 mortgage insurance program. Begun in 1942, the program had been conceived of as an emergency measure, first to help meet the need for war-worker housing and then to provide accommodations for veterans. It was set to expire in 1949, when Congress extended it for another six months. It lapsed on March 1, 1950.[1]

The willingness to allow the 608 program to expire reflected a sense in Congress and the FHA that the postwar housing crisis was coming to an end, and with it the need for government support for rental housing. Plenty of veterans and their families were still living in Quonset huts and other temporary quarters, and would be for years to come, but housing construction had massively geared up since the end of the war. From a mere 325,000 private housing starts in 1945, the building industry started over a million units in 1946 and 1.9 million in 1950, more than doubling the prewar annual peak.[2]

Doubts about the FHA program also came into play. Real estate industry figures claimed that as other forms of housing drew off customers, some section 608–insured developments were facing financial trouble. Saul Bennett, a Miami Beach broker, pointed to "the pressure of Government competition with itself" in the form of Veterans' Administration (VA) loans allowing home purchases with no down payment. As of late 1950, out of more than 400,000 units that had been built with section 608 insurance, only 4,000 had been taken over by the FHA as a result of default. But the fear of more foreclosures lurked.[3]

The drop-off in garden apartment construction was not immediate. When developers realized that the 608 program was about to expire, they flooded the FHA with proposals for new projects. The agency continued to insure apartment complexes if their applications had been submitted before March 1, 1950. Also in 1950, Congress liberalized another FHA mortgage insurance program for multifamily homes, section 207, which subsequently was used to develop some garden apartments. However, its terms were less favorable than section 608 and its cap on unit costs made it difficult to use in high-cost parts of the country.[4]

The Truman administration recognized that with the expiration of section 608 there would be underserved "lower-middle-income" families, with incomes too high for public housing but too low to buy homes. Its main proposal to meet their needs was a provision in a 1950 housing bill to provide fifty-year, low-cost loans for cooperative housing, a modification of a plan put forward the previous year by Senator John Sparkman. Under the plan, the government would directly provide mortgage money, not simply insure private loans. The long amortization period, low interest rates, and elimination of profits would make possible housing at a significantly lower cost than commercial developments.

Lenders and real estate interests launched a fierce campaign against the co-op proposal, making free use of the rhetoric of the emerging Cold War. Among other things, the cooperative feature of the 1950 bill was

Figure 7.1. Brochure for Deepdale Gardens, in Queens, New York, an FHA section 213–insured cooperative for veterans built in 1952.

called "pure socialism," following "the Moscow party line." In the end, Congress stripped the cooperative loan program from the 1950 bill and instead amended an FHA program, section 213, to provide mortgage insurance for cooperative developments on terms similar to those provided for commercial developments. But the cooperative garden apartments built under section 213 were nowhere near the number needed to make up for the end of section 608. From 220,000 multifamily private home starts (including but not only garden apartments) in 1950, construction dropped to 135,000 in 1954, as the last of the 608 projects finished up, and 130,000 in 1956.[5]

Revelations in 1954 of abuses in the section 608 program killed any possibility of a revival of large-scale federal support for garden apartment construction. What became a major scandal began quietly with an investigation by the Federal Bureau of Investigation and the Internal Revenue Service into section 608 activity and another FHA program, Title 1, which insured small loans for home improvements. For 608, the focus was on the "windfall profits" made through mortgaging out, a practice that was well known in the real estate industry and among federal officials but which had not received much public attention. The FHA had been warned, even before Congress enacted section 608, about potential problems with permitting "building operators to cash out with a profit from the loan proceeds before [a] house is sold or rented," but the agency had ignored the issue. After the program ended, federal officials, no longer so complacent, claimed that developers of 1,149 section 608–insured projects (out of a total of 7,070) together had taken more than $65 million dollars in excess mortgages. Though not necessarily illegal, unless the applications were fraudulent, the tax treatment of these profits was challenged by the IRS. Many developers treated the extra mortgage money they kept as a long-term capital gain, taxed at 25 percent. The IRS said that such windfalls should have been treated as ordinary income, which could be taxed at a rate as high as 75 percent.[6]

The scandal burst into public view on April 12, 1954, when Guy T. O. Hollyday, who President Dwight Eisenhower had appointed to head the FHA, was pushed into resigning for failing to act on information about the abuses and alleged fraud. Almost immediately, congressional committees fell over one another to launch investigations. By the fall, the FHA official in charge of multifamily housing had taken the Fifth Amendment before a Senate committee (an act, in that era, more associated with investigations into communism than housing); twenty-one FHA officials, including the general counsel, had been fired and eleven more suspended; and more than two hundred indictments had been issued (many for Title 1 frauds).[7]

The Senate Committee on Banking and Currency, which at the time was considering a new housing bill, won support for a major investigation of the FHA. It became something of a political extravaganza, with forty-three days of public hearings in Washington, DC, New York, Los Angeles, New Orleans, Chicago, Detroit, and Indianapolis. The inquiry, while not overtly partisan—most of the 608 abuses had taken place during the Truman administration, but many of the Title 1 problems occurred under Eisenhower—nonetheless represented a major attack on government support for rental housing. Developers and government officials brought before the committee came across as greedy, dishonest, or incompetent, as a tone of moral outrage pervaded the public sessions. Investigators revealed some instances of outright corruption and a general aura of coziness between FHA officials and developers.[8]

The Republican committee majority—which included conservative luminaries John Bricker and Barry Goldwater, as well as moderates Irving Ives and Prescott Bush—put the blame for the problems with section 608 not so much on the statute itself but on its "maladministration by FHA."[9] A few witnesses and outside observers argued that the provision worked pretty much as it was intended to, stimulating the rapid construction of a great deal of affordable housing by offering builders generous incentives with loose regulation. Committee Democrats, who included J. William Fulbright, John Sparkman, Paul Douglas, and Herbert Lehman, conceded that abuses and corruption occurred and that excess mortgages pushed up rents at some projects. Nonetheless, they argued, most projects did not have such problems and, broadly speaking, section 608 proved to be a success. As the post-1950 construction drop-off suggested, it was difficult to make a profit building affordable housing without government-provided "windfalls."[10]

The Senate hearings and the report that came out of them had little immediate impact on private garden apartment construction, since section 608 already had expired. But the work of the committee contributed to a somewhat unsavory image for 608 projects, both at the time and later, for sleazy operators, shoddy construction (one issue the committee hearings explored), and financial shakiness.[11] The assault on section 608 also dampened support for public housing. After the passage of the Housing Act of 1949, public housing remained a divisive issue. The FHA scandal unfolded just as what ultimately became the Housing Act of 1954 was being debated. The law, delayed by the FHA hearings, as finally passed diminished the total number of public housing units to be produced and reoriented their primary purpose from a way to house low-income families to an adjunct of urban renewal. It gave priority in public housing to people displaced by federally supported urban renewal projects that brought commercial and higher-end residential developments to areas that had housed working-class and poor residents. From an average of nearly 50,000 new units of public housing a year in the early 1950s, production fell to an annual average of not much more than 20,000 units from 1955 to 1964. Many of these apartments were in high-rise developments. In the public as well as the private sector, garden apartment construction wound down.[12]

Single-Family Homes

While the federal government all but withdrew its support for garden apartments, it continued to promote single-family homeownership. Every year during the 1950s, private developers built at least 1.3 million units of housing, the vast majority of which were single-family homes (depending on the year, between 80 and 92 percent). Many of these new dwellings were in large suburban tracts, like Lakewood, in Los Angeles County, with 17,500 homes; Oak Forest, near Houston, with 5,000; Park Forest, outside of Chicago, with 8,000; Levittown, New York, with 17,400; and Levittown, Pennsylvania, with 16,000. The cost of buying a small suburban tract home often was the same or less than renting an equivalent-sized city apartment, making these houses accessible to many families that might otherwise have moved into or stayed in a garden apartment.[13]

Builders kept the prices of tract houses low by utilizing methods Catherine Bauer had identified back in 1934 as key to the affordability of European social housing: large-scale planning, mass production, and cheap financing. Constructing whole communities at once, rather than individual houses; using standardized building plans; introducing an intense division of construction labor; and making extensive use of off-site prefabrication all lowered costs. Developers saw much greater potential for profit in these endeavors than in urban, multifamily rental complexes, where, among other things, they faced the possibility of rent controls.

Many tract housing developers, like William and Alfred Levitt, learned how to build quickly and cheaply during World War II, when they erected defense-worker housing. Their expertise could be used to build postwar suburban housing because the federal government backed their efforts. In a break from prewar practices, the FHA guaranteed construction loans for large-scale developments, not just mortgages to buy completed structures. Individual purchasers could then get guarantees from the FHA or VA for loans that required low or no down payments from banks that faced no risks.[14]

Even some labor and left-wing groups critical of commercial real estate practices embraced single-family homes. During World War II, the United Automobile Workers (UAW) promoted planned communities, collective ownership, and advanced production methods to bring the cost of decent housing down to a level its members could afford. But it seemed to take for granted the freestanding, single-family home as their preferred mode of living. The aborted union proposal for a "Defense City" of garden apartment–type structures was something of an exception from a general orientation toward detached homes. For the UAW, cooperative ownership and innovative production techniques were not necessarily linked to multifamily approaches to affordable housing. When in 1947 the Philadelphia branch of the American Veterans Committee (AVC), a left-liberal organization of World War II veterans, proposed a cooperative housing project for a suburban area north of the city, it envisioned three-bedroom bungalows—not multifamily buildings—laid out on what had been a large private estate.[15]

Blocking Affordable Housing

The Philadelphia AVC project was never built. Neighboring homeowners used zoning and political maneuvers to delay the project for so long

Figure 7.2. "Design for Living," from the 1943 UAW pamphlet *Homes for Workers in Planned Communities through Collective Action.*

that its sponsors abandoned it. Such opposition to affordable housing construction—including garden apartments—was not unusual. Sometimes it came from real estate interests or political conservatives. Other times, existing community residents did not want to see working-class or poor families or different kind of folks moving nearby. In the case of the Philadelphia cooperative, which had a substantial number of Jewish veterans committed to moving in, antisemitism played a major role.[16]

The fiercest pushback to garden apartment construction occurred against public projects, part of a widespread effort to stop public housing of any sort. A favorite tactic of real estate interests and other public housing opponents was to win state or local laws that required each proposed development to be put on the ballot for public approval. Between the passage of the Housing Act of 1949 and the end of 1951, thirty-eight such votes were held, with projects rejected in twenty-five cases.[17]

A 1949 California law that required voter approval for any new housing project proved a major impediment in Los Angeles, where conservatives, real estate interests, and the *Los Angeles Times* launched a ferocious, red-baiting campaign against public housing and the local housing authority. Several proposed developments (not all garden apartments) were blocked and the large Mar Vista Gardens garden apartment development, on the west side of the city, was delayed for several years. Completed in 1954, it turned out to be one of the last public housing projects built in Los Angeles.[18]

Private garden apartment developments faced opposition, too. In the early 1950s, in Whitestone, Queens, local real estate interests and homeowners' groups were unable to block a large cooperative garden apartment development sponsored by the Brooklyn and Queens chapters of the Disabled American Veterans using FHA section 213 mortgage insurance, but they did succeed in denying it a city tax exemption. Deepdale Gardens, another Queens cooperative garden apartment complex, faced similar opposition. Later, as manufacturers began building suburban plants, nearby upscale communities resisted efforts to build affordable housing for workers, such as a proposed garden apartment complex near a large IBM facility in Franklin Lakes, New Jersey. One of the landmark fair housing cases, *Southern Burlington County NAACP v. Township of Mt. Laurel*, decided by the New Jersey Supreme Court in 1975, began when local officials used zoning to block an effort by local black residents to build a small garden apartment development.[19]

It is impossible to know how many more garden apartments might have been built without such opposition. In many cases the motives of opponents were simply pecuniary; real estate interests and their allies saw public housing and garden apartments as competition. Other times fears of neighborhood change, distaste for low-income families, or outright racism came into play. And so did anticommunism. Even stripped of their radical roots and more daring features, garden apartments represented a challenge to long traditions of the private housing market and the valorization of individual ownership.

Decay and Renewal in New York

As the garden apartment faded from visions of the future, it remained very much part of the present for millions of Americans who lived in such dwellings. While garden apartment living often remained a positive experience, problems increasingly plagued many developments. By the 1970s, conditions at some projects had so deteriorated that questions arose over their survival.

Physical deterioration took its toll on structures that in many cases had been built quickly and cheaply. Section 608 developers had an incentive to keep labor and other construction costs down, because to the extent they came in below the estimates in their loan applications they could profit through mortgaging out. Multifamily residential projects with FHA insurance were required to pay construction workers "not less than the wages prevailing in the locality" for "construction of a similar character," which generally meant the equivalent of union wages. But a 1954 FHA report found the requirement frequently had not been enforced for section 608 developments. An FHA official testified that "in cases where labor was underpaid, construction very often was poor." Problems included peeling paint and plaster, drainage backups that caused moisture to seep through walls, leaks around gas vents, and the use of nonstandard plumbing and fixtures.[20]

Properly maintaining garden apartments required ongoing investment, but many private owners of such projects skimped. Some may not have been looking at their properties as long-term investments, having already made their money through mortgaging out or other financial maneuvers. In parts of the country, like New York City, that had kept some form of rent control, landlords, with limited ability to raise their income, tried to maintain profits by cutting costs. A 1980 New York City government study of Queens garden apartments found among the rental units "nearly 40 percent in the beginning stages of deterioration, with an additional 20 percent in poor condition." By contrast, "all of the cooperative and condominium units appeared to be in good condition." Resident-owners were willing to pay for needed upkeep to preserve their quality of life and protect their investments.[21]

Some common design features of garden apartments proved problematic. Mostly built during an era of low fuel prices, many garden apartments had uninsulated ceilings and casement windows that did little to preserve heat. It was also the general practice to build central heating facilities rather than boilers for individual buildings, seen as a more efficient design requiring less initial investment and less space. But once fuel prices rose, the lost heat from long runs of uninsulated hot water and steam pipes proved very expensive. Also, the spread-out design of garden apartment complexes necessitated more maintenance workers than other types of residences.[22]

By the late 1970s, soaring heating costs, rising labor costs, backlogs of deferred maintenance, and, in some locations, caps on rents pushed many privately owned garden apartments into physical deterioration and onto shaky financial grounds. In Queens, Joyce Apartments, foreclosed and in receivership, looked neglected, badly in need of painting and repointing, with cellar windows boarded up. American Gardens was in worse shape, as it was vacant, sealed up, and about to be taken over by the federal government for nonpayment on its section 608–insured mortgage.[23]

As deterioration occurred, some projects responded with new investment. Clearview Gardens, a section 213 cooperative in Queens, replaced all of its boilers using a reserve fund that it had accumulated and installed a pilot solar hot water heating system. The bank that foreclosed on Grand Central Apartments, which had fallen into disrepair, invested in renovations.[24] But more commonly, Queens garden apartment owners began looking for exit strategies.

A few tried to sell off apartments individually, converting rental projects to condominiums. Some investors bought garden apartment complexes with that goal in mind. It proved to be a difficult process. To make units attractive enough to get buyers, significant capital investments were needed. Furthermore, under the New York City Rent Stabilization Law, owners needed permission from the city's Conciliation and Appeals Board to withdraw apartments from the rental market. A few conversions to condominiums did take place, successfully at the Villas of Laurelton and less successfully at Jewel Gardens (renamed Robin Este Estates) and a section of Heather Gardens (renamed Parkridge). But the challenges of this route discouraged most owners from following it.[25]

Co-op conversion proved more popular. In the late 1970s, owners of New York City rental buildings of all sorts, facing financial challenges and uncertain prospects, began looking to cash out by converting their buildings to cooperatives. The process entailed getting existing tenants to buy shares in a corporation, which in turn would buy the property from the current owner. Renters who did not purchase could be evicted.

Initially, renters resisted such conversions. In the face of their opposition, which included political mobilization, building owners improved the deals they offered, lowering prices and promising capital investments and improvements. The state government, for its part, began requiring, in most cases, "non-eviction" plans that allowed tenants who chose not to buy to remain in their homes as renters.[26]

For both garden apartment complex owners and their tenants, non-eviction cooperative conversions proved an attractive solution to deteriorating physical conditions and uncertain profit prospects. In a matter of just a few years, a wave of conversions swept through Gotham's garden apartment empire. In Queens alone, owners undertook cooperative conversions at Hollis Court Gardens, Cloverdale Gardens, Windsor Oaks, Campus Hall Apartments (renamed Georgetown Mews), Alley Pond, Parkway Village, Glen Oaks Village, and Grand Central Apartments (renamed Parkwood Estates). Garden apartments complexes in Westchester and Rockland counties saw conversions as well.[27]

Renters who became cooperative owners faced multiple challenges. Often with little or no experience in property ownership or management, they needed to set up governance structures, elect boards of directors,

Figure 7.3. Rooftop solar panels at Georgetown Mews, with a chimney for a central heating plant in the background. Note also the added through-wall air conditioners.

and hire firms to take care of day-to-day operations. Also, in most cases, they needed to raise funds to meet the backlog of maintenance and modernization issues that led the previous owners to sell. In an environment of very high interest rates—in October 1981 the average thirty-year fixed mortgage rate hit an all-time high of 18.63 percent—borrowing was costly. Increasing income also was difficult, as remaining renters were still protected by rent regulations, limiting hikes. Co-op boards could raise maintenance fees or impose assessments on co-op owners, but doing so in a poor economy meant imposing real pain.

It took time for most newly converted cooperatives to work their way out of their financial difficulties and improve physical facilities. Associations of cooperatives provided technical advice, spread the word about best practices, and advocated on their behalf with local and state authorities. Eventually, at most projects, physical conditions improved and financial conditions stabilized. Some projects even invested in major capital enhancements, like the installation of rooftop solar panels at Georgetown Mews.[28]

Through a series of unanticipated developments, the section 608 garden apartments that converted to cooperatives went the full circle. Begun as federally supported, quick-profit enterprises, they joined existing cooperative garden apartments in a property form much closer to Ebenezer Howard's vision for garden cities than the individually owned, rental, or public dwellings that made up the vast majority of housing in the United

States. In their modest way, they at least partially fulfilled long-standing ideas, coming from reformers and social critics, about how to solve the perpetual need for decent, affordable housing.

Preserving Garden Apartments in Los Angeles

New York City was unique in the extent of its garden apartment–cooperative conversions. It had a very large number of privately owned garden apartments, a rent control system that limited future profits, and a strong tradition of and legal structure for cooperative ownership. But owners of rental garden apartment complexes elsewhere also faced serious challenges and sought new arrangements to realize gains from their investments.

Struggles over the future of garden apartments were particularly intense in Los Angeles. It, too, had numerous privately owned garden apartments and a rent stabilization ordinance (which went into effect in 1979) that limited the ability of landlords to raise rents or evict tenants.[29] Efforts by project owners to sell or demolish garden apartments set off fierce battles.

The longest and bitterest fight took place at Lincoln Place, in Venice, a modest-rent, exceptionally well-designed development in what became a gentrified part of Los Angeles.[30] The struggle began in 1972, when one of the original project owners arranged a sale to a company that intended to sell the 795 apartments as condominiums. However, when the city government announced it would impose substantial fees for the sell-off, the owner backed off.

The battle resumed in 1986 when the complex was sold to a large real estate company, TransAction. The new owner tried to use a loophole in the Los Angeles rent control law, claiming it was going to undertake major renovations, to evict tenants and re-rent their units at higher rates. Outraged and fearful, tenants, many older and with modest incomes, organized a tenants' association and pressured political leaders to make changes in the rent control ordinance that thwarted the plan.

In 1990 TransAction came up with a new strategy to profit off its purchase. Now it proposed a complete redevelopment that would entail demolishing most of the existing buildings. In their place, it planned to build townhouses, most of which would be sold on the open market. The tenants' association rejected the plan. Instead, it sought to buy the complex and convert it into a cooperative.

An extended battle followed in planning agencies, the political arena, the courts, and the local media, as TransAction tried to win the permissions it needed to proceed with large-scale evictions and demolitions. In 1995 the tenants' association succeeded in blocking TransAction's efforts, but it was just a temporary reprieve. In 2003, the owners, who through threats and inducements had begun moving out residents, knocked down seven of the fifty-two buildings in the complex. Two years later, with the help of the sheriff's department, it forced fifty-two families out of their homes, the largest one-day eviction in Los Angeles history.

By 2007 things looked very grim for the future of Lincoln Place. A deep-pocketed minority owner, AIMCO, a Colorado-based developer, had bought out TransAction. It aggressively pushed to empty out the remaining buildings and demolish them. At the low point, only eleven households, all with senior or disabled members, lived on the thirty-eight-acre grounds, a ghost yard of boarded-up buildings.

But after defeat after defeat, the still-active tenants' group won a series of legal victories, including a ban on further evictions. In 2008, with the tenants threatening a suit for damages and the economy tanking, AIMCO gave up, accepting a settlement that gave the tenants almost everything they wanted. It agreed to stop the evictions, preserve and renovate the remaining buildings, and allow all the tenants who had been evicted or otherwise forced out to return at their old rents. In return, it would be allowed to put up new rental buildings on the sites of the demolished structures.

After fighting tooth and nail to keep Lincoln Place from being designated a historically significant development, AIMCO itself eventually applied for its listing on the National Register of Historic Places. As part of its turnaround, the company worked hard to preserve the original designs and details in its renovations, which, ironically, were financed with a $190 million FHA-insured loan. As a result of the epic defense of the complex by its tenants, today Lincoln Place stands as a remarkably attractive, well-preserved community, more economically accessible—if not cheap—than much of the surrounding area, a testament to section 608 housing at its best.[31]

Similar, if less extended, struggles took place elsewhere in Los Angeles. Chase Knolls Garden Apartments in the San Fernando Valley, like Lincoln Place, had been designed by Heth Wharton and Ralph Vaughn, with modernist touches and an attractive layout. In 2000, its owner unveiled a plan to demolish the 260-unit complex and build 403 luxury apartments. Residents of the project and of nearby buildings mobilized to block the scheme. With backing from the Los Angeles Conservancy and the local city councilman, they convinced the Los Angeles City Council to declare Chase Knolls a "Historical-Cultural Monument." The designation put restrictions on redevelopment possibilities for ten years. After an ownership change, TransAction—the same company that had owned Lincoln Place—agreed to preserve the existing buildings, in return for a tax break and the right to replace carports on the site with additional units. (See plate 17.)[32]

At Wyvernwood, the large, prewar garden apartment complex in Boyle

Heights, yet another plan for demolition and luxury rebuilding was put forth. In 1998, a Miami-based investment firm, Fifteen Group, bought the complex, which housed 6,000 residents, overwhelmingly Latino and mostly working class. A decade later it announced plans for a massive, $2 billion redevelopment that would knock down all the existing buildings and replace them with well over three times as many condominium and rental apartments, as well as stores, offices, restaurants, and recreational facilities. The new buildings would be as tall as twenty-four stories. The number of parking spaces would jump from 1,799 to 9,048.

In response, Wyvernwood residents organized a tenants' association, El Comité de la Esperanza, which retained one of the lawyers involved in the fight to save Lincoln Place. Disagreements about tactics divided the tenants, but the support they won from their city councilman, as at Chase Knolls, proved decisive. Under intense community pressure, the city council never granted the permissions the owner needed to rebuild the community. Though, in contrast to Lincoln Place and Chase Knolls, Wyvernwood did not receive a thorough restoration after its tenants defeated the demolition plan, it remained a vibrant community of people who, for the most part, would have been unable to afford decent housing elsewhere in Los Angeles. (See plate 18.)[33]

Not all garden apartments fared as well as those in New York and Los Angeles. In Prince George's County, Maryland, outside of Washington, DC, at one point two out of every five families lived in a garden apartment. But by the start of the twenty-first century, many of the projects put up in the 1950s and '60s were being torn down, to be replaced by mixed-income developments, luxury townhouses, or single-family homes. "In the process," noted a *Washington Post* article, "one of the last sources of housing for the working poor is disappearing, often without an affordable replacement."[34] Deterioration and redevelopment took their toll in other parts of the country, too. Still, though there is no way to be certain, it seems that the bulk of privately owned mid-twentieth-century garden apartments remain occupied and functional seventy or more years later.

Demolishing Public Housing

Publicly owned garden apartments suffered a grimmer fate. The problems they faced had little to do with their specific design but rather reflected a general crisis of public housing. Government policy, racism, and changed social priorities led to widespread deterioration of public housing of all sorts. Many public garden apartments ultimately were demolished.

Public housing had been introduced during the New Deal as a way to employ construction workers and material producers and house families that could not afford decent housing in the private market. In many cases, those families experienced what turned out to be temporary setbacks as a result of unemployment during the Great Depression. With the World War II–stimulated revival of the economy and then an extended period of postwar economic growth, many of these families had rising income and, with it, potentially greater options for housing.

The dynamic played out differently for white families than it did for everyone else. Many white families, as their economic circumstances improved, chose to leave public housing to rent apartments elsewhere or buy homes. In some cases, they had to leave when their incomes rose past ceilings for public housing residency. Even families with level incomes sometimes had to leave when housing authorities lowered their income caps.

African Americans and other non-white Americans had fewer options. For one thing, their incomes continued to lag behind those of white residents with similar backgrounds and qualifications, even as, on average, theirs went up, too. For another thing, discrimination in housing markets meant that they could not move into many neighborhoods, including new suburban developments that offered relatively affordable houses for purchase. Racial discrimination in both employment and housing thus made public housing a choice that over time drew more and more black residents.[35]

Until the early 1950s, most local housing authorities segregated their projects by race. A 1952 lawsuit challenged that policy as carried out by the San Francisco Housing Authority, winning in the California courts and upheld in 1954 by the US Supreme Court. But change came slowly, with other cities continuing discrimination for another decade. Even in San Francisco, in practice racial segregation continued for years. A 1962 executive order from President John F. Kennedy prohibiting racial discrimination in the sale, leasing, or rental of properties owned, funded, or insured by the federal government accelerated desegregation, though in some cities it still took several more years for the process to begin.

Ironically, the end of discriminatory bars often did not lead to integration but simply flipped the racial makeup of a project. As black families began moving into formerly all-white projects, many white residents left. By 2000, in some cities, including Washington, DC, New Orleans, Memphis, and Detroit, virtually all public housing residents—99 percent—were African American. Nationally, 48 percent of public housing residents were black.[36]

Public housing residents also became, on average, poorer. Prior to 1949, many housing authorities rejected the poorest applicants. That practice changed when the Housing Act of 1949 forbid keeping out tenants because they received welfare payments and required authorities "to give preference to families having the most urgent needs." With better-off families, especially white families, leaving public housing and poorer families moving in, the percentage of the median national income that public housing residents earned fell from 57 percent in 1950 to 41 percent in 1960. In the decade that followed, many housing authorities began giving priority to families receiving public assistance, in many cases single-parent households. By 1970, the earnings of public housing residents lay at just 29 percent of the national median, and the percentage kept dropping thereafter.[37]

Techwood, the very first public housing project, provides a good example of these processes at work. The Atlanta Housing Authority kept the pioneer project all white until the end of the 1960s, but by late 1974 half the residents were African American. By 1990, African Americans made up over 95 percent of the project population, with some 90 percent of the households headed by a woman. Sixty-two percent of the households received Aid to Families with Dependent Children, 13 percent disability income, and nearly 9 percent Social Security retirement benefits.[38]

Poorer families reduced the rental income available to maintain and operate housing projects. A 1969 congressional measure, designed to help the poorest residents, capped their rent at 25 percent of their income. As African Americans, very poor families, and families receiving some sort of state income benefit made up an ever-larger proportion of the public housing population, public housing became increasingly stigmatized, reducing political support for adequate funding. Poor management, sometimes the result of politicians using housing authorities for patronage, added to the problem. The result could be seen in the physical deterioration of individual apartments and whole buildings, in broken playground equipment and unkept grounds, in broken lights and uncleared garbage, in the end of various programs for residents, and in the failure to provide adequate security. Public housing residents also suffered from general social ills of the late twentieth century that most impacted the poor, including racial discrimination, deindustrialization, and crime. The multiple problems that made life hard for public housing residents received the greatest notice at high-rise projects like Pruitt-Igoe in St. Louis and the Robert Taylor Homes in Chicago, which became notorious symbols of public housing failure, but they could be found at garden apartment complexes as well.[39]

At Clason Point Gardens in the Bronx, New York, buildings were run down and the grounds shabby by 1969. Interracial and intergenerational disputes were common among the residents, a mixture of elderly whites and younger African American and Puerto Rican families. Residents, fearful of gangs and drug dealers, felt safe only inside or immediately around their apartments. Thirty percent of the four hundred units lay vacant.[40]

The publicly owned garden apartments in New Orleans suffered from similar but worse problems. At the Desire project, shoddy construction and poor maintenance meant collapsed ceilings, clogged sewers, and insect infestations. During the 1970s and '80s, a high level of crime, much of it linked to drugs, made residents fearful of leaving their homes. At the older but better constructed Lafitte project, an elevated interstate highway destroyed many nearby black-owned businesses and blighted the area, while containerization eliminated many longshore jobs once held by residents.

The 1980s crack epidemic brought a spike in crime and violence at New Orleans garden apartment projects, including Lafitte and Calliope (which had been home to a host of musical prodigies, including the Dixie Cups, the Neville family, and Master P). Simultaneously, a decrease in federal subsidies reduced the budget for maintenance. Short of funds, the Housing Authority of New Orleans (HANO) kept vacant a growing inventory of apartments it allowed to fall into disrepair.[41]

As public housing living conditions worsened, and housing authorities and public officials seemed indifferent or incompetent, residents pressed for formal roles in project management. An unusual success took place at Racine Courts, a small garden apartment complex in Chicago. In the early 1960s, distressed by crime and other problems, tenants began organizing. In 1968, residents of 85 of the 121 units, along with some "over-income" residents being forced out of other Chicago housing projects and a few outsiders, purchased the project from the Chicago Housing Authority to run as a cooperative, as it continues to operate to this day. (See plate 19.)[42]

More commonly, with the US Department of Housing and Urban Development (HUD)—by then the federal agency in charge of public housing—mandating increased resident participation in project management, tenants formed advisory councils or resident management corporations that pressed housing authorities for better services and took over some management functions. Most of these efforts were led by women. At Wentworth Gardens in Chicago, residents launched crime prevention initiatives and children's food programs, provided social services, and successfully pressed for the renovation of the laundromat and field house. At Nickerson Gardens in Los Angeles, residents obtained housing authority funds and foundation grants to renovate "tot lots" that had been allowed to deteriorate to the point of endangering children. At the Lafitte project in New Orleans, the residential council successfully pressed for the construction of the Sojourner Truth Community Center. But given the scale of problems at many public housing developments, the gains won by organized tenants represented only modest improvements in often inhuman conditions.[43]

In a few cases, housing authorities undertook large-scale renovations. In 1969, the New York City Housing Authority (NYCHA), after at one point deciding to demolish Clason Point Gardens to build high-rises, instead went ahead with a previously authorized redesign by architect Oscar

Newman. Newman fenced off some public spaces for use by particular clusters of apartments, redid recreational areas, added new lighting and benches, and had the buildings resurfaced. In the aftermath, crime in the project dropped significantly and all the vacant apartments were rented.[44]

In Atlanta, in the early 1980s, Mayor Maynard Jackson ordered inspections of the Techwood and adjacent Clark Howell housing projects that found some ten thousand housing code violations. He then won $17.2 million from HUD to replace the roofs, windows, and plumbing, heating, and electrical systems and to upgrade kitchens and bathrooms. But as historians Larry Keating and Carol A. Flores noted, the "physical rehabilitation could not prevent the effects of the drug epidemic that pervaded cities across the country during the late 1980s," with both projects plagued by high crime rates and turf battles between drug dealers.[45]

By the 1980s, the drift of public policy was away from rehabilitating public housing toward simply demolishing it. The opening shot in the campaign to terminate public housing came in 1972 with the literal blowing up of part of the huge, high-rise Pruitt-Igoe project in St. Louis, a deeply troubled complex no longer needed in a shrinking city. For many commentators, demolishing Pruitt-Igoe represented a healthy step away from a social experiment that had failed. Patricia Harris, who served as Secretary of HUD under Jimmy Carter, said that the incoming administration "should make it clear that we're abandoning the whole notion of public housing." Other demolitions were slow to follow because of provisions in the Housing Act of 1937 limiting removals. But some housing authorities turned to "de facto demolition," leaving units vacant and unrepaired, to degrade a project to the point that demolishment could be justified.[46]

The "discourse of disaster" that characterized discussions of public housing among politicians, planners, and social scientists and in popular culture was used to justify demolition. High-rise developments dominated its imagery, even though they contained only about a quarter of all public housing units. Critics greatly exaggerated the degree of crisis. In its 1992 report, the National Commission on Severely Distressed Public Housing, created by Congress, found that only 6 percent of public housing units fell into that category because of high crime, physical deterioration, management problems, or distressed families.[47]

Nonetheless, federal policy became increasingly amenable to demolition through HUD's 1992 HOPE VI program and other vehicles, which generally called for the replacement of existing public housing with mixed-income, privately developed, low-rise projects. In 1996, Congress furthered the processes when it directed that all large public housing projects with 10 percent or more vacant units be assessed to see if it would be cheaper to demolish them and give displaced tenants vouchers to use on the private market than to repair and rehabilitate them. By 2010, over a quarter of a million of the nation's 1.4 million public housing units had been taken down.[48]

While depictions of crime-ridden, partially vacant, decaying high-rises provided the ostensible logic and political punch for the destruction of public housing, many garden apartments, including ones in reasonably good shape, became victims of the bulldozer, too. Some housing authorities genuinely saw demolition and redevelopment or tenant dispersal as a way to improve the lives of public housing residents, but other factors also came into play. Some public garden apartments had been built in central city areas as part of slum clearance projects. Years later, as those areas gentrified, the projects themselves came to be seen as obstacles to upgrading and profit opportunities. Many business, political, and real estate leaders saw public housing residents, especially African Americans, as an undesirable element in increasingly well-off residential and commercial districts. Also, private-public, mixed-income projects were a better political and ideological fit for a neoliberal age, disdainful of expansive government and welfare programs, than traditional public housing.[49]

Residents of public garden apartments resisted demolition plans, but rarely successfully. In Atlanta, business and civic leaders who long wanted to get rid of Techwood Homes, including the heads of Coca-Cola and Georgia Tech, both located nearby, allied with political officials to use preparations for the 1996 Olympics, with its Olympic Village to be built across the street from Techwood, as the justification to demolish it, even though a study indicated that its buildings were capable of another sixty years of use. Atlanta went on to become the first city to demolish all its public housing.[50]

In 2005 Hurricane Katrina provided the opportunity for New Orleans leaders, seeking to fundamentally transform the city, to rid it of landmark public housing projects. Before the storm, HANO had decided to demolish all of its large projects and proceeded to knock down Desire and several other developments. But it faced considerable resistance from residents of four of its biggest projects. After tenants evacuated those complexes during Katrina, HANO—which HUD had taken over in 1996 because of its severe maintenance failures—refused to allow them to return to their homes, which in many cases had suffered only minor damage. A prolonged fight followed, but dispossession proved to be nine-tenths of the law. Except for a few buildings at the Calliope project, kept as tokens of historic preservation, all the structures at the four projects, including Lafitte, were taken down.[51]

By the early years of the twenty-first century, cities across the country were knocking down publicly owned garden apartments. In San Francisco, in 1997, the housing authority applied to HUD for a HOPE VI grant to redevelop Valencia Gardens, a mid-sized project built in the Mission District during World War II. It stood out for its high-quality design by Harry Thomsen Jr. and William W. Wurster (a prominent architect married to Catherine Bauer) and for the sculptures in its courtyards by WPA artist Beniamino Bufano. In spite of extensive input from residents who expressed their desire to have the existing buildings refurbished and upgraded, the housing authority, in a move common in the HOPE VI program, switched plans and in 2003 relocated the last remaining tenants and knocked down their homes.[52]

New York City generally was the exception when it came to public housing, including in keeping virtually all its inventory. But in 2005 NYCHA joined the demolition derby when it announced plans to knock down the Edwin Markham Houses on Staten Island, one of its two garden apartment complexes (along with Clason Point Gardens). Like Valencia Gardens, Markham Houses had been built during World War II as temporary housing for war workers. Six decades later, NYCHA decided the buildings were too decayed to repair. So it razed them and handed over the land to a private company for redevelopment.[53]

In 2016 the Macon Housing Authority began knocking down Tindall Heights, where Otis Redding had lived. According to the head of the agency, after seventy years the complex "became functionally obsolete." To replace it, the agency put up a combination of senior and mixed-income housing, with fewer total units than were demolished. The Chicago Housing Authority announced a similar plan for LeClaire Courts, which were completely demolished by 2011, but it then left the site empty.[54]

Replacing Public Housing

In most cases, housing authorities replaced the garden apartments they knocked down with housing for varied income groups, sometimes as part of mixed-use developments that included commercial space. Reformers argued that the concentration of exclusively poor residents was a major reason why public housing failed. Having better-off families living alongside poorer ones, they contended, would provide behavioral models for poor residents, who, it was assumed—if not always openly stated—had cultural deficiencies. Shifting the income profile of residents also usually meant having fewer African Americans.

A wealthier income mix served private interests. For one thing, it could increase business and property values in the vicinity of a project. For another thing, it provided a larger cash flow for the projects themselves, which in many cases were privately owned or managed. Public-private

Figure 7.4. Edwin Markham Houses, Staten Island, New York, before demolition.

partnerships of one sort or another became the new norm. Markham Gardens, which replaced the original Edwin Markham Houses, was run by a for-profit company, with twelve different sources of financing, including from Citibank, two large real estate investment firms, and a variety of New York City, New York State, and HUD loan and subsidy programs. It also had a city tax abatement. Despite the very substantial government investment in the project, it was, according to an NYCHA spokesman, "a private development."[55]

Homes built to replace public garden apartments varied in quality. Many proved to be attractive and well designed, if rarely outstanding. Some included features suggested by tenants of the projects they replaced. The new Valencia Gardens, at the insistence of residents of its former iteration, once again featured the Bufano sculptures. It also had a community room, a children's play area, day care, and washer and dryer hookups in every apartment. Returning residents, however, believed the construction to be shoddy compared to the original project. (See plate 20.)[56]

Most residents of the original Valencia Gardens, and of most demolished public housing, never lived in the buildings that replaced their homes. Various factors conspired to maintain a low rate of return, which was only 24 percent nationwide in 2008. For one thing, the new projects usually had fewer apartments than the developments they replaced, very dramatically so when high-rises were demolished, even in the case of many garden apartments. Markham Gardens replaced 360 apartments with 240 rental units and 25 two-family homes for sale. Furthermore, usually only some of the new units were for public housing. The new Valencia

Gardens had slightly more units than the old one, but only 148 of the 260 apartments were for public housing, with the rest reserved for seniors, holders of section 8 vouchers, or families with incomes too high to qualify for public housing. Creating mixed-income communities necessarily meant fewer slots for the poor.[57]

HUD gave discretion to housing authorities about what procedures and guarantees they provided for displaced residents to return to replacement projects. But even when an authority chose to give former residents priority, most never came back. Usually it was at least several years between when residents were forced to leave their old homes and when new ones became available. In the interim, they moved to other public housing projects or into units they rented with section 8 vouchers, which might be quite far away, or simply disappeared from the rolls of subsidized housing. Many chose not to return or could not be found when replacement projects opened. Some who did want to come back were barred because, even if their income still made them eligible, new requirements, like credit checks, kept them out. In Atlanta, preferential rights to return were granted to 693 residents of the Techwood and Clark Howell projects, but only sixty-eight ended up moving to Centennial Place, the development that replaced their old homes. Rebuilding public housing often improved neighborhoods while doing little to benefit their one-time residents.[58]

Figure 7.5. Markham Gardens, Staten Island, New York.

When replacing public housing, housing authorities and their private partners typically erected low-rise buildings. For some authorities, especially in big cities, this represented a turnaround, a repudiation of a previous movement away from garden apartments to high-rises. When in 1961 HANO was planning a new project, the William J. Guste Sr. Homes, it commissioned a review of earlier New Orleans garden apartment–style public housing. Architect Arthur Q. Davis found that those projects had "many operational weaknesses based upon [a] desire to create intimacy in design." Courtyards and clustered buildings, Davis wrote, made policing "a gigantic task." Having many small buildings increased the cost of utility infrastructure, streets, parking areas, and construction. Small courtyards proved hard to maintain and not big enough to serve as play areas. And the distribution of apartments made it difficult to distance seniors from large, boisterous families. HANO accepted Davis's recommendation for "a completely new approach" for the Guste Homes, one that combined long low-rise buildings with a twelve-story senior residence.[59] The Chicago Housing Authority, after experimenting with high-rise buildings, decided lower buildings worked better. Nonetheless, it kept building high-rises because federal officials rejected its proposals for low-rise structures as too expensive.[60] But negative experiences with high-rise, elevator buildings led many housing authorities, including in New Orleans and Chicago, to later revert to low-rise, walk-up structures when they had a chance.

When low-rise, mixed-income developments replaced high-rise public housing, the differences between the new and old projects were dramatic in number of units, density, site layout, and building design. When garden apartments were replaced, there were many continuities as well as changes. Generally, the population density of sites did not greatly change. Typically, replacement buildings followed the garden apartment model of low-rise, walk-up buildings with direct street access to entranceways for just a few apartments, rather than internal hallways. Like garden apartments, many of the new projects had outdoor recreational facilities and some indoor common spaces. However, buildings in new projects, whether row houses or closely spaced detached homes, were generally arrayed in continuous lines along the street grid with minimal setbacks and no interrupting courtyards. Often, designers tried to visually distinguish individual buildings from their neighbors through varied external colors and decorative elements to make it seem—rarely successfully—as though they were not part of large, institutional developments. Some projects adopted neo-traditional designs, while others used a generic, postmodern design vocabulary, including offset building fronts, small cantilevered extensions, and varied fenestration. Some look like cousins of the shopping malls cloaked as "commons" that were constructed around the country at roughly the same time.[61]

Many of the public housing replacements adhered to "New Urbanist" design ideas meant to promote community and re-create values and social interactions attributed to earlier forms of neighborhood and town layout. Porches were a favorite gesture in that direction—virtually a fetish of Hope VI—though in an age of air-conditioning, they were less necessary and less likely to be used than in an earlier era. (See plate 21.) Of course, many decades earlier garden apartments had expressed many of the ideas claimed by the New Urbanists about community, neighborliness, and scale. *The City*, produced by key figures in bringing garden city/garden apartment ideas to the United States, presented those design approaches as a way to restore village life (or a highly romanticized conception of villageness).

Still, there were important differences. The originators of garden apartments saw shared spaces and facilities as a way to build democratic communities. New Urbanist designs and the buildings that replaced public garden apartments sought to individuate living quarters and associated spaces in a renunciation of shared facilities and communal approaches. Rather than having common laundry rooms, individual apartments typically had washers and dryers (and often dishwashers and air-conditioning, too). Following the ideas of Oscar Newman, worked out at Clason Point Gardens and elsewhere and promoted in his highly influential book *Defensible Space*, sponsors of public housing replacements believed that people would better maintain and protect spaces and structures about which they felt a sense of ownership than they would common grounds, whether or not they actually owned them. Accordingly, replacements for garden apartments featured private yards, stoops, porches, entryways, and individually distinguished buildings, all seen as devices to shape tenant behavior and increase security. Some projects had strict regulations to further the effort. At Faubourg Lafitte (see plate 22), the replacement for the demolished Lafitte project, there were rules about how many residents could congregate outside at one time and curfews for children. With public housing replacements, the trajectory of the garden apartment went the full distance from its origins in radical communal experiments to the American cult of the individual.[62]

Neo-Garden Apartments

The demolition and replacement of public housing occurred after a revival of low-rise, multiunit private construction already had begun. For a half dozen years after the end of the section 608 program, construction of private apartment buildings, large and small, remained depressed. In 1957, it began to rise again and continued to grow, with some ups and downs, until the early 1970s, in both absolute numbers and as a percentage of all private residential construction. One study found that nearly half of all housing built during this period consisted of what it defined as garden apartments, rental units in low-rise, non-elevator buildings, which occupied only modest parts of landscaped sites. Another burst of multiunit construction occurred in the mid-1980s, before dropping again.[63]

Some of the construction in the 1960s consisted of suburban infill, garden apartment developments on small sites in areas that already had single-family tract homes and shopping. More significantly, the era saw the proliferation, first in California and then elsewhere, of "condos," multiunit complexes where residents owned their individual dwellings and shared responsibility for whatever common spaces there might be (unlike in co-ops, where the residents collectively owned the entire development). These communities looked different from classic garden apartments but shared some characteristics. Many consisted of row houses, with garages behind or beneath them, accessed by driveways or alleys. Often they included shared amenities, like outdoor swimming pools and landscaped open areas, if not the courtyards so characteristic of earlier garden apartments. Some offered extensive services to young families, including on-site nursery schools, much like some postwar garden apartment complexes had done. But, like the mixed-income developments that replaced public housing, the typical condo development, compared to older garden apartments, had a much more individual orientation; they were not designed to promote community or communal experience but simply to provide convenient, pleasant living at lower cost than freestanding homes.[64]

During the last decades of the twentieth century and the first decades of the twenty-first, "garden-style" rental and condominium units, including townhouses (with one family inhabiting multiple floors), came to rival the detached single-family home as the typical residence in large swaths of the country. Builders, brokers, and public authorities often labeled such dwellings "garden apartments," though the term became so loosely used that it encompassed a wide variety of types of low-rise multifamily complexes. The new garden-style residences served a more diverse group of residents than had mid-twentieth-century garden apartments, including single people, childless couples, and the elderly. As in the past, for many they served as a stepping stone toward single-family homeownership.

Cost was a major factor in the spread of neo-garden apartments. In 1950, the median cost of a freestanding single-family home was less than twice the median annual family income. By 2000, it was nearly three times as much. A typical house in 2000 was larger and had many more appliances and conveniences than a house a half century earlier, but that made no difference if you could not afford it. Townhouses and attached condo units cost substantially less than freestanding homes and, of course, rental units did not require any capital outlay, making these alternatives increasingly attractive to the nonrich.[65]

As their popularity grew, neo-garden apartments became a major investment vehicle for giant financial institutions. Real Estate Investment Trusts (REITs) did not put big money into garden apartments until the mid-2010s. One researcher for a large asset management company commented, "Garden apartments are not glamorous. They don't show well in photographs." But investors began to realize that compared to higher-rise, upscale, central city properties, garden apartments could be obtained at a comparatively cheap cost, with the promise of good profits, especially for rental complexes. In 2022, investors spent $57.4 billion to buy garden apartments in the second quarter alone. Nearly a third of the spending consisted of "giant acquisitions of portfolios."

Blackstone Inc. led the way. In December 2021 an REIT organized by Blackstone, which already owned tens of thousands of garden apartments, purchased for $3.6 billion another REIT that owned 11,000 units concentrated in garden apartment–like structures. The next month it spent $3.7 billion for a portfolio of "multifamily, garden-style assets," forty-two complexes with more than 12,600 apartments featuring "significant green space and amenities." Smaller (though not small) investment firms got in on the action, too, like Turner Impact Capital, which bought a 1,155-unit garden apartment complex in Glendale Heights, Illinois, in the largest real estate transaction on record in suburban Chicago. Some REITs went beyond simply purchasing garden apartments to build them. By one estimate, "institutional capital" in early 2022 owned portfolios of garden-style apartments worth $60 billion. The garden apartment, or at least the "garden-style" apartment, once a fringe, reformist innovation, found its resting place in the heart of modern capitalism.[66]

The garden apartment survived the Cold War, the section 608 scandal, the rise of mass suburban single-family tract housing, and the implosion of public housing to morph into a central "asset" in the for-profit housing market. This is not the garden apartment as first conceived of in the early twentieth century or as built during its mid-twentieth-century heyday. Yet it is a type of housing serving tens of millions of Americans that in all likelihood would not have come about without that earlier vehicle for dreams of utopia and dreams of profit.

CONCLUSION *Garden Apartments and the Politics of Change*

For many years I worked at Queens College, on a modest, urban campus, with garden apartments along one of its sides and more nearby. Every time I went to work, I walked or drove past these dwellings but gave them little thought. They were simply a familiar part of the background, something I took for granted. After all, I had grown up in garden apartments until the age of nine and through high school many of my friends had lived in them. My lack of interest in them, as I was to learn, was the norm, even among scholars and practitioners of housing and design.

One day, walking to a bus stop to get myself home, I began wondering why there were so many garden apartments in Queens. Who built them? Why do they all look so similar? And why were they no longer being built? Only then did it occur to me that garden apartments had a history, and I had no idea what it was.

As I began to look more closely, I noticed that the apartments I so frequently passed were in good repair, well kept, and functional, even though they were over sixty years old. Living in a city, like much of the United States, plagued by insufficient, exorbitantly expensive housing, it belatedly occurred to me, a bit like Dorothy in Kansas, that one solution to the problem of affordable housing had been there all along, right in front of my eyes. Garden apartments had been, and still were, a source of decent, attractive housing for people of limited means.

Out of those moments, this book originated. At first, I imagined a modest project, an article about the burst of garden apartment construction in the decade after World War II. It would be a history of housing and architecture, with a bit of social history thrown in. But as I began tracing the origins of the type of building I so frequently passed, it became evident that I would have to go further back in time, to the start of the twentieth century. It was in that era, I discovered, that the roots of the garden apartment could be found. To my surprise, they lay in efforts to address not only a pervasive housing crisis but also broad inequalities in society. The history of garden apartments turns out to be, above all else, a history of politics.

Political ideas and actions, to a great extent, created the garden apartment and led to its dissemination in the United States. Its successes and limitations reflected balances of political and social power at particular moments. Even seemingly technical issues of design—the size of rooms, the layout of sites, the choice of building materials—turned out to be physical manifestations of political circumstances.

The politics of the garden apartment make its history more than a niche concern. Unless you live or lived in a garden apartment, the subject might seem peculiar or arcane. Though substantial in number, garden apartments never challenged the detached, single-family, owner-occupied home for a central place in the American imagination and in the twentieth-century remaking of the national landscape. But the story of garden apartments can help us see how change happens in society and how it doesn't, how radical challenges to the status quo can win and lose at the same time.

When radical critics like Henry George, Edward Bellamy, Friedrich Engels, and Ebenezer Howard criticized capitalism for its failure to provide for basic human needs, including housing, they seemed very much outsiders. Yet within a surprisingly few years, their ideas yielded material changes in the form of new types of homes and communities, first in Europe and eventually in the United States.

In Europe, the development of social housing stemmed from seemingly contradictory forces. Growing working-class, reform, and socialist movements made affordable housing an important part of their programs. In instances where they achieved political power, they vigorously pursued its creation. In the process, these movements, and the architects they worked with, generated new ideas about housing design, layout, construction, financing, and management. They gave concrete reality to visions of new ways of life. At the same time, the specter of worker unrest and, especially after 1917, of socialist revolution, led middle-class reformers and business and political leaders to promote social housing as a means of creating social stability. Decent housing for working people might serve as a buffer against radical transformation. From the start, the housing forms from which the garden apartment derived were simultaneously promoted as ways to move beyond capitalism and as ways to bolster it.

In the United States, the housing question played out somewhat differently, largely because, compared to Europe, of the relative weakness of the political left and the strength of the real estate industry. In the twentieth century, anticapitalist movements in the United States were not on the scale found in Europe, nor did the political left generally make housing creation a major focus. Episodically, until the Great Depression, middle-class reformers and businessmen—in some cases fearing worker unrest and radical challenges—launched affordable housing efforts, but on a very modest scale.

The New Deal brought mass social housing to the United States. Its housing programs were not the result of popular demand. Nonetheless, New Deal leaders embraced housing as a state function, a way to generate jobs and part of a broader vision of a more secure, democratic society, without the large pockets of need that had long characterized the country. Once initiated, government involvement in housing won enthusiastic backing from key components of the coalition that sustained the New Deal: urban voters, especially first- and second-generation immigrants; African Americans; labor; and Southern Democrats. Their support allowed the garden apartment to become a mass form of housing. Housing reformers and architects who had operated on the margins of politics, architecture, and urban development suddenly found themselves with substantial influence, able to carry out even some of their more radical visions. The garden apartment emerged as one of the leading physical forms for their goal of providing well-designed, affordable housing. For many, garden apartments were not simply a relatively inexpensive way to provide decent dwellings but, with common spaces and shared amenities, a physical framework for promoting democratic communities.

Even at the height of the New Deal, however, the forces opposing substantial state involvement in housing (except to promote privately owned, single-family homes) remained extremely powerful. Many had pecuniary concerns, their fear that government programs would diminish the profit-making potential in housing. Others were more ideologically driven, wedded to a conception of small government and individual self-reliance. The Housing Act of 1937, while making public housing an ongoing part of the emerging welfare state, did so in ways that severely restricted its quality and the universe it could serve.

At the start of World War II, for a tantalizing moment, an extraordinary alliance emerged, bringing together housing reformers, left-wing New Dealers, modernist architects, innovative material producers, and organized labor. The garden apartment, whose physical design had lagged behind its social purpose, blossomed in new shapes, layouts, and appearances. For a blink of the eye, there seemed to be the possibility that a new social and aesthetic landscape would emerge after the war.

But it was just for a blink. Aesthetically, pushback came from architectural traditionalists and elected officials, who saw in European modernist influences not a vision of a better life but an intrusion of alien forms into communities that had little if any say over their construction. Politically, momentum shifted to real estate interests and conservatives who had no interest in seeing a new wave of public housing succeed, setting a template for postwar development. With congressional and public support for the New Deal waning and military needs paramount, it was no contest.

When Allied victory came, jostling intensified over the direction of postwar politics and policy. Despite a massive wave of labor militancy, the overall trajectory of national politics was away from the left-liberalism that had animated the New Deal, toward what Arthur Schlesinger famously termed "the vital center," which was not very vital at all. The revival of the economy ended the sense of crisis and the view that capitalism had exhausted itself, which had allowed for expanded state functions and new political and social departures. Business and conservative forces, discredited by the Depression, regained legitimacy and political power. And there was the Cold War. The wave of repression that accompanied it aimed not just at communists and their allies but also at all sorts of progressive and nonconforming movements, people, and initiatives.

It was at this moment of political retreat for social reformers that the garden apartment became a major component of the national housing stock. One effort after another to extend the New Deal went down to defeat in the immediate postwar years: national health insurance, new regional authorities along the lines of the Tennessee Valley Authority, a federal commitment to provide a job for everyone seeking one, federal aid to education, and federal protection of the rights of African Americans. Housing was one of the few areas in which there was a major expansion of progressive state action in the period between the end of World War II and the Great Society of the mid-1960s.

The severity of the postwar housing crisis helps explain the initiation of new federal housing programs in the half decade after World War II. So do the moral and political claims of the millions of ill-housed veterans. But housing laws passed only because they were structured to make sure they did not challenge real estate interests or capitalist markets. In the case of private rental garden apartments, section 608 provided a bonanza for developers, who had no reason to oppose it. In the case of public garden apartments, the Housing Act of 1949 ensured that only people too poor to afford new or well-kept private-sector housing would be eligible for state dwellings, while private developers could take advantage of the urban renewal opportunities the law created.

In this sense, social housing, like other progressive initiatives, suffered defeat in the years immediately after World War II. And yet, after defeat, even out of defeat, came a great deal of decent, affordable housing that made millions of people's lives better. Specific social circumstances and compromises with the dominant economic and political forces allowed the garden apartment not only to survive but to flourish, at least for a while.

The history of the garden apartment is not an argument for incrementalism, for modest programs that do not rock the boat or challenge the status quo. Quite the opposite. The garden apartment came into being only because of the audacity of early twentieth-century housing reformers. In the United States, it took some time for their ideas to be manifested on more than a token scale, and very quickly limits were placed on the possibilities for truly innovative housing in the public realm. Still, though the bulk of garden apartments fell short of earlier notions in their quantity, quality of design, shared facilities, and cost to residents, they represented a major achievement. Even with its declension, the garden apartment was a utopian project.

Or at least sort of. To call the garden apartment a utopia, even a low-rent utopia, perhaps is an exaggeration. In some ways, its achievements were modest. The template for a jump in living standards for the "middle majority" of Americans preceded the mass construction of garden apartments rather than flowed from it: indoor bathrooms with a toilet, sink, and bathing facilities; electricity and gas from utility networks; gas or electric stoves and other kitchen appliances; private bedrooms; larger homes.[1] But the garden apartment brought such now taken-for-granted conditions to millions of Americans who had never experienced them. Add to that safe play areas for children, lawns and trees to enjoy and look out at, shared amenities, and the communities all these fostered, and understandably it could make a garden apartment seem like a utopia for someone coming from a run-down city tenement or a rural shack.

It is remarkable how little has changed in housing since the post–World War II heyday of garden apartment construction. There has been nothing even approaching the dramatic difference between having an outdoor toilet or an indoor one, between not having electricity or gas and having it. Adding a microwave or a dishwasher to the arsenal of kitchen appliances seems puny compared to freeing cooks from wood or coal stoves and providing them with refrigerators. Homes have gotten on average larger and larger (at least until quite recently) but there has not been any fundamental change in their internal organization. Arguably only air-conditioning in warm climates represents an existential improvement.[2]

What is most distressing, perhaps, is not the lack of progress in housing design, technology, and access over the past eighty years but the lack of any animating vision of the future. Utopias are never real places, corporal entities, but are visions imagined and possibilities yearned for. Radical housing reformers had a vision out of which the garden apartment arose.

As realized, most garden apartments do not look like much, have names that disguise their actuality, and carry little cultural or social weight. But at a moment when society seems to have so few visions or expectations of a different and better future, in their humble way they seem utopian indeed.

Today, there is a housing crisis in the United States that is in some ways as severe as the one at the end of World War II. Tens of millions of Americans cannot afford decent housing where they want to live. For some, the solution is to commute long distances from far-outlying communities. For others, it means living with parents long after achieving adulthood or spending an inordinate proportion of their income on housing. And for still others, there simply is no decent housing, just cramped quarters, dangerous neighborhoods, run-down buildings, repeated evictions, or homelessness. The solutions of 1935 or 1945 may not be solutions appropriate for today. But the history of the garden apartment demonstrates the capacity of a mobilized society to quickly use public resources, directly and indirectly, to go a long way toward solving social problems. With a bit of boldness and some political will, we might find the intractable is not as intractable as it seems.

ACKNOWLEDGMENTS

As the author of a book in what for me was a largely new field of study, I am especially grateful for the advice and assistance I received from colleagues. Members of the Faculty Research Group at the City University of New York School of Labor and Urban Studies gave me rich feedback on an early, short manuscript about garden apartments and convinced me to expand it into a book. Jeffrey Kroessler and Matthew Gordon Lasner provided advice and encouragement. Marta Gutman and Daniel Bluestone read a draft of the book with great care and insight, providing a wealth of suggestions, drawing on their deep expertise. Debbie Bell and Jack Metzgar have read in manuscript almost everything I have written, and as usual provided invaluable comments. At moments when I felt uncertain and discouraged about this project, they pushed me on. As always, Steve Fraser provided sage advice. I also owe a debt to the anonymous readers for the *Journal of Urban History* (for an earlier version of this project) and the University of Chicago Press, whose criticism and suggestions I did not always agree with, but which made this a better book.

I am extremely appreciative of Timothy Gilfoyle, an editor of the series in which this book appears, for his enthusiasm, editing, and smart suggestions. Working with Timothy Mennel at the University of Chicago Press has been a pleasure. Andrea Blatz unflappably and knowledgably answered my flood of questions about illustrations and manuscript preparation. Copyediting by Lindsy Rice made *Garden Apartments* a much more readable book.

Because there is very little written about garden apartments, researching this book proved challenging. What I learned as an undergraduate from a course I took with J. B. Jackson proved fundamental: look at the things not normally thought worth looking at. More specifically, on housing, I benefited enormously from the work of Gail Radford, who I once nominally advised. Chandni Tariq provided research help at the very beginning of my work. National Register of Historic Places Registration Forms, submitted to the National Park Service, enlightened me about many, often obscure, buildings. These are gems of architectural, social, and political history, whose authors usually remain unsung.

Paul Milkman, Jan Oxenberg, and Jesús Hermosillo generously discussed their recollections of garden apartment living with me, and Jack Metzgar wrote to me about his. Jesús also gave me a revelatory tour of the Wyvernwood Garden Apartments. I benefited, too, from oral histories and filmed interviews of garden apartment residents conducted by others, which are cited in my notes. Amy Shearn kindly sent me a copy of the book, *The Little Bastard*, her grandmother, Frances Schutze, wrote based on her experience living in Neighborhood Gardens.

I could not have provided the illustrations in this volume without the assistance and generosity of a large number of archivists, librarians, photographers, preservationists, historical consultants, and government officials. The extent to which so many of them went out of their way to help me was heartwarming. To list everyone who provided assistance would take up way too much space, but some people deserve special recognition.

To my delight, Kerry James Marshall gave me permission to reproduce his extraordinary painting *Watts 1963*, which perhaps more than any other image captures what this book is about. Bo Cabell, David Schalliol, Adrian Scott Fine, and Harry Connolly contributed their terrific photographs. Tina Lincer made available family photographs. Leopoldo Villardi, at *Architectural Record*, provided historical images.

Patrick Choy, at the Housing Authority of the City of Los Angeles, repeatedly helped me secure photographs of local public housing. Jennifer Navarre, at the Historic New Orleans Collection, did not give up until she found a photograph I was fruitlessly trying to locate, and then suggested a better one. Sarah Henry, at the Museum of the City of New York; Tim Askin, at the Historic Preservation Commission, City of Milwaukee; Amanda Fallis, at the City Archives and Special Collections, New Orleans Public Library; Chira Daab, at the Institut für Stadtgeschichte in Frankfurt; and Sabine Ambrosius, at Landesdenkmalamt Berlin, made it possible for me to present wonderful photographs of social and public housing in those cities. Amanda Yoder Duane, at GPA Consulting, and Julie Abell Horn, at Historical Perspectives, Inc., tracked down photographs from reports they prepared years ago. The staff at Avery Architectural and Fine Arts Library, Columbia University, was especially helpful. My thanks, too, to the Interlibrary Loan office at the Graduate Center of the City University of New York, which obtained for me many obscure publications with images I wanted to reproduce. Daniel Esterman and Stefano Morello graciously took the time and care to scan those and other illustrations.

I hope this volume does justice to the efforts of the many people who made it possible. My heartfelt thanks to all of them.

NOTES

Introduction

1. The complex is still owned by the Memphis Housing Authority but has since been renamed Uptown Square Apartments. Peter Guralnick, *Last Train to Memphis: The Rise of Elvis Presley* (Little Brown, 1994), 32–34; "Memphis Housing Authority/Hope VI Development 2017 Property Portfolio," Memphis Housing Authority, https://cms5.revize.com/revize/memphisha/property%20portfolio/2017-MHA-Property-Portfolio.pdf.

2. Betty Friedan, *Life So Far: A Memoir* (Simon & Schuster, 2006), 76; Betty Friedan, *"It Changed My Life": Writings on the Women's Movement* (Laurel, 1991), 14.

3. The painting of Nickerson Gardens, *Watts 1963*, is in the Saint Louis Art Museum, https://www.slam.org/collection/objects/28619/; Calvin Tomkins, "On an Epic Scale: How Kerry James Marshall Takes on the Western Canon," *New Yorker*, August 9, 2021.

4. See, for example, Gwendolyn Wright, *Building the Dream: A Social History of Housing in America* (Pantheon Books, 1981), and Dell Upton, *Architecture in the United States* (Oxford University Press, 1998). Jane C. Busch, Mark Edward Braun, and Brenda Kayzar, *The Greenwood Encyclopedia of Homes through American History: Volume Four 1946–Present* (Greenwood Press, 2008) has only two paragraphs on garden apartments in nearly five hundred pages of text.

5. Architect Daniel Parolek, who coined the term "missing middle housing," has a widely reproduced illustration of the types of such housing that includes duplex, triplex, and fourplex buildings, bungalow courts, townhouses, live/work buildings, and courtyard apartments, but not garden apartments, in "Missing Middle Housing: Responding to the Demand for Walkable Urban Living," https://www.nahbclassic.org/assets/docs/ises/DanParolek_MissingMiddleHousingfinal_20140127095017.pdf. See also Sarah Button, "Missing Middle Housing," *Municipal World*, May 2017, 27–29, 44.

6. The generally comprehensive, 1,561-page *The Encyclopedia of New York City: Second Edition*, edited by Kenneth T. Jackson, Lisa Keller, and Nancy V. Flood (Yale University Press, 2010), has no entry for garden apartments, nor are they included in the general entry on "housing." A few individual projects are mentioned. Similarly, the 1,376-page *New York 1960: Architecture and Urbanism Between the Second World War and the Bicentennial*, 2nd ed., by Robert A. M. Stern, David Fishman, and Thomas Mellins (Monacelli Press, 1997), discusses a few individual garden apartment developments, but overall gives them scant attention. In his pathbreaking *A History of*

Housing in New York City, rev. ed. (Columbia University Press, 2016), Richard Plunz unearthed the history of the multistory apartment buildings in Jackson Heights built in the 1910s and 1920s, which were the first buildings in the United States to be dubbed "garden apartments," but completely ignored the history of the more numerous low-rise garden apartments constructed during the 1940s and 1950s.

7. Lucia Anaya, "Former Leclaire Courts Residents Are Still Fighting to Go Home," *Chicago Reader*, August 4, 2016, https://www.chicagoreader.com/chicago/leclaire-courts-redevelopment-controversy-cha/Content?oid=23039100; Marina Budhos, "Friedan's Village," *The Awl*, May 20, 2015, https://www.theawl.com/2015/05/friedans-village/.

8. Sylvie Murray, *The Progressive Housewife: Community Activism in Suburban Queens, 1945–1965* (University of Pennsylvania Press, 2003), 25, 27, which includes the quote from Mumford. For his full review, see Lewis Mumford, "The Sky Line: From Utopia Parkway Turn East," *New Yorker*, October 22, 1949, 102–6.

9. Quoted in Stern, Fishman, and Mellins, *New York 1960*, 1004.

10. Some garden apartment residents living in public housing fell below Hubka's "middle majority." Thomas C. Hubka, *How the Working-Class Home Became Modern, 1900–1940* (University of Minnesota Press, 2020). Ironically Hubka himself ignores garden apartments in this pathbreaking study that covers a period when they were beginning to be built in significant numbers.

11. Residents of garden apartment public housing, starting in the 1960s, were something of an exception and were sometimes seen as problematic. The classic investigation into the ills of the tenement is Jacob A. Riis, *How the Other Half Lives: Studies among the Tenements of New York* (Charles Scribner's Sons, 1890). For a fine recent study of tenement housing in New York and Boston, see Zachary J. Violette, *The Decorated Tenement: How Immigrant Builders and Architects Transformed the Slum in the Gilded Age* (University of Minnesota Press, 2019). Herbert J. Gans, *The Levittowners: Ways of Life in a New Suburban Community* (Pantheon, 1967), and Bennett M. Berger, *Working-Class Suburb: A Study of Auto Workers in Suburbia* (University of California Press, 1960), are among the best-known early suburb studies.

12. Herbert Hoover, "Address to the White House Conference on Home Building and Home Ownership," December 2, 1931, online by Gerhard Peters and John T. Woolley, The American Presidency Project, https://www.presidency.ucsb.edu/node/206990.

13. Joshua B. Freeman, *American Empire, 1945–2000: The Rise of a Global Power; the Democratic Revolution at Home* (Viking, 2012), 125–42; Chloe N. Thurston, *At the Boundaries of Homeownership: Credit, Discrimination, and the American State* (Cambridge University Press, 2018), 30; Elaine Tyler May, *Homeward Bound: American Families in the Cold War Era*, rev. ed. (Basic Books, 2017).

14. Thurston, *At the Boundaries of Homeownership*, 6–7.

15. More recently, such buildings are sometimes called clustered developments. Sometimes the term *garden apartment* is used to refer to a ground floor or basement apartment in a large building or in a two-family house that has direct access to the outside, typically to a garden or lawn. These types of apartments are not the subject of this study, except to the extent that some may be part of complexes with the characteristics of garden apartments, as defined above. *OED* Online, "garden apartment," last modified July 2023, http://www.oed.com/dictionary/garden-apartment_n; Gail Radford, "The Federal Government and Housing During the Great Depression," in

From Tenements to the Taylor Homes: In Search of an Urban Housing Policy in Twentieth-Century America, ed. John F. Bauman, Roger Biles, and Kristin M. Szylvian (Penn State University Press, 2000), 103.

16. For the first wave of large "garden apartment" buildings, see Plunz, *A History of Housing in New York City*, 122–63, and Matthew Gordon Lasner, *High Life: Condo Living in the Suburban Century* (Yale University Press, 2012), 66–76.

17. The largest categories of privately owned garden apartments were those receiving mortgage insurance from the Federal Housing Administration (FHA). Two FHA programs, section 207, begun in 1934 and primarily aimed at government-owned rental housing, and section 213, enacted in 1950 for cooperatively owned projects, had insured 107,527 units by 1954, including but not restricted to garden apartments. By the time the much larger section 608 program, begun in 1942 to insure privately built apartments, wound down in the mid-1950s, it had insured mortgages for 7,045 projects containing 465,633 apartments. Most of these were garden apartments, though there were some taller, elevator buildings in high-density urban areas. *FHA Investigation Before the Senate Committee on Banking and Currency*, 84th Cong. 1st sess. (January 6, 1955), 127. In addition, there were some garden apartments built under different federal programs and some built with no government support. For public housing garden apartments, see "Public Housing: Images Versus Facts," *U.S. Housing Market Conditions* (US Department of Housing and Urban Development, Office of Policy Development and Research) (Spring 1995), https://www.huduser.gov/periodicals/ushmc/spring95/spring95.html. Estimate of number of garden apartment residents calculated using US Bureau of the Census, "Current Population Reports: Population Estimates," September 27, 1956, https://www2.census.gov/library/publications/1955/demographics/P25-121.pdf, and (for average family size) "Size of U.S. Family Continues to Drop, Census Bureau Says," *New York Times*, June 2, 1988.

18. Carl F. Horowitz, *The New Garden Apartment: Current Market Realities of an American Housing Form* (Center for Urban Policy Research, 1983), 16–17, 22. Horowitz determined the number of garden apartments using data from the federal census and annual housing surveys. Though garden apartments do not appear as a category in the data, he used a cluster of variables to separate them out from other types of housing. The resulting figures should be considered only approximate. For his justification of his method, see 51–53.

19. Roosevelt's phrase comes from his "Economic Bill of Rights," part of his 1944 State of the Union Message to Congress, which can be viewed at http://www.fdrlibrary.marist.edu/archives/address_text.html. Catherine Bauer, *Modern Housing* (1934; repr., University of Minnesota Press, 2020), 136 (includes quote), 242. Many critiques of housing under capitalism take as their starting point arguments laid out in Friedrich Engels, *The Housing Question* (1872; repr., International Publishers, 1935). See, for example, David Harvey, "Capitalism Is Not the Solution to Urban America's Problems—Capitalism Itself Is the Problem," *Jacobin*, June 2, 2020, https://davidharvey.org/2020/06/capitalism-is-not-the-solution-to-urban-americas-problems-capitalism-itself-is-the-problem/.

20. Jackson's first collection of essays, J. B. Jackson, *Landscapes* (University of Massachusetts Press, 1970), is a good place to begin exploring his work.

21. Robert Fishman, *Urban Utopias in the Twentieth Century: Ebenezer Howard, Frank Lloyd Wright, Le Corbusier* (Basic Books, 1977); Eve Blau, *The Architecture of Red Vienna*

1919–1934 (MIT Press, 1999); Susan R. Henderson, *Building Culture: Ernst May and the New Frankfurt Initiative, 1926–1931* (Peter Lang, 2013); Owen Hatherley, *Red Metropolis: Socialism and the Government of London* (Repeater Books, 2020); Stanley Buder, *Visionaries and Planners: The Garden City Movement and the Modern Community* (Oxford University Press, 1990).

22. Plunz, *A History of Housing in New York City*.

23. Gail Radford, *Modern Housing for America: Policy Struggles in the New Deal Era* (University of Chicago Press, 1996); Kristin M. Szylvian, *The Mutual Housing Experiment: New Deal Communities for the Urban Middle Class* (Temple University Press, 2015); Kristin M. Szylvian, "The Federal Housing Program During World War II," in *From Tenements to the Taylor Homes,* ed. Bauman, Biles, and Szylvian.

24. See, among their other works, D. Bradford Hunt, "Public Housing in Urban America," *Oxford Research Encyclopedia of American History*, https://oxfordre.com/americanhistory/view/10.1093/acrefore/9780199329175.001.0001/acrefore-9780199329175-e-61?rskey=iq3AiF&result=1; Joseph Heathcott, "The Strange Career of Public Housing: Policy, Planning, and the American Metropolis in the Twentieth Century," *Journal of the American Planning Association* 78, no. 4 (2012): 360–75; Nicholas Dagen Bloom, *Public Housing That Worked: New York in the Twentieth Century* (University of Pennsylvania Press, 2008); Edward G. Goetz, *New Deal Ruins: Race, Economic Justice, and Public Housing Policy* (Cornell University Press, 2013); Lawrence J. Vale and Yonah Freemark, "From Public Housing to Public-Private Housing: 75 Years of American Social Experimentation," *Journal of the American Planning Association* 78, no. 4 (2012): 379–402; and Lawrence W. Vale, *Purging the Poorest: Public Housing and Design Politics of Twice-Cleared Communities* (University of Chicago, 2013).

25. Murray, *The Progressive Housewife*.

26. See, especially, Lasner, *High Life*; Matthew Gordon Lasner, "Bell Park Gardens," *SAH Archipedia*, https://sah-archipedia.org/buildings/NY-01-081-0001; and Matthew Gordon Lasner, "Architect as Developer and the Postwar U.S. Apartment, 1945–60," *Buildings & Landscapes* 21, no. 1 (2014): 27–55.

27. For a good discussion of scholarly critiques of the New Deal, especially with regard to race, see Katie Rader, "Race and the New Deal," *Catalyst* 8, no. 1 (2024): 81–118.

Chapter 1

1. In Southern California, some garden apartment developers preferred names meant to evoke Mexican-controlled "Old California," like Rancho San Pedro and Pueblo del Rio, but besides a few landscaping touches these projects had as little to do with Mexican architecture as garden apartments elsewhere had to do with traditional English buildings. Los Angeles Conservancy, "Garden Apartments of Los Angeles: Historic Context Statement," October 2012, 38.

2. Ebenezer Howard, *To-Morrow: A Peaceful Path to Real Reform* (Swan Sonnenchein & Co., 1898); Ebenezer Howard, *Garden Cities of To-Morrow* (1902; repr., Faber and Faber, 1946).

3. Joshua B. Freeman, *Behemoth: A History of the Factory and the Making of the Modern World* (W. W. Norton, 2018), 27–30; Claire Lévy-Vroelant, Christoph Reinprecht, Douglas Robertson, and Frank Wassenberg, "Learning from History: Path Dependency

and Change in the Social Housing Sectors of Austria, France, the Netherlands, and Scotland, 1889–2013," in *Social Housing in Europe*, ed. Kathleen Scanlon, Christine Whitehead, and Melissa Fernández Arrigoitia (John Wiley & Sons, 2014), 277–81; Fredrick Engels, *The Housing Question* (1872; repr., Progress Publishers, 1970), esp. 30–31; Maureen A. Flanagan, *Constructing the Patriarchal City: Gender and the Built Environments of London, Dublin, Toronto, and Chicago, 1870s into the 1940s* (Temple University Press, 2018), 15–18. In the United States, the most influential discussion of the dangers of slum housing to the broader society was Jacob A. Riis, *How the Other Half Lives: Studies among the Tenements of New York* (Charles Scribner's Sons, 1890).

4. Bellamy knew firsthand the wonders and ills of industrialization, spending his whole life in Chicopee Falls, Massachusetts, a textile manufacturing center. Howard grew wary of the idea of a powerful national administrative state, as imagined by Bellamy, instead suggesting a decentralization of power to local communities. Dugald Macfadyen, *Sir Ebenezer Howard and the Town Planning Movement* (MIT Press, 1970); Edward Bellamy, *Looking Backward: 2000–1887* (Ticknor & Co., 1888); Robert Fishman, *Urban Utopias in the Twentieth Century: Ebenezer Howard, Frank Lloyd Wright, Le Corbusier* (Basic Books, 1977), 36–37.

5. In essentially calling for the end of private land ownership, at least in urban areas, Howard went beyond George and most middle-class reformers. Henry George, *Progress and Poverty: An Inquiry into the Cause of Industrial Depressions and of Increase of Want with Increase of Wealth: The Remedy* (D. Appleton and Company, 1879); Fishman, *Urban Utopias*, 47–48.

6. Charles Fourier, *Design for Utopia: Selected Writings of Charles Fourier* (1901; repr., Schocken Books, 1971); Robert Owen, "Report to the County of Lanark, of a Plan for Relieving Public Distress and Removing Discontent" (1820), in *A New View of Society* (J. M. Dent, 1927).

7. Engels, *The Housing Question*, 49. See also Fredrick Engels, *Socialism: Scientific and Utopian* (International Publishers, 1935).

8. Macfadyen, *Sir Ebenezer Howard*, 44–79; Fishman, *Urban Utopias*, 59–63, 69–71; Edgar Bonham-Carter, "Planning and Development of Letchworth Garden City," *Town Planning Review* 21, no. 4 (1951): 362–76; Louis H. Pink, *The New Day in Housing* (John Day Company, 1928), 68–70; Dolores Hayden, *The Grand Domestic Revolution: A History of Feminist Designs for American Homes, Neighborhoods, and Cities* (MIT Press, 1981), 230–37.

9. Bonham-Carter. "Planning and Development of Letchworth Garden City," 372; Macfadyen, *Sir Ebenezer Howard*, 119–43; Jeffrey A. Kroessler, *Sunnyside Gardens: Planning and Preservation in a Historic Garden Suburb* (Fordham University Press, 2021), 23–24, 26.

10. Peter Hall, *Cities of Tomorrow: An Intellectual History of Urban Planning and Design in the Twentieth Century* (Basil Blackwell, 1988), 101–8.

11. Kenneth T. Jackson, *Crabgrass Frontier: The Suburbanization of the United States* (Oxford University Press, 1985), 76–86; Hall, *Cities of Tomorrow*, 89. For a monumental survey of garden suburbs, see Robert A. M. Stern, David Fishman, and Jacob Tilove, *Paradise Planned: The Garden Suburb and the Modern City* (Monacelli Press, 2013). In South Africa, garden city design was used to create whites-only communities, with greenbelts insulating them from Black and mixed-race settlements. Matthew Maganga, "Ecological Control and the Garden City: Utopia

for Whom?," *ArchDaily*, June 22, 2022, www.archdaily.com/983622/ecological-control-and-the-garden-city-utopia-for-whom.

12. Michael Harloe, *The People's Home?: Social Rented Housing in Europe and America* (Basil Blackwell, 1995), 26–27, 30–35, 39, 42, 52; Lévy-Vroelant, Reinprecht, Robertson, and Wassenberg, "Learning from History," 279–81; Claire Lévy-Vroelant and Christoph Reinprecht, "Housing the Poor in Paris and Vienna: The Changing Understanding of the 'Social,'" in *Social Housing in Europe*, ed. Scanlon, Whitehead, and Arrigoitia, 298; Edith Elmer Wood, *Housing Progress in Western Europe* (E. P. Dutton & Company, 1923); Catherine Bauer, *Modern Housing* (1934; repr., University of Minnesota Press, 2020), xlix, 94.

13. Harloe, *The People's Home?*, 80–147; Wood, *Housing Progress*, 67.

14. Bauer, *Modern Housing*, 124–27.

15. Harloe, *The People's Home?*, 107–12. On council housing in London, see Pink, *The New Day in Housing*, 15–24 (*Spectator* quote on 16); Owen Hatherley, *Red Metropolis: Socialism and the Government of London* (Repeater Books, 2000), 47–58; Bauer, *Modern Housing*, 132.

16. Bauer, *Modern Housing*, 100, 130–33, 225; Harloe, *The People's Home?*, 117–19, 139; Lévy-Vroelant, Reinprecht, Robertson, and Wassenberg, "Learning from History," 282–83.

17. Louis H. Pink's 1928 *The New Day in Housing*, which discusses European social housing along with the housing challenges in the United States, includes (pp. 58–66) an early account of the Vienna housing.

18. The low rents in Vienna's municipal housing not only aided workers but also their employers, allowing them to pay lower wages than otherwise would be necessary. This, in turn, helped promote exports, on which the city and country depended. Pink, *The New Day in Housing*, 62–63; Eve Blau, *The Architecture of Red Vienna 1919–1934* (MIT Press, 1999); Bauer, *Modern Housing*, 130–31, 225; Helmut Gruber, *Red Vienna: Experiment in Working-Class Culture 1919–1934* (Oxford University Press, 1991), 38, 49, 51–52, 55, 59–60. For comparative apartment sizes, see Blau, 181, and Adina Dragos, "National Average Apartment Size Shrinking as Studios & 1-Bedroom Apartments Gain in Share," RentCafe, March 16, 2023, https://www.rentcafe.com/blog/rental-market/market-snapshots/national-average-apartment-size/.

19. Hatherley, *Red Metropolis*, 47–48; Christopher Grey, "Built in 1931 by Idealism, Threatened Now by Reality," *New York Times*, July 3, 1994; "Our History," Amalgamated Dwellings, https://www.amalgamateddwellings.coop/history.

20. Harloe, *The People's Home?*, 85–86, 108; Lévy-Vroelant, Reinprecht, Robertson, and Wassenberg, "Learning from History," 281–82; Pink, *The New Day in Housing*, 25–45.

21. Kristianna Hartman, "The Berlin Garden City of Falkenberg: A Successful Example of Planning from the German Garden City Movement," in *Berlin/New York: Like and Unlike; Essays on Architecture and Art from 1870 to Present*, ed. Josef Paul Kleihues and Christina Rathgeber (Rizzoli, 1993), 83–84; Jörg Haspel and Annemarie Jaeggi, eds., *Housing Estates in the Berlin Modern Style* (Deutscher Kunstverlag, 2007), 20; Bauer, *Modern Housing*, 93, 98–100, 271–72; Harloe, *The People's Home?*, 117–19.

22. In the 1930s, while working as a city planner in the Soviet Union, May, closely following Howard's original conception of the garden city, went so far as to

propose the creation of a series of new satellite cities surrounding Moscow, allowing the depopulation and radical redesign of the capital, a scheme the Soviet leadership quickly rejected. The most comprehensive English-language study of Frankfurt social housing is Susan R. Henderson, *Building Culture: Ernst May and the New Frankfurt Initiative, 1926–1931* (Peter Lang, 2013). See also Eckhard Herrel, "'Constant Maturing': Student Years, House-Building in Frankfurt and War Memorials on the Front," 15, 19; Beate Störtkuhl, "Ernst May and the Schleisische Heimstätte," 33–46; Christoph Mohr, "The New Frankfurt: Housing Construction and the City 1925–30," 51–53; and Thomas Flierl, "'Possibly the Greatest Task an Architect Ever Faced': Ernst May in the Soviet Union (1930–1933)," 180–86, all in Claudia Quiing, Wolfgang Voight, Peter Cachola Schmal, and Eckhard Herrel, eds., *Ernst May 1886–1970* (Prestel, 2011).

23. Hall, *Cities of Tomorrow*, 117–19; Mohr, "The New Frankfurt," 53–65; Harloe, *The People's Home?*, 118; Gruber, *Red Vienna*, 60; Museum of Modern Art, "The Frankfurt Kitchen," Counter-Space: Design + The Modern Kitchen, exhibit, https://www.moma.org/interactives/exhibitions/2010/counter_space/the_frankfurt_kitchen/; Bauer, *Modern Housing*, 229. Apartment size from John Robert Mullin, "City Planning in Frankfurt, 1925–1932: A Study in Practical Utopianism," *Journal of Urban History* 4, no. 1 (1977): 20. As building costs rose, apartments shrank in size, with four-room units averaging only 807 square feet in 1930.

24. Much of the construction of the Berlin projects was carried out by special social building companies, including one sponsored by trade unions. Hartman, "The Berlin Garden City of Falkenberg," 87–88; Haspel and Jaeggi, *Housing Estates*; Hall, *Cities of Tomorrow*, 118–22; Natallia Barykina, "'The Dissolution of Cities': The Horseshoe Settlement in Weimar Berlin," *Urban History* 45, no. 3 (2018): 471–88. Information about the individual Berlin *Siedlungen* and photographs of them also can be found at "Siedlungen der Berliner Moderne," Landesdenkmalamt Berlin, https://www.berlin.de/landesdenkmalamt/welterbe/welterbestaetten/siedlungen-der-berliner-moderne/.

25. Pink served as one of the first members of the New York City Housing Authority. The Louis H. Pink Houses are in East New York, Brooklyn. Wood, *Housing Progress*, 186–87; Pink, *The New Day in Housing*, 15.

26. Gail Radford, *Modern Housing for America: Policy Struggles in the New Deal Era* (University of Chicago Press, 1996), 64–81; Bauer, *Modern Housing*, xlix (includes quotes).

27. Wood, *Housing Progress*, 180. See, also, Bauer, *Modern Housing*, 153.

Chapter 2

1. Richard Plunz was the first scholar to bring attention to these garden apartments in *A History of Housing in New York City* (Columbia University Press, 2016), on which my account draws heavily. See especially, 128, 130. See also James Nevius, "The Transformation of Jackson Heights," *Curbed New York*, April 19, 2017, https://ny.curbed.com/2017/4/19/15328342/jackson-heights-queens-history.

2. Mike Wallace, *Greater Gotham: A History of New York City from 1898 to 1919* (Oxford University Press, 2017), 202; Stanley Buder, *Visionaries and Planners: The Garden City Movement and the Modern Community* (Oxford University Press, 1990), 158–59; Jon A. Peterson, *The Birth of City Planning in the United States, 1840–1917*

(Johns Hopkins University Press, 2003), 235; "Cities for Workingmen," *New York Times*, December 3, 1906.

3. Wallace, *Greater Gotham*, 287–88; Buder, *Visionaries and Planners*, 164.

4. Siemens continued to build housing in what came to be called Siemensstadt, where it had large factories and administrative offices. Later a large *Siedlung*, Großsiedlung Siemensstadt, was built there as well. John Taylor Boyd Jr., "Garden Apartments in Cities," pt. II, *Architectural Record*, August 1920, 122; Plunz, *A History of Housing in New York City*, 138–39; Martin Münzel, *Building for the Future: Siemensstadt* (Siemens, 2019), 67, https://assets.new.siemens.com/siemens/assets/api/uuid:9ddcc6aa-ee37-4fef-a3db-1920537295ec/104-201912-journeys-through-history-1-siemensstadt-english-pdf.pdf.

5. The Queensboro buildings are still standing and have not been heavily modified. Ines M. Miyares, "From Exclusionary Covenant to Ethnic Hyperdiversity in Jackson Heights, Queens," *Geographical Review* 94, no. 4 (2004): 469–72; Plunz, *A History of Housing in New York City*, 139–48; Nevius, "The Transformation of Jackson Heights"; Matthew Gordon Lasner, *High Life: Condo Living in the Suburban Century* (Yale University Press, 2012), 66–76.

6. The Finnish cooperative building still stands at 816 43rd Street in Sunset Park. Miyares, "From Exclusionary Covenant to Ethnic Hyperdiversity," 469; Lasner, *High Life*, 35–39, 45, 60–63; Wallace, *Greater Gotham*, 275; [New York City] Landmarks Preservation Commission, "United Workers' Cooperative Colony," Designation List 245, June 2, 1992, 3.

7. The Garden Homes district is now a designated historic district. All the original homes survive, but some of the street names have been changed. National Register of Historic Places Registration Form for Garden Homes Historic District, 1990, National Park Service, United States Department of the Interior, https://npgallery.nps.gov/NRHP/GetAsset/NRHP/90000669_text; Katherine Kaliszewski, "The Garden Homes Community," National Park Service, https://www.nps.gov/articles/the-garden-homes-community.htm; Marsha Weisiger et al., "Garden Homes Historic District," *SAH Archipedia*, https://sah-archipedia.org/buildings/WI-01-MI120; Louis H. Pink, *The New Day in Housing* (John Day Company, 1928), 162. For 1940s efforts, see chapter 5 of this book.

8. Daniel Bluestone, "Framing Landscape While Building Density: Chicago Courtyard Apartments, 1891–1929," *Journal of the Society of Architectural Historians* 76, no. 4 (2017): 506–31; Carla Yanni, *Living on Campus: An Architectural History of the American Dormitory* (University of Minnesota Press, 2019), 4, 16, 128; John Nelson Tarn, *Five Per Cent Philanthropy: An Account of Housing in Urban Areas between 1840 and 1914* (Cambridge University Press, 1974), 18–21.

9. The second phase of the Coops had some modernist touches, which, though fairly subdued, set it off from the other projects. Later additions to the Amalgamated Houses included elevators. Plunz, *A History of Housing in New York City*, 151–63; Landmarks Preservation Commission, "United Workers' Cooperative Colony"; Melech Epstein, *The Jew and Communism: The Story of Early Communist Victories and Ultimate Defeats in the Jewish Community, U.S.A., 1919–1941* (Trade Union Sponsoring Committee, 1959), 216. For the early history of limited-dividend housing in London and Dublin, see Tarn, *Five Per Cent Philanthropy*, 22–23; Maureen A. Flanagan, *Constructing*

the Patriarchal City: Gender and the Built Environments of London, Dublin, Toronto, and Chicago, 1870s into the 1940s (Temple University Press, 2018), 26–29.

10. The newspaper argued that zoning should be used to limit building heights, which would keep land values from going so high that affordable housing would be impossible in dense areas like the Lower East Side. The articles were collected in a booklet *Garden Apartments to Replace Slums* (n.p., 1924). A copy can be found in box 20, Edith Elmer Wood papers, Department of Drawings & Archives, Avery Architectural and Fine Arts Library, Columbia University, New York.

11. Thomas designed yet another limited-dividend New York courtyard project, the Brooklyn Garden Apartments, a mile and a half from the first Finnish cooperative. Organized by Louis Pink, it had financing from, among others, New York Governor Alfred E. Smith, a local Democratic Party boss, and Rockefeller. Apartments cost about eleven dollars a room per month. Plunz, *A History of Housing in New York City*, 155–56, 159–60; Lasner, *High Life*, 99–106, 108–9; Reminiscences of Louis Heaton Pink, 1949, Columbia Center for Oral History, Columbia University, New York, 34–36; "Brooklyn Garden Apartments," *One More Folded Sunset* (blog), December 20, 2015, https://www.onemorefoldedsunset.com/2015/12/brooklyn-garden-apartments.html.

12. National Register of Historic Places Registration Form for Marshall Field Garden Apartments, National Park Service, United States Department of the Interior, https://web.archive.org/web/20151222080447/http://gis.hpa.state.il.us/pdfs/200892.pdf.

13. *Five-Year Report of the Michigan Boulevard Garden Apartments Building Corporation* (n.p., 1934); *Rosenwald Court Apartments Landmark Designation Report* (City of Chicago, September 7, 2017).

14. Plunz, *A History of Housing in New York City*, 168–73; Lewis Mumford, introduction to *Toward New Towns for America*, by Clarence Stein (MIT Press, 1957), 14–16; Jeffrey A. Kroessler, *Sunnyside Gardens: The Planning and Preservation in a Historic Garden Suburb* (Fordham University Press, 2021), 52–54. On the RPAA, see Edward K. Spann, *Designing Modern America: The Regional Planning Association of American and its Members* (Ohio State University Press, 1996).

15. Kroessler, *Sunnyside Gardens*, 29–31, 47–52; Gail Radford, *Modern Housing for America: Policy Struggles in the New Deal Era* (University of Chicago Press, 1996), 38–44.

16. Pink, *The New Day in Housing*, 98–114; Clarence Stein, *Toward New Towns for America* (MIT Press, 1957), 19–22; Kristin E. Larsen, *Community Architect: The Life and Vision of Clarence S. Stein* (Cornell University Press, 2016), 70; Henry Wright, "Housing—Why, When, and How?," pt. 2, *Architecture* 68 (1933), 85–86.

17. Kroessler, *Sunnyside Gardens*, 55–57; Stein, *Toward New Towns for America*, 23–24, 34 (includes quotes); Pink, *The New Day in Housing*, 111.

18. Spann, *Designing Modern America*, 14; Raymond Unwin, *Nothing Gained by Overcrowding!: How the Garden City Type of Development May Benefit Both Owner and Occupier* (Garden Cities & Town Planning Association, 1912); Henry Wright, "The Fallacy of Tall Building: A Swing of the Pendulum"; Wright to Clarence S. Stein, April 7, 1932; and Wright, "Will a New Dwelling Type Solve the Problem of Providing Low Rentals for the Lower-Income Groups?," all in box 3, Henry Wright Papers, Division

of Rare and Manuscript Collections, Cornell University Library, Ithaca, NY; *Rosenwald Court Apartments Landmark Designation Report*, 6. For Stein's taller buildings, see Stein, *Toward New Towns for America*, 77–95.

19. Stein, *Toward New Towns for America*, 21–33; Henry Churchill, "Henry Wright: 1878–1936," *Journal of the American Institute of Planners* 2, no. 4 (1960): 293; Nader Vossoughian and Matthew Gordon Lasner, "Sunnyside Gardens," in *Affordable Housing in New York: The People, Places, and Policies that Transformed a City*, ed. Nicholas Dagen Bloom and Matthew Gordon Lasner (Princeton University Press, 2016), 58–62; Kroessler, *Sunnyside Gardens*, 67–82; Plunz, *A History of Housing in New York City*, 171; Wright, "Housing—Why, When, and How?," 87.

20. The first three-story apartment building in Sunnyside Gardens also had 700-square-foot units, in a deliberate effort to make cost comparisons possible. There were somewhat larger units in two-story, two-family buildings at block ends and in two-story, single-family homes, which, at 1,086 square feet, were comparable in size to municipal apartments in Frankfurt. Sunnyside Gardens unit sizes calculated from Stein, *Toward New Towns for America*, 31.

21. Kroessler, *Sunnyside Gardens*, 62–66; Vossoughian and Lasner, "Sunnyside Gardens," 59–60; Larsen, *Community Architect*, 76–77.

22. Kroessler, *Sunnyside Gardens*, 82; Andrew Dolkart, *Biography of a Tenement House in New York City: An Architectural History of 97 Orchard Street*, 2nd ed. (University of Virginia Press, 2017), 24, 34–37, 79; Zachary J. Violette, *The Decorated Tenement; How Immigrant Builders and Architects Transformed the Slum in the Gilded Age* (University of Minnesota Press, 2019), 57–86; Stein, *Toward New Towns for America*, 29.

23. Kroessler, *Sunnyside Gardens*, 58, 82–84; Stein, *Toward New Towns for America*, 30.

24. For the later history of Sunnyside Gardens, see Kroessler, *Sunnyside Gardens*, esp. chapters 6, 9, and 10.

25. Stein, *Toward New Towns for America*, 37–69; Larsen, *Community Architect*, 85; Kroessler, *Sunnyside Gardens*, 88.

26. Clarence Arthur Perry, "The Neighborhood Unit: A Scheme for Arrangement of Family-Life Community," in *Neighborhood and Community Planning, Regional Survey*, vol. VI (Regional Plan of New York and Its Environs, 1929). For earlier ideas that Perry drew on, see Donald Leslie Johnson, "Origin of the Neighbourhood Unit," *Planning Perspectives* 17 (2002); 227–45, and Lewis Mumford, "The Neighborhood and the Neighborhood Unit," *Town Planning Review* 24 (1954): 256–70.

27. James Dahir, *The Neighborhood Unit Plan, Its Spread and Acceptance* (Russell Sage Foundation, 1947), esp. 27–83; A. T. Erickson and A. R. Highsmith, "The Neighborhood Unit: Schools, Segregation, and the Shaping of the Modern Metropolitan Landscape," *Teachers College Record* 120, no. 3 (2018): 1–36.

28. Perry endorsed the idea that "the tendency toward segregation along racial, cultural, and economic lines is a natural phenomenon of urban life" and applauded approaches to urban development that "accelerated and improved in character" that tendency. Clarence Arthur Perry, "The Tangible Aspects of Community Organization," *Social Forces* 8, no. 4 (1930): 563; Perry, "The Neighborhood Unit," 25.

29. Catherine Bauer, who joined the RPAA sometime after its initiation, was a notable dissenter. Stein apparently was not, though he himself was Jewish. Larsen, *Community Architect*, 84.

30. Mumford, "The Neighborhood and the Neighborhood Unit," 263; Wright, "Housing—Why, When, and How?," 95–97; Henry Wright, "Study of Application of Sunnyside Planning Principles to a Larger City Area," box 3, Henry Wright Papers; Stein, *Toward New Towns for America*, 38–39, 44.

31. Unwin consulted with the RPAA group during the early stages of design and construction of Radburn. Larsen, *Community Architect*, 89, 91; Stein, *Toward New Towns for America*, 41, 56, 64; Spann, *Designing Modern America*, 115.

32. Stein, *Toward New Towns for America*, 77–85; Angelique Bamberg, *Chatham Village: Pittsburgh's Garden City* (University of Pittsburgh Press, 2014), Ingham quote on 85.

33. Bamberg, *Chatham Village*, 134; Jane Jacobs, *The Death and Life of Great American Cities* (Random House, 1961), 64–65, 73, 79–80, 84.

34. National Register of Historic Places Multiple Property Documentation Form: "Garden Apartments, Apartment Houses and Apartment Complexes in Arlington County, Virginia: 1934–1954," 2002, National Park Service, United States Department of the Interior, 10.

35. In 1931, there were 245,000 housing starts, about one-third the yearly average during the 1920s. Radford, *Modern Housing*, 86.

36. Avi Garelick and Andrew Schustek, "The Rise and Fall of the Coops," *Jewish Currents*, December 7, 2020, https://jewishcurrents.org/the-rise-and-fall-of-the-coops; "Rockefeller Block Auctioned in Bronx," *New York Times*, October 28, 1936; Lasner, "Housing to Remember: The Paul Laurence Dunbar Apartments," Gotham Center for New York City History, March 28, 2017, https://www.gothamcenter.org/blog/housing-to-remember-the-paul-laurence-dunbar-apartments.

37. Kroessler, *Sunnyside Gardens*, 101–14; Stein, *Toward New Towns for America*, 64–67.

38. Lasner, "Housing to Remember"; Thomas Lee Philpott, *The Slum and the Ghetto: Neighborhood Deterioration and Middle-Class Reform, Chicago, 1880–1930* (Oxford University Press, 1978), 267–68; Stephen Becker, *Marshall Field III: A Biography* (Simon & Schuster, 1964), 113–14; Stein, *Toward New Towns for America*, 67.

Chapter 3

1. "Address of the President, Grant Field, Atlanta, Georgia" and "Informal Extemporaneous Remarks of the President, Atlanta University," both November 29, 1935, box 23, Franklin D. Roosevelt Master Speech File, 1898–1945, Franklin D. Roosevelt Presidential Library and Museum, Hyde Park, New York (hereafter FDR Library); "Hoover's 'Corner' Gets into Roosevelt Speech," *New York Times*, November 30, 1935; "Roosevelt Rose Bush for Housing Project," *New York Times*, August 30, 1936.

2. Edith Elmer Wood, "Public Housing and/or Private," *Survey Graphic* 24, no. 1 (1935): 5.

3. Wolfgang M. Rudorf, "The Housing Division of the Public Works Administration in its Architectural Context" (master's thesis, MIT, 1984), 13–14; C. W. Short and R. Stanley-Brown, *Public Buildings: A Survey of Architecture of Projects Constructed by Federal and Other Governmental Bodies Between the Years 1933 and 1939 with the Assistance of the Public Works Administration* (US Government Printing Office, 1939), 654; Edward K. Spann, *Designing Modern America: The Regional Planning Association*

of American and its Members (Ohio State University Press, 1996), 145; Richard Plunz, *A History of Housing in New York City: Dwelling Type and Social Change in the American Metropolis* (Columbia University Press, 1990), 225; Harold L. Ickes, *The Secret Diary of Harold L. Ickes: The First Thousand Days, 1933–1936* (Simon & Schuster, 1953), 673.

4. Rudorf, "The Housing Division of the Public Works Administration," 15, 34–35.

5. Spann, *Designing Modern America*, 137, 140, 188–89; Gail Radford, *Modern Housing for America: Policy Struggles in the New Deal Era* (University of Chicago Press, 1996), 101; "Summary of Discussion at the Housing Conference, Before Hon. Harold L. Ickes," September 30, 1937, copy in folder 3, box 8, Edith Elmer Wood papers, Department of Drawings & Archives, Avery Architectural and Fine Arts Library, Columbia University, New York.

6. Playwright William Inge was among the early Neighborhood Gardens residents. Joseph Heathcott, "'In the Nature of a Clinic': The Design of Early Public Housing in St. Louis," *Journal of the Society of Architectural Historians* 70, no. 1 (2011): 82–103; Frances Schutze, *The Little Bastard* (Anchor & Plume Press, 2014).

7. Radford, *Modern Housing for America*, 97–98, 110–44; Gail Radford, "The Federal Government and Housing During the Great Depression," in *From Tenements to the Taylor Homes: In Search of an Urban Housing Policy in Twentieth-Century America*, ed. John F. Bauman, Roger Biles, and Kristin M. Szylvian (Penn State University Press, 2000), 105; Richard Pommer, "The Architecture of Urban Housing in the United States during the Early 1930s," *Journal of the Society of Architectural Historians* 36, no. 4 (1978): 239–42.

8. Of the other five PWA limited-dividend projects, two were small row house projects and one a small apartment project. The biggest projects by far were two apartment complexes in New York City: Hillside Homes, designed by Clarence Stein, and Boulevard Gardens, developed by the Dick-Meyer Corporation. Radford, *Modern Housing for America*, 93; Clarence Stein, *Toward New Towns for America* (MIT Press, 1957), 93–107; "Historical Overview," Boulevard Gardens, https://boulevardgardens.nyc/history.

9. Henry Wright, *Rehousing Urban America* (Columbia University Press, 1935), "remarkable attainments" on 96; National Association of Housing Officials, *Program for the United States* (National Association of Housing Officials, 1934); Ernest J. Bohn to Col. Louis McHenry Howe, November 13, 1934, Franklin D. Roosevelt, Papers as President: The President's Official File, Part 1, OF 63, Housing, box 1, FDR Library; Horace W. Peaslee to Edith Elmer Wood, June 12, 1936, and William V. Reed, "European Housing, A Series of Confidential Reports to The Housing Division, P.W.A.," folder 2, box 8, Wood papers; Stewart McDonald to Stephen F. Early, February 19, 1937, and M. H. McIntyre to McDonald, February 27, 1937, Franklin D. Roosevelt, Papers as President: The President's Official File, OF 1091, Federal Housing Administration, FDR Library.

10. Though the government supervised the construction of these projects, local architects and constructions companies were hired to carry them out. Radford, *Modern Housing for America*, 99–101.

11. [New York City] Landmarks Preservation Commission, "Williamsburg Houses," Designation List 348, June 24, 2003; Radford, *Modern Housing for America*, 100–101.

12. For a sense of the depth of central PWA involvement in specific projects, see Public Housing Administration Project Files (1933–1937), Project H-1000 General

Folders, boxes 1 and 2, Record Group 196, National Archives at College Park, College Park, MD, which deal with PWA housing projects in Cleveland, Ohio. See also Radford, *Modern Housing for America*, 102; Rudorf, "The Housing Division of the Public Works Administration," 55–57, 65–67, 75, 77, 111, 168–69; Shannon Clark, *The Making of the American Creative Class: New York's Culture Workers and Twentieth-Century Consumer Capitalism* (Oxford University Press, 2021), 167.

13. Reed, "European Housing"; Stonorov letter quoted in Pommer, "The Architecture of Urban Housing," 242–43; Rudorf, "The Housing Division of the Public Works Administration," 137. The public housing program in Frankfurt also moved toward greater simplification and standardization in its last phase, not because of the lack of skilled designers but because of decreased funding. See Susan R. Henderson, *Building Culture: Ernst May and the New Frankfurt Initiative* (Peter Lang, 2013), 397–418.

14. Techwood and University Homes began as limited-dividend projects but were taken over by the PWA after it turned to direct-built housing. Robert D. Kohn to Henry M. Waite, October 12, 1933, and Max Dunning and M. D. Carrel to C. E. Pynchon, January 15, 1934, H-1101 file 3 of 3, General Folders, box 28, Public Housing Administration Project Files (1933–1937), RG 196, National Archives at College Park; Frank Ruechel, "New Deal Public Housing, Urban Poverty, and Jim Crow: Techwood and University Homes in Atlanta," *Georgia Historical Quarterly* 81, no. 4 (1997): 915–37; Irene Holliman, "Techwood Homes," *New Georgia Encyclopedia*, https://www.georgiaencyclopedia.org/articles/arts-culture/techwood-homes/; Federal Emergency Administration of Public Works, *Homes for Workers: Housing Division Bulletin No. 3* (US Government Printing Office, 1937), 56–57, 76; Lawrence W. Vale, *Purging the Poorest: Public Housing and Design Politics of Twice-Cleared Communities* (University of Chicago Press, 2013), 68–69, 75; "Ickes Hits Rents on PWA Housing," *New York Times*, July 10, 1936.

15. Radford, *Modern Housing for America*, 104–5; Ruechel, "New Deal Public Housing," 927; T. H. Watkins, *Righteous Pilgrim: The Life and Times of Harold L. Ickes, 1874–1952* (Henry Holt, 1990), 645–46; Short and Stanley-Brown, *Public Buildings*, 656.

16. Ruechel, "New Deal Public Housing," 922–24; M. H. McIntyre to Secretary Ickes, November 19, 1938, Ickes to Mr. President, December 2, 1935, and A. R. Clas, Memorandum to the Administrator, November 27, 1935, all in OF 63, box 2, FDR Library.

17. In 1933 Ickes, following up on a suggestion from FDR, hired Clark Foreman from the Rosenwald Fund to oversee the treatment of African Americans throughout the federal government. Following pushback from the NAACP and in the black community about employing a white Southerner in the post, Ickes hired Robert Weaver as Foreman's assistant. In 1934 Foreman moved to the Power Division of the PWA and Weaver took over his position. Watkins, *Righteous Pilgrim*, 645–46; Heathcott, "'In the Nature of a Clinic,'" 87–88; Ruechel, "New Deal Public Housing," 929–31; Robert C. Weaver, "Note on the Techwood Drive Project," H-1101 file 3 of 3, and William G. Rogers, "Dear Sirs," June 22, 1934, and Frances L. Kenny, "Dear Mr. President," file 1101.02, box 28, Public Housing Administration Project Files (1933–1937), RG 196, National Archives at College Park.

18. "Public Housing," *Architectural Forum*, May 1938, 350, 360–414.

19. United States Department of Agriculture, Resettlement Administration, *Report of the Administrator of the Resettlement Administration, 1937* (US Government Printing

Office, 1937), 1–2; Daniel T. Rodgers, *Atlantic Crossings: Social Politics in a Progressive Age* (Harvard University Press, 2000), 454–55; Stein, *Toward New Towns for America*, 119–20; Stanley Buder, *Visionaries and Planners: The Garden City Movement and the Modern Community* (Oxford University Press,1990), 176 (first quote); Rexford Tugwell to Franklin D. Roosevelt, December 12, 1935 (second quote), President's Secretary File, container 53, FDR Library.

20. For the sake of clarity, the name FSA is used throughout, even in connection with developments that occurred when it was still called the RA. During World War II, additional housing was constructed in the greenbelt towns for war workers. After the war, the federal government sold Greenbelt and Greenhills to cooperative associations of their tenants. Divisions among Greendale residents led to the piecemeal sale of its individual buildings and vacant lots. Rodgers, *Atlantic Crossings*, 469–70; Rexford Tugwell to Franklin D. Roosevelt, March 12, 1936, and accompanying "Memorandum, Re: Litigation—Bound Brook Suburban Resettlement Project," President's Secretary File, container 53, FDR Library; Gourney and Sies, "Greenbelt, Maryland," 207, 212–13; Stein, *Toward New Towns for America*, 119–20, 136–37; "Greenhills Historic District," *SAH Archipedia*; National Register of Historic Places Registration Form for Greendale Historic District, 18–19, 49, 64; Starner-Heffron, "The Story of Greendale," 49; United States Department of Agriculture, Resettlement Administration, *Report of the Administrator of the Resettlement Administration, 1938* (US Government Printing Office, 1938), 20; Federal Writers' Project, *The WPA Guide to Washington, D.C.* (1942; repr., Pantheon, 1983), 478.

21. Stein, *Toward New Towns for America*, 119, 121, 128, 150; Isabelle Gourney and Mary Corbin Sies, "Greenbelt, Maryland: Beyond the Iconic Legacy," in *Housing Washington: Two Centuries of Residential Development and Planning in the National Capital Area*, ed. Richard Longstreth (Center for American Places at Columbia College Chicago, 2010); Alex Baca, "The New Deal Landmark That's Cannibalizing Itself," CityLab, *Bloomberg*, January 31, 2018, https://www.bloomberg.com/news/articles/2018-01-31/the-utopian-vision-of-greenhills-ohio-is-crumbling; "Greenhills Historic District," *SAH Archipedia*, https://sah-archipedia.org/buildings/OH-01-061-0074; National Register of Historic Places Registration Form for Greendale Historic District, 2005, National Park Service, United States Department of the Interior, https://npgallery.nps.gov/NRHP/GetAsset/NRHP/05000763_text; Sierra Starner-Heffron, "The Story of Greendale: A Utopia Unrealized," *e.polis* 7 (2015): 82–100.

22. Stein, *Toward New Towns for America*, 8; National Register of Historic Places Registration Form for Greendale Historic District, 65–66.

23. See, for example, Ronald Lawson, ed., *The Tenant Movement in New York City, 1904–1984* (Rutgers University Press, 1986), 39–133; Annie Howard, "When the Unemployed Fought Back," *Shelterforce*, February 24, 2022, https://shelterforce.org/2022/02/24/when-the-unemployed-fought-back/.

24. Ralph Steiner and Willard Van Dyke, *The City* (American Documentary Film Inc., 1939), 43 min.; H. Peter Oberlander and Eva M Newbrun, *Houser: The Life and Work of Catherine Bauer, 1905–64* (University of British Columbia Press, 1999), 151–52; Howard Gillette Jr., "Film as Artifact: *The City* (1939)," *American Studies* 18, no. 2 (1977): 71–85.

25. For a classic study of antiurbanism in US life, see Morton White and Lucia

White, *The Intellectual Versus the City: From Thomas Jefferson to Frank Lloyd Wright* (Harvard University Press, 1962). On the New Deal, see Joshua Freeman et al., *Who Built America? Working People and the Nation's Economy, Politics, Culture, and Society Vol. II* (Pantheon, 1992), 345–54; Michael Denning, *The Cultural Front: The Laboring of American Culture in the Twentieth Century* (Verso, 1997).

26. Radford, *Modern Housing for America*, 184–86. For labor backing of the 1937 housing bill, see "1937 May" and "1937 June" folders, box 4, OF 63 Housing, FDR Library.

27. M. H. McIntyre to Frank Crowther, March 13, 1937, OF 63, box 2, FDR Library; Short and Stanley-Brown, *Public Buildings*, 655.

28. Radford, *Modern Housing for America*, 181–90; John H. Mollenkopf, *The Contested City* (Princeton University Press, 1983), 68–69; Miles L. Colean, *American Housing: Problems and Prospects* (Twentieth Century Fund, 1944), 279–80; "Public Housing and the USHA," *Architectural Forum*, January 1940, 6.

29. Lower average land costs also reduced the cost of USHA housing compared to PWA projects. Radford, *Modern Housing for America*, 189–92; Colean, *American Housing*, 281, 439; Mason B. Williams, *City of Ambition: FDR, La Guardia, and the Making of Modern New York* (W. W. Norton, 2013), 186–87.

30. The USHA obtained funds to lend for construction by selling bonds. Many local housing authorities also used bond funding for their share of capital costs. Catherine Bauer estimated that in 1940 the operating subsidies for USHA housing averaged $20 per person per year from the federal government and $5 per person per year from local tax exemptions ($457 and $114 in 2025 dollars). Catherine Bauer, *A Citizen's Guide to Public Housing* (Vassar College, 1940), 24–25, 28–29, 80–81; "Public Housing and the USHA," 3–4; Colean, *American Housing*, 279.

31. "Public Housing," *Architectural Forum*, May 1938, 347, 349.

32. Federal Works Agency, United States Housing Authority, "Design of Low-Rent Housing Projects: Architectural Planning and Design Checking List," August 1939, https://www.huduser.gov/portal/publications/Design-of-Low-Rent-Housing-Projects-Architectural-Planning-and-Designhtml.

33. Plunz, *History of Housing in New York City*, 240; Gwendolyn Wright, *Building the Dream: A Social History of Housing in America* (Pantheon, 1981), 235–36; Federal Works Agency, *First Annual Report, 1940* (US Government Printing Office, 1940), 358–78; Joseph Heathcott, "Planning Note: Pruitt-Igoe and the Critique of Public Housing," *Journal of the American Planning Association* 78, no. 4 (2012): 450–51; D. Bradford Hunt, "What Went Wrong with Public Housing in Chicago? A History of the Robert Taylor Homes," *Journal of the Illinois State Historical Society* 94, no. 1 (2001): 101–7, 116–17; Bauer, *A Citizen's Guide to Public Housing*, 40.

34. National Register of Historic Places Registration Form for Rosewood Courts Historic District, National Park Service, United States Department of the Interior, https://atlas.thc.texas.gov/NR/pdfs/14000549/14000549.pdf (no longer available); "Santa Rita Courts," Housing Authority of the City of Austin, https://www.hacanet.org/location/santa-rita-courts/; Federal Works Agency, United States Housing Authority, *Terms, Covenants, and Conditions Compromising Part Two of Contract for Loan and Annual Contributions between Local Authority and the United States Housing Authority* (1940), copy in Housing Authority of the City of Los Angeles (HACLA), "Resolutions 7.2.40–7.19.40," digital file, HACLA.

35. Jared Kofsky, "Newark's Seth Boyden Terrace Site Could Become 'Area in Need of Redevelopment,'" *Jersey Digs*, June 15, 2020, https://jerseydigs.com/seth-boyden-terrace-newark-could-become-area-in-need-of-redevelopment/; Karen Yi, "Newark's Demolition of South Ward Housing Project Comes with Promises of New Development," *Gothamist*, February 18, 2022, https://gothamist.com/news/newarks-demolition-of-south-ward-housing-project-comes-with-promises-of-new-development; William B. Helmreich, *The Enduring Community; The Jews of Newark and MetroWest* (Transaction Publishers, 1999), 56.

36. *Report of the Housing Authority of New Orleans: For The Period March 15, 1937 to December 31, 1938*, 17, 19, 26, and *Report of the Housing Authority of New Orleans: For The Year Ending December 31, 1942*, 5, City Archives & Special Collections, New Orleans Public Library, New Orleans, LA. National plumbing figures calculated from US Bureau of the Census, *Sixteenth Census of the United States: 1940; Housing, Volume II, Part I* (US Government Printing Office, 1943), 18.

37. "The Building of the Lafitte Housing Project—1941," *Creolegen*, August 20, 2014, http://www.creolegen.org/2014/08/20/the-building-of-the-lafitte-housing-project-1941/; Nicolai Ouroussoff, "All Fall Down," *New York Times*, November 19, 2006; *Report of the Housing Authority of New Orleans: For The Year Ending December 31, 1940*, 13, 22, City Archives & Special Collections, New Orleans Public Library, New Orleans, LA.

38. New York City Housing Authority, *Clason Point Gardens* (New York City Housing Authority, 1942), 3-5.

39. New York City Housing Authority, *Clason Point Gardens*, Straus quote, 2–3; "One-Family Houses with Individual Yards Included in Calson Point Housing Project," *New York Times*, October 21, 1940; "Defense May Halt City Housing Plan," *New York Times*, September 30, 1941; Maria Newman, "Clason Point Gardens Journal; For 50 Years a Home, a Real Home," *New York Times*, August 6, 1992; Hunt, "What Went Wrong with Public Housing in Chicago?"; Nicholas Dagen Bloom, *Public Housing That Worked: New York in the Twentieth Century* (University of Pennsylvania Press, 2008), 1–10.

40. Stanley Dunlap, "Tindall Heights Transformation to Begin in May," *The Telegraph* (Macon, Georgia), April 30, 2016, https://www.macon.com/news/local/article74943697.html; Jonathan Gould, *Otis Redding: An Unfinished Life* (Crown, 2017), 47–48.

41. Lana Robert in "The Building of the Lafitte Housing Project—1941."

42. Mollenkopf, *The Contested City*, 69–70; Kenneth T. Jackson, *Crabgrass Frontier: The Suburbanization of the United States* (Oxford University Press, 1985), 203–18; Richard Rothstein, *The Color of Law: A Forgotten History of How Our Government Segregated America* (Norton, 2017); Lizabeth Cohen, *A Consumer's Republic: The Politics of Mass Consumption in Postwar America* (Vintage Books, 2004), 194–256.

43. "Garden Apartments," *Architectural Forum*, May 1940, 309; Laura Bobeczko and Richard Longstreth, "Housing Reform Meets the Marketplace: Washington and the Federal Housing Administration's Contribution to Apartment Building Design, 1935–1940," in *Housing Washington*, ed. Longstreth, 159, 178; Lasner, *High Life*, 120.

44. Colean, *American Housing*, 268.

45. *Third Annual Report of the Federal Housing Administration* (US Government Printing Office, 1937), 5, 15, 23; "Progress Report on FHA-Insured Rental Housing Program," *Real Estate Record*, October 1938, 34.

46. Bobeczko and Longstreth, "Housing Reform Meets the Marketplace," 165; Henry Churchill, "Henry Wright: 1878–1936," *Journal of the American Institute of Planners* 2, no. 4 (1960): 298.

47. In New York, Rosario Candela, who in the 1920s had been the most prominent architect of apartment buildings for the rich and the very rich, setting the standard for Park Avenue luxury, designed Regency Park, an FHA-insured apartment complex in Kew Gardens, Queens. Though the Regency Park structures had some characteristics of traditional apartment buildings, notably apartment access via internal public hallways, in scale and site layout they shared much with garden apartments. National Register of Historic Places Multiple Property Documentation Form: "Garden Apartments, Apartment Houses and Apartment Complexes in Arlington County, Virginia, 1934–1954," National Park Service, United States Department of the Interior, 16–17; Lasner, *High Life*, 120–22; Bobeczko and Longstreth, "Housing Reform Meets the Marketplace," 167–70; *QueensBorough*, June–July 1939.

48. Lasner, *High Life*, 120–22; Bobeczko and Longstreth, "Housing Reform Meets the Marketplace," 167, 169–72, 174.

49. National Register of Historic Places Registration Form for Buckingham Historic District, December 14, 1998, National Park Service, United States Department of the Interior; "Henry Wright, 58, Architect, Dead," *New York Times*, July 10, 1936.

50. Exposed heat risers were a cheap way to heat bathrooms and kitchens. Instead of installing radiators, pipes bringing hot water or steam from one floor to another were left exposed, rather than put inside walls. While these risers provided heat, they could not be turned on or off and anyone who touched a pipe could be burned. Bobeczko and Longstreth, "Housing Reform Meets the Marketplace," 170–72, 174, 178–79; "Garden Apartments, Apartment Houses and Apartment Complexes in Arlington County, Virginia, 1934–1954," 13–14, 17–19; Miles L. Colean, "Multiple Housing Under FHA," *Architectural Record*, September 1938, 96–132; Eugene H. Klaber to All Chief Zone Architects, February 20, 1940, and FHA Rental Housing Division Architectural Bulletins #1–19, copies in vol. 4, Eugene H. Klaber papers, Department of Drawings and Archives, Avery Library, Columbia University. For USHA room sizes, see Federal Works Agency, United States Housing Authority, "Design of Low-Rent Housing Projects," 2.

51. The FHA review and inspection process can be followed in the files for "Third Buckingham," in Projects Files for Multi-Unit Housing Developments, 1936–1946, boxes 1–4, RG 31, National Archives at College Park. Mr. Field to Mr. Dusenberry, "Final Landscape Inspection," October 12, 1938, is in box 4.

52. As of the end of 1941, New York State had the most units of FHA-insured rental housing, followed by Virginia, Maryland, New Jersey, California, the District of Columbia, Pennsylvania, Illinois, North Carolina, and Missouri. *Eighth Annual Report of the Federal Housing Administration* (US Government Printing Office, 1942), 36–37.

53. Bauer, *A Citizen's Guide to Public Housing*, 39; Carol Crotta, "L.A. Fertile Ground for Garden Apartments," *Los Angeles Times*, October 24, 2014.

54. David J. Witmer served as chief architectural supervisor for the FHA in Southern California before resigning to design Wyvernwood. Harry Bennett, "Wyvernwood and Its Rental Policies," [FHA] *Insured Mortgage Portfolio* 4, no. 8 (1940): 8–10, 19; Colean, "Multiple Housing Under FHA," 120; "Garden Apartments," *Architectural Forum*, May 1940, 311–13; Steven Keylon, "The Complete Wyvernwood Series," *Baldwin*

Village . . . and the Village Green (blog), http://baldwinhillsvillageandthevillagegreen.blogspot.com/2011/09/complete-wyvernwood-series.html.

55. Los Angeles Conservancy, "We Love Garden Apartments," https://www.laconservancy.org/wp-content/uploads/2022/11/GardenAptsTourBk_Final2webLR.pdf; Hector Becerra, "For Garden Complex in Boyle Heights, a Season of Change," *Los Angeles Times*, December 5, 2009; Federal Housing Administration, *Underwriting Manual* (US Government Printing Office, 1936), pt. II, para. 233; Federal Housing Administration, *Underwriting Manual* (US Government Printing Office, 1938), para. 980 (3); LaDale C. Winling and Todd M. Michney, "The Roots of Redlining: Academic, Governmental, and Professional Networks in the Making of the New Deal Lending Regime," *Journal of American History* 108, no. 1 (2021): 42–69; F.D.R., "Memorandum for Hon. Stewart McDonald," June 20, 1936, and McDonald to The President, July 7, 1936, OF 1091, box 3, FDR Library.

56. When it opened, monthly rents per room at Baldwin Hills Village averaged $12.27, compared to $7.66–$9.83, depending on apartment size, at Wyvernwood. Stein, *Toward New Towns for America*, 189; Colean, "Multiple Housing Under FHA," 120.

57. *Seventh Annual Report of the Federal Housing Administration* (US Government Printing Office, 1941), 86, 95; "Garden Apartments," *The Architectural Forum*, May 1940, 309.

58. Westmoreland Gardens sales brochure, Avery Library, Columbia University, https://dlc.library.columbia.edu/nyre/cul:fbg79cnqm0; "Little Neck Suites to be Opened Today: Suburban Apartments with Small Garden-Court Units," *New York Times*, August 18, 1940.

Chapter 4

1. "Chair from Channel Heights Housing Project, San Pedro," Los Angeles County Museum of Art, https://collections.lacma.org/node/172663; "Richard Neutra Channel Heights Stool," Uber-Modern, https://richard-neutra.uber-modern.com/en/richard-neutra/91-channel-heights-stool-neutra.html (no longer available); "Neutra Furniture Collection by VS," https://neutra.vs.de/show/neutra-produkte (no longer available); Barbara Lamprecht, "Neutra's Boomerang Chair: Fanfare for the Common Man," *Modern Resources* (blog), July 6, 2013, https://barbaralamprecht.com/2013/07/06/neutras-boomerang-chair-fanfare-for-the-common-man/.

2. Federal Works Agency, *First Annual Report, 1940* (US Government Printing Office, 1940), 42–45; National Housing Agency, Office of the Administrator, "History of the Administration of War Housing During World War II," August 11, 1945, https://www.huduser.gov/portal/sites/default/files/pdf/History-of-the-Administration-of-War-Housing-During-World-War-II.pdf; National Housing Agency, *War Housing in the United States* (1945), copy in file "War Housing in the United States," Records Pertaining to Title VI and Title VII of the National Housing Act, Record Group 31, National Archives at College Park, College Park, MD; Kristin M. Szylvian, "The Federal Housing Program During World War II," in *From Tenements to the Taylor Homes: In Search of an Urban Housing Policy in Twentieth-Century America*, ed. Kristin M. Szylvian, John F. Bauman, and Roger Biles (Penn State University Press, 2000), 121–38. The divide between defense and nondefense housing was porous. Some public housing,

built for low-income families, was converted for the duration of the war into quarters for workers in the defense industry or was opened to them on a priority basis. In other cases, defense housing was constructed with the specific intention of converting it into civilian housing after the war. In still other cases, projects designed to house war workers, not completed in time for wartime service, were recast as low-income housing. See, for example, Minutes of an Adjourned Regular Meeting of the Commissioners of the Housing Authority of the City of Los Angeles, California, Held on October 17, 1941, and Minutes of a Regular Meeting of the Commissioners of the Housing Authority of the City of Los Angeles, California, Held on November 18, 1941, Housing Authority of the City of Los Angeles (HACLA) records (digital); *New York Housing Authority News*, October 15, 1942; *Report of the Housing Authority of New Orleans For The Period December 31, 1942 Through September 30, 1944*, 95, and *Report of the Housing Authority of New Orleans For the Year Ending September 30, 1950*, 11, City Archives & Special Collections, New Orleans Public Library, New Orleans, LA.

3. The Lanham Act appropriated $140 million for defense housing, to be built by the FWA. In 1941 Congress authorized another $450 million. Jason E. Taylor, "The New Deal Goes to War: The Role of the Alphabet Agencies in World War II Mobilization," *Essays in Economic and Business History* 22 (2004): 241–49; Szylvian, "The Federal Housing Program During World War II," 123–27 (Carmody quote on 125).

4. McLean Gardens had thirty-one garden apartment buildings and nine dormitories. Holly K. Chamberlain, "Permanence in Time of War: Three Defense Homes Corporation Projects in the Washington Metropolitan Area," in *Housing Washington: Two Centuries of Residential Development and Planning in the National Capitol Area*, ed. Richard Longstreth (Center for American Places at Columbia College Chicago, 2010); McLean Gardens, http://www.mcleangardens.com/home.asp; "History of McLean Gardens," *McLean Gardens Today* (blog), https://mcleangardenshomes.wordpress.com/history-of-mclean-gardens/.

5. Clarence Stein, *Toward New Towns for America* (MIT Press, 1957), 113, 120–22.

6. Glenayr and Kenmore Apartments are both still standing and occupied. National Register of Historic Places Multiple Property Documentation Form: "Garden Apartments, Apartment Houses and Apartment Complexes in Arlington County, Virginia, 1934–1954," National Park Service, United States Department of the Interior, 20–23.

7. Brehon Somervell, Memorandum for Major General Edwin M. Watson, August 26, 1941, and F.D.R., Memorandum for Pa, September 6, 1941, Franklin D. Roosevelt, Papers as President: The President's Official File, OF 63, Housing, box 7, FDR Library; Laura L. Bobeczko, "A Study in Decentralized Living: Parkfairfax, Alexandria, Virginia," *Historic Alexandria Quarterly* (Spring 1997): 1–17; Jeffrey S. Gurock, *Parkchester: A Bronx Tale of Race and Ethnicity* (New York University Press, 2019); Los Angeles Conservancy, "Garden Apartments of Los Angeles: Historic Context Statement," October 2012, 39; Woody LaBounty, "Parkmerced," OutsideLands.Org, June 2006, http://www.outsidelands.org/parkmerced.php/; *Fairlington Villages Handbook*, 8th ed., January 2021, 18–19, https://smallpdf.com/file#s=a4e8c6f2-e7b3-4f34-92ff-1b6a9d8f3eef.

8. Lindsay Peterson, "Building the Home Front: The Lanham Act and the Modernization of American Housing, 1940–1945" (PhD diss., New York University, 2017), 114–74; Taylor, "The New Deal Goes to War," 249; Szylvian, "The Federal Housing Program During World War II," 134–35.

9. Kristin M. Szylvian, “Bauhaus on Trial: Aluminum City Terrace and Federal Defence Housing Policy during World War II,” *Planning Perspectives* 9, no. 3 (1994): 230; Peter S. Reed, “Enlisting Modernism,” in *World War II and the American Dream: How Wartime Building Changed a Nation*, ed. Donald Albrecht (National Building Museum and MIT Press, 1995), 11; Peterson, “Building the Home Front,” 76–78, 87–91.

10. For examples of local resistance to central control of defense housing, see Minutes of a Regular Meeting of the Commissioners of the Housing Authority of the City of Los Angeles, California, Held on October 7, 1941, 2–3, HACLA records (digital); *Report of the Housing Authority of New Orleans: For The Year Ending December 31, 1941*, 21–25, City Archives & Special Collections, New Orleans Public Library, New Orleans, LA; Zenia Kotval, “Opportunity Lost: A Clash between Politics, Planning, and Design in Defense Housing for Pittsfield, Massachusetts,” *Journal of Planning History* 2, no. 1 (2003): 29–30.

11. “Dessau-Törten Housing Estate (1926–28),” Bauhaus Dessau, https://www.bauhaus-dessau.de/en/architecture/bauhaus-buildings-in-dessau/dessau-toerten-housing-estate.html; Anthony Paletta, “The Dream of the Bauhaus Is Alive Just Outside Pittsburgh,” CityLab, *Bloomberg*, March 12, 2019, https://www.citylab.com/design/2019/03/bauhaus-pennsylvania-gropius-breuer-aluminum-city-terrace/584485/; “Aluminum City Terrace,” Pittsburgh Art Places, http://www.pittsburghartplaces.org/accounts/view/504; Szylvian, “Bauhaus on Trial,” 229–54.

12. Donald Albrecht and Eeva-Liisa Pelkonen, eds., *Eero Saarinen: Shaping the Future* (Yale University Press, 2006), 139; Eric Follo, “Kramer Homes: A Community, Not a Complex,” *Michigan History Magazine*, May–June 2013; “What Is Required to Begin the Process of Becoming a Member?,” Kramer Homes Co-Operative, https://kramerhomesco-op.com/requirements/.

13. On labor support for defense housing, see Memorandum submitted by the Housing Committee of the Congress of Industrial Organizations to the Office for Emergency Management on April 12, 1941, The President’s Official File, OF 63, Housing, box 7, FDR Library; Kristin M. Szylvian, *The Mutual Housing Experiment: New Deal Communities for the Urban Middle Class* (Temple University Press, 2015), 4, 38, 76; Peterson, “Building the Home Front,” 35–36, 47–51, 78.

14. After the war, the Carver Court units were sold off individually. In the years that followed, most owners added gabled roofs, all of them covered the wood siding with vinyl or other material, and some enclosed the “Plan C” carports and porches, so the buildings no longer retain their original look and are less visually striking. Szylvian, *Mutual Housing Experiment*, 104–5; Urs Büttiker, *Louis I. Kahn: Light and Space* (Whitney Library of Design, 1994), 12, 45; Wendy Lesser, *You Say to Brick: The Life of Louis Kahn* (Farrar, Straus and Giroux, 2017), 105; Sarah Williams Goldhagen, *Louis Kahn’s Situated Modernism* (Yale University Press, 2001), 19–20; National Register of Historic Places Registration Form for Carver Court, National Park Service, United States Department of the Interior, https://steelmuseum.org/uploads/NRHP%20Registration%20Form%2016000310.pdf; Robert McCarter, *Louis I. Kahn* (Phaidon Press, 2003), 35.

15. Thomas J. Sugrue, *The Origins of the Urban Crisis: Race and Inequality in Postwar Detroit*, rev. ed. (Princeton University Press, 2014), 72–73; Gerald Van Dusen, *Detroit’s Sojourner Truth Housing Riot of 1942: Prelude to the Race Riot of 1943* (History Press, 2020); Interview with Clark Foreman, November 16, 1974, Southern Oral History

Program Collection (#4007), https://docsouth.unc.edu/sohp/html_use/B-0003.html; National Register of Historic Places Registration Form for Sojourner Truth Homes, August 3, 2022, National Park Service, United States Department of the Interior, https://www.miplace.org/4ab2e9/globalassets/documents/shpo/programs-and-services/civil-rights-project/sojourner-truth-homes_detroit_wayne-county_nps-scan.pdf.

16. The Mutual Ownership Defense Housing Division built a total of eight projects. For a definitive history of the effort, see Szylvian, *Mutual Housing Experiment*. See, also, Lawrence Westbrook Papers, box 5, folder 3, The Texas Collection, Baylor University, and John M. Carmody to Lawrence Westbrook, August 24, 1942, John M. Carmody Papers, Box 81, FDR Library. For Audubon Village, see "Building for Defense . . . Government Housing in a Hurry," *Architectural Forum*, May 1941, 341–44.

17. Avion Village remains occupied and cooperatively owned. Szylvian, *Mutual Housing Experiment*, 57–61; Thomas S. Hines, *Richard Neutra and the Search for Modern Architecture* (Oxford University Press, 1982), 174–79; "Lost and Found: Avion Village," AIA Dallas Springboard, https://www.aiadallas.org/v/columns-detail/Lost-Found-Avion-Village/pb (no longer available).

18. The executive director of the Los Angeles housing authority explained in April 1941 that "it is the policy . . . to select tenants from the same racial groups as are now living on sites, in the same proportion as exists at the present time. . . . If you have an area where there is no segregation, we expect to maintain that status quo in that area. On the other hand, if you have an area where racial groups are presently segregated, we expect to maintain that status quo in the area." Minutes of an Adjourned Regular Meeting of the Commissioners of the Housing Authority of the City of Los Angeles, California, Held on April 9, 1942, HACLA records (digital). Henry Kraus, a former UAW journalist, lived in Channel Heights during World War II and its aftermath and wrote about the experience, with particular attention to race relations, in *In the City was a Garden* (Renaissance Press, 1951). See also Minutes of a Regular Meeting of the Commissioners of the Housing Authority of the City of Los Angeles, California, Held on April 7, 1942, 6–7, and Minutes of a Regular Meeting Held on November 17, 1942, 3, HACLA records (digital); Scott Gold, "At an Impoverished Housing Complex, a Reflection of South L.A.," *Los Angeles Times*, July 14, 2009; "Pueblo del Rio Historic District," Los Angeles Historic Resources Inventory, Historic Places LA, http://historicplacesla.org/reports/3b706ba6-ffad-47d3-9dc9-f782a4b2ba6b; Hines, *Richard Neutra*, 179–86; Peterson, "Building the Home Front," 150–57; and Los Angeles Conservancy, "Garden Apartments of Los Angeles," 42–43.

19. *A Bill to Establish a National Housing Policy and Provide for Its Execution Part 2: Hearings on S. 1592 Before the Senate Committee on Banking and Currency*, 79th Cong. 1st sess. (December 6, 7, 11, 12, 13, 14, 17, 18, 1945, and January 24 and 25, 1946) [Revised] (US Government Printing Office, 1946), 890; Bobeczko, "A Study in Decentralized Living," 10–11.

20. Szylvian, *Mutual Housing Experiment*, 5, 38, 47–49; Hines, *Richard Neutra*, 196.

21. Peterson, "Building the Home Front," 25–26, 34; John M. Carmody to Lawrence Westbrook, March 23, 1948, John M. Carmody Papers, Box 81, FDR Library.

22. Kotval, "Opportunity Lost," 31–39, which includes the quotes from Lanham and Truman. Wright's Pittsfield design built on a plan he developed in 1913 for siting four single-family homes on a block, each facing a different direction. The project was never constructed. Daniel Bluestone, "Framing Landscape While Building

Density: Chicago Courtyard Apartments, 1891–1929," *Journal of the Society of Architectural Historians* 76, no. 4 (2017): 527–28. In a parallel dynamic, in Frankfurt local architects complained that Ernst May did not make sufficient use of their services, hiring architects from outside the area. They were particularly critical of the hiring of Austrian architects to work on Frankfurt projects. Susan R. Henderson, *Building Culture: Ernst May and the New Frankfurt Initiative, 1926–1931* (Peter Lang, 2013), 66.

23. "Calls Job Bungled in Defense Housing," *New York Times*, October 30, 1941; "Carmody is Named to Maritime Body," *New York Times*, November 20, 1941; Thomas J. Hamilton, "House Bars Vote on Housing Funds," *New York Times*, December 2, 1941; Winifred Mallon, "Straus Quits Post as Head of USHA," *New York Times*, January 6, 1942; "Straus Says Foes Seek to Kill USHA," *New York Times*, February 18, 1942; Interview with Clark Foreman, November 16, 1974; Robert F. Wagner to President Roosevelt, November 23, 1941, and Samuel I. Rosenman to Mr. President [n.d.], President's Official File, OF 63, Housing, box 7, FDR Library.

24. Samuel I. Rosenman to Mr. President [n.d.] (includes "complete reorganization"); Sammy the Rose [Rosenman], Memorandum for the President, December 1, 1941; and Robert F. Wagner to President Roosevelt, February 4, 1942, all in President's Official File, OF 63, Housing, box 7, FDR Library; W. H. Lawrence, "President Merges Housing Agencies," *New York Times*, February 25, 1942; Peterson, "Building the Home Front," 34–40 (quote from *Architectural Record* on 40); Szylvian, *Mutual Housing Experiment*, 102–3, 105–7; Franklin D. Roosevelt, "Excerpts from the Press Conference," December 28, 1943, The American Presidency Project, https://www.presidency.ucsb.edu/documents/excerpts-from-the-press-conference-8.

25. Federal Housing Administration (FHA), *Insured Mortgage Portfolio*, 3rd quarter 1945, 14–15, 32, and 4th quarter 1945, 23; "Summary of 1942 Amendments to the National Housing Act," file "Interoffice Memorandum Title VI," Records Pertaining to Title VI and Title VII of the National Housing Act, Record Group 31, National Archives.

26. National Housing Agency, *War Housing in the United States*, 6.

27. The politics of Defense City can be followed in folder "1942 Jan-May," President's Official File, OF 63, Housing, box 7, FDR Library. See also Sarah Jo Peterson, *Planning the Home Front: Building Bombers and Communities at Willow Run* (University of Chicago Press, 2013); National Register of Historic Places Registration Form for Carver Court, National Park Service, United States Department of the Interior, 21; Szylvian, *Mutual Housing Experiment*, 82–87, 94–97.

Chapter 5

1. This account is based on family documents in possession of the author.

2. United States Department of Labor, Bureau of Labor Statistics, *Nonfarm Housing Starts 1889–1958*, Bulletin 1260 (US Government Printing Office, 1959), 15–16; New York State Division of Housing, *Annual Report of the Commission of Housing to the Governor and the Legislature for the Year ending March 31, 1951*, 140–43; Federal Housing Administration (FHA), *Insured Mortgage Portfolio*, 1st quarter 1946, 3–4; Laura McEnaney, *Postwar: Waging Peace in Chicago* (University of Pennsylvania Press, 2018), 42.

3. See, for example, Guy Greer and Alvin H Hansen, *Urban Redevelopment and Housing: A Program for Post-War* (National Planning Association, 1941); National

Association of Housing Officials, *Housing for the United States after the War* (National Association of Housing Officials, 1944); National Housing Agency, *Housing Needs: A Preliminary Estimate* (National Housing Agency, November 1944), "Housing Needs: A Preliminary Estimate" file, Records Pertaining to Post-World War II Housing 02/24/1942-1950 container # 1, Record Group 31, National Archives at College Park, College Park, MD; Hilary Botein, "Labor Unions and Affordable Housing; An Uneasy Relationship," *Urban Affairs Review* 42, no. 6 (2007): 802.

4. There is an extensive literature on the GI bill, including Michael J. Bennett, *When Dreams Came True: The GI Bill and the Making of Modern America* (Brassey's, 1996); Suzanne Mettler, *Soldiers to Citizens: The G.I. Bill and the Making of the Greatest Generation* (Oxford University Press, 2005); and Glenn C. Altschuler and Stuart M. Blumin, *The GI Bill: A New Deal for Veterans* (Oxford University Press, 2009). *A Bill to Establish a National Housing Policy and Provide for Its Execution Part 2: Hearings on S. 1592 Before the Senate Committee on Banking and Currency*, 79th Cong. 1st sess. (December 6, 7, 11, 12, 13, 14, 17, 18, 1945, and January 24 and 25, 1946) [Revised] (US Government Printing Office, 1946); Rosalind Tough, "What's Behind Housing," *Social Science Review* 23, no. 1 (1949): 26–31; Bill Mauldin, *Back Home* (William Sloane Associates, 1947), 77; FHA, *Insured Mortgage Portfolio*, 3rd quarter 1945, 1, 4.

5. Tim O'Neil, "A Look Back: Returning WWII Vets Picketed City Hall to Protest the Tight Housing Market," *St. Louis Post-Dispatch*, December 28, 2022; Joshua B. Freeman, *Working-Class New York: Life and Labor since World War II* (New Press, 2000), 105–8; "Veterans Picket Here," *New York Times*, March 10, 1946; "Veterans Seize New York State Senate Chamber," *The Sunday Star*, October 20, 1946; Minutes of a Regular Meeting of the Commissioners of the Housing Authority of the City of Los Angeles, California, Held on January 15, 1946, 2, and Minutes of a Regular Meeting of the Commissioners of the Housing Authority of the City of Los Angeles, California, Held on June 10, 1946, 2, Housing Authority of the City of Los Angeles (HACLA) records (digital); Jack Smith, "Give Me Shelter: L.A.'s Post-WWII Housing Shortage Foreshadowed the Crisis of the 1980s," *Los Angeles Times*, September 17, 1989; "Veterans Camp in Park to Protest Housing Shortage," *The Key West Citizen*, January 11, 1947.

6. Chloe N. Thurston, *At the Boundaries of Homeownership: Credit, Discrimination, and the American State* (Cambridge University Press, 2018), 30–33, 58; Richard O. Davies, *Housing Reform During the Truman Administration* (University of Missouri Press, 1966), 40; US Bureau of the Census, *Historical Statistics of the United States, Colonial Times to 1970*, bicentennial ed., pt. 2 (US Government Printing Office, 1975), 639; FHA, *Insured Mortgage Portfolio*, 1st quarter 1946, 29, and 1st quarter 1947, 3.

7. *FHA Investigation Before the Senate Committee on Banking and Currency*, 84th Cong. 1st sess. (January 6, 1955), 8–10; *United States Statutes at Large*, vol. 60 (US Government Printing Office, 1947), 207–15 ("veterans" on 214); Office of Housing Expediter, National Housing Agency, *Rental Housing: Opportunities for Builders & Investors* (US Government Printing Office, [1947?]), includes all other quotes; National Register of Historic Places Registration Form for Lincoln Place Apartments (draft) National Park Service, United States Department of the Interior, 14–15.

8. Roberta Gold, *When Tenants Claimed the City: The Struggle for Citizenship in New York City Housing* (University of Illinois Press, 2014), 21–22, 28–29; "Apartment Boom," *Architectural Forum*, January 1950, 98; *FHA Investigation*, 9, 47; *FHA*

Investigation: Hearings, Part 1, Before the Senate Committee on Banking and Currency, 83rd Cong. 2nd sess. (1954), 104.

9. Federal Housing Administration, *Administrative Rules and Regulations for Rental Housing Insurance Under Section 608 of the National Housing Act* (US Government Printing Office, 1946), 3, 12. The use and abuse of section 608 are discussed extensively in Committee on Banking and Currency, *FHA Investigation* and *FHA Investigation: Hearings, Part 1*.

10. The National Housing Act limited FHA mortgage insurance to $5 million per project. To evade the limit, several different corporations were set up to borrow money to build Glen Oaks Village in sections. *FHA Investigation: Hearings, Part 1*, 53, 559–61.

11. *FHA Investigation: Hearings, Part 1*, 52, 57; Ira S. Robbins and Marian Sameth, eds., *Directory of Large-Scale Rental and Cooperative Housing* (Citizens' Housing and Planning Council of New York, 1957), 23.

12. The National Archives has a copy of *Story of Glen Oaks Village* (Record Group 306, MAID 49415, Local ID 306.3063), but it was unavailable for viewing at the time of this writing. The script of the movie and information about its distribution can be found in "Glen Oaks Village Motion Picture" file, container 12, and "Story of Glen Oaks Village" file, container 41, US Information Agency, Motion Picture and Television Service, Laboratory Services, Film Versions, 1953?–1965?, Record Group 306: Records of the US Information Agency, National Archives at College Park.

13. FHA, *Insured Mortgage Portfolio*, 4th quarter 1946, 5, 3rd quarter 1947, 22, 32, 2nd quarter 1948, 2, Fall 1953, 6, and Winter 1953–54, 31 (number 608 units); Department of Housing and Urban Development, Office of Policy Development and Research, "Assisted Housing: National and Local," https://www.huduser.gov/portal/datasets/assthsg.html#year2009-2022 (public housing units); Marc Perry, Brian Mendez-Smith, and Lynda Laughlin, "National Archives Will Soon Release 1950 Census, Offering a Look at a Defining Time in Modern U.S. History," US Bureau of the Census, March 28, 2022, https://www.census.gov/library/stories/2022/03/1950-census-records-window-to-history.html.

14. Richard White, *Railroaded: The Transcontinentals and the Making of Modern America* (Norton, 2011), 26–36; James Wolfinger, *Running the Rails: Capital and Labor in the Philadelphia Transit Industry* (Cornell University Press, 2016), 25–26; Nelson Lichtenstein and Judith Stein, *A Fabulous Failure: The Clinton Presidency and the Transformation of American Capitalism* (Princeton University Press, 2023), 390–91; "Apartment Boom," *Architectural Forum*, January 1950, 97; *FHA Investigation: Hearings, Part 1*, 545.

15. *FHA Investigation*, 11; International Union, United Automobile, Aircraft and Agricultural Implement Workers of America, *Homes for Workers in Planned Communities Thru Collective Action* (International Union, 1943); *A Bill to Establish a National Housing Policy and Provide for Its Execution Part 2*, 685–66, 697–98, 723–24, 730.

16. New York State Division of Housing, *Annual Report of the Commission, 1951*, 61–64; "How It All Began . . . ," *Bell Park Gardens Yearbook*, 1950–51, 5, http://bpg.50megs.com/YEARBOOK/yearbook.html; Joshua B. Freeman, *American Empire, 1945–2000: The Rise of a Global Power; the Democratic Revolution at Home* (Viking, 2012), 32–35.

17. The original Electchester complex consisted of a mixture of three-story walk-up and six-story elevator buildings, laid out in a typical garden apartment arrangement. Two high-rise buildings were later added. Thomas E. Dewey to A. Lincoln Bush and Harry Van Arsdale, Jr., September 15, 1949, reprinted in James R. Harley, "Electchester," unpublished paper, July 10, 1971, copy in possession of the author.

18. New York State and California together accounted for about 90 percent of the section 213 projects. *FHA Investigation: Hearings, Part 1*, 12; Davies, *Housing Reform During the Truman Administration*, 117–21, 149; FHA, *Insured Mortgage Portfolio*, Winter 1953–54, 23, 31. For a list of section 213 garden apartments in New York City, see Robbins and Sameth, *Directory of Large-Scale Rental and Cooperative Housing*, 18–23.

19. *FHA Investigation*, 70, 73–74; "Apartment Boom," *Architectural Forum*, January 1950, 100–101; Robbins and Sameth, *Directory of Large-Scale Rental and Cooperative Housing*, 21; John A. Bradley, "900 Garden Suites Started in Queens by Gross-Morton," *New York Times*, December 12, 1950; Diana Shaman, "Born in the Postwar Era," *New York Times*, August 22, 1999; "Saratoga Will Get Garden Apartments," *New York Times*, October 5, 1947.

20. Figures derived from a database of garden apartments developed by the author. Because some data is missing, the total number of units is an undercount. Fresh Meadows and Electchester, both of which had a mixture of two- or three-story buildings and larger apartment buildings, are not included. The low-rise components of those developments have several thousand apartments. Database sources: Robbins and Sameth, *Directory of Large-Scale Rental and Cooperative Housing*; "279-Unit Housing Sold at Bayside," *New York Times*, January 21, 1951; "Investor Acquires Housing in Queens," *New York Times*, May 21, 1951; "Investors Acquire Bayside Housing," *New York Times*, December 22, 1952; "Garden Apartments Converted," *New York Times*, November 26, 1978; Alan S. Oser, "About Real Estate; Condominium Restoring Life to a Queens Complex," *New York Times*, July 16, 1982; Alan S. Oser, "Perspectives: Conversions; Upgrading Queens Garden Apartments," *New York Times*, May 19, 1985; Matthew Gordon Lasner, *High Life: Condo Living in the Suburban Century* (Yale University Press, 2012), 151; "Featured Properties," Esquire Management Corporation, https://www.esquiremanagement.com/featured-properties.php.

21. From database described in note 20.

22. Lasner, *High Life*, 151; George Barrett, "550 Apartments Will Be Erected In Flushing Meadow Area for U.N.," *New York Times*, April 28, 1946; "$4,000,000 Suites Started in Queens," *New York Times*, June 18, 1950; Alan S. Oser, "Clearview: A Sense of Cooperative Living in Queens," *New York Times*, March 31, 1978; *Kew Gardens Post*, April 12, 1940; Claudia Gryvatz Copquin, *The Neighborhoods of Queens* (Yale University Press, 2007), 79–80; *New York Daily News*, September 17, 1986. Examples of section 608 garden apartments can be found in Federal Housing Administration, *Neighborhoods Built for Rental Housing: Examples of Rental Housing Developments Built and Financed by Private Enterprise with Mortgages Insured by FHA* (Federal Housing Administration, 1947). See also FHA, *Insured Mortgage Portfolio*, which often profiled garden apartment complexes. On Los Angeles, see Los Angeles Conservancy, "Garden Apartments of Los Angeles: Historic Context Statement," October 2012.

23. US Bureau of the Census, *U.S. Census of Housing: 1950. Vol. I, General Characteristics, Part 1: U. S. Summary* (US Government Printing Office, 1953), 90, 94; *Long Island Press*, January 21, 1957; Oser, "Clearview."

24. "About Great Neck Terrace," Great Neck Terrace, http://www.greatneckterrace.com/about.html; "Garden Village Owners Corp.," Richland Management Company, https://www.richlandmgmt.com/village-garden-owners-corp.

25. Garden apartment complexes in Westchester include Bryn Mawr Ridge and Greystone-in-Westchester in Yonkers, Ridgewood Gardens in Rye, Country Club Ridge in Hartsdale, Interlaken Gardens in Eastchester, and Cooper Hill Apartments in New Rochelle.

26. Kathleen Lynn, "Garden Apartments Help Shape the N.J. Landscape," *northjersey.com*, August 28, 2016, https://www.northjersey.com/story/news/2016/08/28/garden-apartments-help-shape-the-nj-landscape/92965962/.

27. Robert Schafer, *The Suburbanization of Multifamily Housing* (Lexington Books, 1974), 6–7; "Apartment Boom," *Architectural Forum*, January 1950, 101; Federal Housing Administration, *Planning Rental Housing Projects*, revised September 1947 (US Government Printing Office, 1947); FHA, *Neighborhoods Built for Rental Housing*. See also FHA, *Insured Mortgage Portfolio*, which regularly published layouts for and examples of garden apartments. For a discussion of the FHA design approval process from the viewpoint of a developer, see *FHA Investigation: Hearings, Part 1*, 560.

28. *FHA Investigation*, 9; "Apartment Boom," *Architectural Forum*, January 1950, 100; FHA, *Planning Rental Housing Projects*, 6–8, 14, 21–22 ("decorative effect" on 6; emphasis in original). Floor plans used to calculate apartment size for Arrowbrook Gardens and Beech Hills are available at the New York Real Estate Brochure Collection, Avery Architectural & Fine Arts Library, Columbia University.

29. FHA, *Planning Rental Housing Projects*, 6–7; Los Angeles Conservancy, "Garden Apartments of Los Angeles," 47; Anders Åman, *Architecture and Ideology in Eastern Europe during the Stalin Era: An Aspect of Cold War History* (MIT Press, 1992).

30. "Architects Score Federal Housing," *New York Times*, June 29, 1950. The Stonorov comments are quoted in Richard Pommer, "The Architecture of Urban Housing in the United States during the Early 1930s," *Journal of the Society of Architectural Historians* 36, no. 4 (1978): 242–43.

31. "Apartment Boom," *Architectural Forum*, January 1950, 101, 104–5. For examples of more modernist 608 projects, see FHA, *Planning Rental Housing Projects*, 61–62.

32. *FHA Investigation*, 3, and *FHA Investigation: Hearings, Part 1*, 188–89, 285–86, 291, 379–82.

33. The architects for New York City garden apartments are listed in Robbins and Sameth, *Directory of Large-Scale Rental and Cooperative Housing*. "Benjamin Braunstein, 79, Dead; Architect of Garden Apartments," *New York Times*, January 22, 1972; Matthew Gordon Lasner, "Bell Park Gardens," *SAH Archipedia*, https://sah-archipedia.org/buildings/NY-01-081-0001; Mathew Gordon Lasner, "Architect as Developer and the Postwar U.S. Apartment, 1945–60," *Buildings & Landscapes* 21, no. 1 (2014): 43–46, 54.

34. At least for some, this was in spite of their continued interest. Richard Neutra designed a major public housing project for Chavez Ravine in Los Angeles, which included garden apartment–style units. The homes of many low-income residents were demolished to clear the site, but a campaign attacking public housing as socialistic

led the city to abandon the project. Thomas S. Hines, *Richard Neutra and the Search for Modern Architecture* (Oxford University Press, 1982), 109, 196; Thomas S. Hines, "The Battle of Chavez Ravine," *Los Angeles Times*, April 20, 1997.

35. Gail Gregory Sansbury, "Lincoln Place: A Case Study of a Multi-Family Rental Complex Built in Los Angeles in 1949–50" (master's thesis, University of California, Los Angeles, 1993), 67–70; National Register of Historic Places Registration Form for Lincoln Place Apartments, 24–27; "Bellrose Suites Ahead of Schedule," *New York Times*, August 26, 1951; "Stanley H. Klein Dies; Housing Architect," *New York Times*, April 17, 1992; "Apartment Boom," *Architectural Forum*, January 1950, 108; Barry Moore, "Building a Houston Practice: The Career of S.I. Morris," *Cite: The Architecture + Design Review of Houston* 43 (1999): 30–31.

36. *FHA Investigation*, 64, 99; Sansbury, "Lincoln Place," 61–62; FHA, *Insured Mortgage Portfolio*, 4th quarter 1947, 5.

37. Arnold R. Hirsch, "Choosing Segregation: Federal Housing Policy Between Shelley and Brown," in *From Tenements to the Taylor Homes: In Search of an Urban Housing Policy in Twentieth-Century America*, ed. John F. Bauman, Roger Biles, and Kristin M. Szylvian (Penn State University Press, 2000), 208–9.

38. Sansbury, "Lincoln Place," 46; Federal Housing Administration, *Underwriting Manual* (Federal Housing Administration, 1947), para. 1320(1) and 1320(2). There apparently are no studies that examine racial practices at garden apartments. Nor are there any studies of African American garden apartment projects, but, for examples, see FHA, *Insured Mortgage Portfolio*, 1st quarter 1947, 13, 2nd quarter 1947, 3, 3rd quarter 1947, 11–12, 27, and Fall 1953, 9–11 (Aiken on 11).

39. Cleveland Rodgers and Rebecca Rankin, *New York: The World's Capital City, Its Development and Contributions to Progress* (Harper, 1948), 300–301; National Register of Historic Places Registration Form for Parkway Village, December 29, 2011, National Park Service, United States Department of the Interior, section 8, 8–9, 21. Parkway Village is a ten-minute drive from the house where Donald Trump grew up in Jamaica Estates.

40. Brafman bought the land for Merrick Park Gardens from the estate of Homer and Langley Collyer, two reclusive brothers who died in 1947 in a booby-trapped Harlem brownstone filled with their hoardings. Some accounts describe Merrick Park Gardens as being built specifically for black families. "Collyer Tract Sold in Court for $92,000," *New York Times*, March 25, 1950; "Cooperative Apartments of 116 Families Started on Old Collyer Reality in Jamaica," *New York Times*, April 8, 1951; "$1,040,300 Loan Set on Queens Housing," *New York Times*, March 28, 1952; Lee E. Cooper, "Site in South Jamaica to Be Improved With Co-Operative Housing for Negroes," *New York Times*, April 25, 1952; Lasner, *High Life*, 151, 155.

41. The 1960 census also listed fifty-five persons of "Other Races" in Queens census tract 1551. US Bureau of the Census, *U.S. Census of Population: 1950*, vol. III, *Census Tract Statistics*, chap. 37 (US Government Printing Office, 1952), 140; US Bureau of the Census, *U.S. Census of Population and Housing: 1960. Census Tracts*, Final Report PHC(1)-104, pt. 1 (US Government Printing Office, 1962), 181. For the 1970 census, the boundaries of the tract were changed, making data thereafter incomparable. For the citywide population, see Kenneth T. Jackson, ed., *The Encyclopedia of New York City* (Yale University Press, 1995), 920.

42. Freeman, *Working-Class New York*, 68–71; Martha Biondi, *To Stand and Fight:*

The Struggle for Civil Rights in Postwar New York City (Harvard University Press, 2003); Joel Schwartz, *The New York Approach: Robert Moses, Urban Liberals, and the Redevelopment of the Inner City* (Ohio State University Press, 1993), 110, 202.

43. There is a very large literature on residential segregation and its effects. See, for example, Douglas S. Massey and Nancy A. Denton, *American Apartheid: Segregation and the Making of the Underclass* (Harvard University Press, 1993); Richard Rothstein, *The Color of Law: A Forgotten History of How Our Government Segregated America* (Liveright, 2017), esp. 168–93; George Lipsitz, *The Possessive Investment in Whiteness: How White People Profit from Identity Politics* (Temple University Press, 2006), 5–15, 108–11; and Mimi Abramovitz and Richard J. Smith, "The Persistence of Residential Segregation by Race, 1940 to 2010: The Role of Federal Housing Policy," *Families in Society: The Journal of Contemporary Social Sciences* 102, no. 1 (2021): 5–32. For an interesting comparison of current analyses of housing discrimination with those from the immediate postwar years, see Preston H. Smith II, "Race and the Housing Question," *Catalyst* 7, no. 1 (2023): 71–117.

44. Davies, *Housing Reform During the Truman Administration*, 104–5, 126–28; D. Bradford Hunt, "Public Housing in Urban America," *Oxford Research Encyclopedia of American History*, https://oxfordre.com/americanhistory/view/10.1093/acrefore/9780199329175.001.0001/acrefore-9780199329175-e-61?rskey=iq3AiF&result=1; Roger Biles, "Public Housing and the Postwar Urban Renaissance, 1949–1973," in *From Tenements to the Taylor Homes*, ed. Bauman, Biles, and Szylvian, 145; National Register of Historic Places Registration Form for Mar Vista Gardens (Draft), National Park Service, United States Department of the Interior, 11.

45. Nicholas Dagen Bloom, *Public Housing That Worked: New York in the Twentieth Century* (University of Pennsylvania Press, 2008), 74.

46. Lucia Anaya, "Former LeClaire Courts Residents Are Still Fighting to Go Home," *Chicago Reader*, August 4, 2016, https://www.chicagoreader.com/chicago/leclaire-courts-redevelopment-controversy-cha/Content?oid=23039100; "Racine Courts," *Chicago Gang History*, https://www.chicagoganghistory.com/housing-project/racine-courts/; "Lowden Homes," Chicago Housing Authority, https://web.archive.org/web/20121115154912/http://www.thecha.org/pages/Lowden_Homes/50.php?devID=261.

47. Los Angeles Conservancy, "Garden Apartments of Los Angeles," 25–27.

48. National Register of Historic Places Registration Form for Mar Vista Gardens (Draft), 4–5, 11, 14–15, 31.

49. Claire Spiegel, "Watts Housing Project Will Be Renovated," *Los Angeles Times*, July 18, 1987; C. Kaye Rawlings, "The Watts Riots, Nickerson Gardens, and Black Lives Matter," *Artillery*, July 15, 2020, https://artillerymag.com/provenance/; Los Angeles Conservancy, "Garden Apartments of Los Angeles," 42–43, 80, 89. In addition to Mar Vista Gardens and Nickerson Gardens, the Housing Authority of the City of Los Angeles also built the smaller San Fernando Gardens in Pacoima.

50. The Housing Authority of New Orleans continued its aggressive building program after World War II, but even it admitted its new projects had deficiencies. *Report of the Housing Authority of New Orleans*: *For Year Ending September 30, 1950*, 5–11, *For Year Ending September 30, 1952*, 7, *For Year Ending September 30, 1953*, 7, and *For Year Ending September 30, 1954*, 9, 35, City Archives & Special Collections, New Orleans Public Library, New Orleans, LA; Laine Kaplan-Levenson, host, *TriPod: New Orleans*

at 300, podcast, "Desire, Louisiana," WWNO 89.9, October 11, 2018, https://www.wwno.org/podcast/tripod-new-orleans-at-300/2018-10-11/desire-louisiana; Michael Matsumaru, "Desire Housing Project, New Orleans, Louisiana (1956–2001)," *Black Past*, September 30, 2010; Takashi Michael Matsumaru, "Defending Desire: Resident Activists in New Orleans' Desire Housing Project, 1956–1980" (master's thesis, University of New Orleans, 2011), quote on 16.

51. Hunt, "Public Housing in Urban America"; *Audit Report, The City of Little Rock Housing Authority, Procurement and Asset Control* (Department of Housing and Urban Development, January 26, 2004), 12–15, https://archives.hud.gov/offices/oig/reports/files/ig461001.pdf; John A. Kirk, "Housing, Urban Development, and the Persistence of Racial Inequality in the Post-Civil Rights Era South," in *The New Black History: Revisiting the Second Reconstruction*, ed. Manning Marable and Elizabeth Kai Hinton (Palgrave, 2011), 21–22; Andy Davis, "LR Housing Project on Way Out," *Arkansas Democratic Gazette*, December 14, 2007; Christopher Silver and John V. Moeser, *The Separate City: Black Communities in the Urban South, 1940–1968* (University Press of Kentucky, 1995), esp. 125–26, 128, 151.

52. "Rental—Midland City Housing Authority Apartments," South Central Alabama Regional Housing Authority, https://www.scarhahousing.com/locations/detail/2653.

53. Franklin D. Roosevelt, "State of the Union Message to Congress," January 11, 1944, http://www.fdrlibrary.marist.edu/archives/address_text.html; Freeman, *American Empire*, 29–32.

54. FHA, *Administrative Rules and Regulations for Rental Housing Insurance*, 23–25; *FHA Investigation*, 72; *Twenty-First Annual Report of the Federal Housing Administration, Year ending December 31, 1954* (US Government Printing Office, 1956), 242–44.

55. Alexander von Hoffman, "A Study in Contradictions: The Origins and Legacy of the Housing Act of 1949," *Housing Policy Debate* 11, no. 2 (2000): 312; US Bureau of the Census, *Historical Statistics of the United States, Colonial Times to 1970*, bicentennial ed., pt. 2, 340.

Chapter 6

1. Marina Budhos, "Summer Nights, Part 1," *The Margins*, June 3, 2014, https://aaww.org/end-everything-part/, and "Summer Nights, Part 2," *The Margins*, June 5, 2014, https://aaww.org/end-everything-part-2/; interview with Jan Oxenberg, March 9, 2023. See also Andrea A. Krest, "The Postwar Garden Apartment: Housing for the Middle-Class in Bell Park Gardens, Queens" (master's thesis, Columbia University, 1984), 63. My own childhood recollections of living in garden apartments until age nine closely correspond with these memories.

2. Randall DeGroat, April 5, 2017, comment on Joann Williams, "Leclaire Courts: The History of a Community in Public Housing," Desktop Documentaries, https://www.desktop-documentaries.com/leclaire-courts-the-history-of-a-community-in-public-housing.html; Laine Kaplan-Levenson, host, *TriPod: New Orleans at 300*, podcast, "Desire, Louisiana," WWNO 89.9, October 11, 2018, https://www.wwno.org/podcast/tripod-new-orleans-at-300/2018-10-11/desire-louisiana.

3. Devereux Bowly Jr., *The Poorhouse: Subsidized Housing in Chicago*, 2nd ed. (Southern Illinois University Press, 2012), 59–62; Lucia Anaya, "Former LeClaire Courts Residents Are Still Fighting to Go Home," *Chicago Reader*, August 4, 2016, https://

www.chicagoreader.com/chicago/leclaire-courts-redevelopment-controversy-cha/Content?oid=23039100.

4. Linda Wheeler, "Fairlington: At 50, A Mature 'Little Town,'" *Washington Post*, May 29, 1993; National Register of Historic Places Registration Form for Carver Court, National Park Service, United States Department of the Interior, 50, https://www.nps.gov/nr/feature/places/pdfs/16000310.pdf; Marina Budhos, "Friedan's Village," *The Awl*, May 20, 2015, https://www.theawl.com/2015/05/friedans-village. Warren interviewed in "To Me It Will Always Be The Calliope: The Oral History of a Housing Project," video, directed by Georges Collinet, 2013, 33 min., 6 sec., https://www.hano.org/media/.

5. Interview with Jesús Hermosillo, 2009, https://vimeo.com/3059245; Kaplan-Levenson, "Desire, Louisiana."

6. Budhos, "Summer Nights, Part 1"; Tina Lincer, "From Foxholes to Bayside Homes," *New York Daily News*, November 11, 2013; Sylvester E. White, August 1, 2014, comment on Williams, "Leclaire Courts: The History of a Community."

7. Matthew Gordon Lasner, *High Life: Condo Living in the Suburban Century* (Yale University Press, 2012), 151; Budhos, "Summer Nights, Part 2."

8. Lewis Mumford, *Sketches from Life: The Autobiography of Lewis Mumford: The Early Years* (Dial Press, 1982), 418–19; Jeffrey A. Kroessler, *Sunnyside Gardens: Planning and Preservation in a Historic Garden Suburb* (Fordham University Press, 2021), 84–85.

9. Herbert J. Gans, "Planning and Social Life," *Journal of the American Institute of City Planners* 37, no. 2 (1961), reprinted in Gans, *People and Plans: Essays on Urban Problems and Solutions* (Basic Books, 1968), 152–54.

10. Lincer, "From Foxholes to Bayside Homes"; Krest, "The Postwar Garden Apartment," 64–65; "If Those Bricks Could Talk," video, produced by Spyboy Production, 25 min., 27 sec., https://www.hano.org/media/.

11. Some Mexicans and Central Americans who lived elsewhere also camped outside after the quake, but at Wyvernwood the arrangement was strongly communal. Interview with Jesús Hermosillo, March 9, 2023; Judy Pasternak, Frederick M. Muir, and Laurie Becklund, "With Resignation, Even Humor, Residents Pick up the Pieces," *Philadelphia Inquirer*, October 2, 1987; Judy Pasternak, "Quake Impact: It Depends on Where You Live," *Los Angeles Times*, October 9, 1987.

12. Lincer, "From Foxholes to Bayside Homes;" Maurice Washington, *My Life: My Awakening* (Jade Media Books, 2017).

13. Washington, *My Life*; interview with Jesús Hermosillo, March 9, 2023; Rachael Breunlin, *If Those Bricks Could Talk: A Collaborative Book Dedicated to the Lafitte Public Housing Development in New Orleans* (Neighborhood Story Project, 2016).

14. *Long Island Daily Press*, January 22, 1957.

15. *Bell Park Gardens Yearbook, 1950–51*, 5, 8–22, http://bpg.50megs.com/YEARBOOK/yearbook.html; Lasner, *High Life*, 2, 126; Mathew Gordon Lasner, "Bell Park Gardens," *SAH Archipedia*, https://sah-archipedia.org/buildings/NY-01-081-0001.

16. Lasner, *High Life*, 151; *Bell Park Gardens Yearbook, 1950–51*, 9–11; Joshua B. Freeman, *Working-Class New York: Life and Labor since World War II* (New Press, 2000), 127, 130–31; Jennifer Klein, *For All These Rights: Business, Labor, and the Shaping of America's Public-Private Welfare State* (Princeton University Press, 2003), 116–17, 208–44, 258–59; Krest, "Postwar Garden Apartment," 71–72. For an example of

community organization and activities in suburban tract housing, see Rosalyn Baxandall and Elizabeth Ewen, *Picture Windows: How the Suburbs Happened* (Basic Books, 2000), 152–57.

17. Budhos, "Friedan's Village"; Budhos, "Summer Nights, Part 2"; Daniel Horowitz, *Betty Friedan and the Making of "The Feminine Mystique": The American Left, the Cold War, and Modern Feminism* (University of Massachusetts Press, 1998), 156; Kayla Levy, "Biography of a Building," *New York Magazine*, January 19, 2023.

18. For interviews with former residents of Lafitte, see the video "If Those Bricks Could Talk." See, also, Breunlin, *If Those Bricks Could Talk*; *Report of the Housing Authority of New Orleans, For Year Ending September 30, 1955*, 8, City Archives & Special Collections, New Orleans Public Library, New Orleans, LA; Ashley Nelson, *The Combination* (Neighborhood Story Project, 2005), 95–100.

19. National Register of Historic Places Registration Form for Mar Vista Gardens (Draft), National Park Service, United States Department of the Interior, 37; Jacqueline Leavitt, "Women under Fire: Public Housing Activism in Los Angeles," *Frontiers: A Journal of Women's Studies* 13, no. 2 (1993): 120–21.

20. Gans, "Planning and Social Life," 155.

21. Krest, "The Postwar Garden Apartment," 55–56; US Bureau of the Census, *U.S. Census of Population: 1950*, vol. III, *Census Tract Statistics*, chap. 37 (US Government Printing Office, 1952), 410; US Bureau of the Census, *U.S. Census of Population and Housing: 1960. Census Tracts*, Final Report PHC(1)-104, pt. 1 (US Government Printing Office, 1962), 502. In 1950, 30.7 percent of the population in Brooklyn and 35.7 percent of Manhattan was age 45 or older, boroughs from where many Queens garden apartment residents had moved. Calculated from US Bureau of the Census, *U.S. Census of Population: 1950*, vol. II, *Characteristics of the Population*, pt. 32, New York (US Government Printing Office, 1952), 145, 147.

22. Jack Metzgar to the author (email), August 27, 2023.

23. *Long Island Daily Press*, January 25, 1957; *Daily News*, September 17, 1986; Minutes of Adjourned 1954 Annual Meeting of the Commissioners of the Housing Authority of the City of Los Angeles, Held on July 29, 1954, 7, Housing Authority of the City of Los Angeles (HACLA) records (digital).

24. Lincer, "From Foxholes to Bayside Homes."

25. Joseph Heathcott, "'In the Nature of a Clinic': The Design of Early Public Housing in St. Louis," *Journal of the Society of Architectural Historians* 70, no. 1 (2011): 101; Jessica Fletcher, "'Where Tenants and Tenets Don't Agree': Elisabeth Coit and the Planning Practices of the New York City Housing Authority (1934–51)," *Buildings & Landscapes: Journal of the Vernacular Architecture Forum* 28, no. 2 (2021): 72–74, 78–80.

26. Interview with Jan Oxenberg; Metzgar to the author, August 27, 2023; interview with Jesús Hermosillo, March 9, 2023; Kaplan-Levenson, "Desire, Louisiana."

27. On homeowner self-construction, see, for example, Baxandall and Ewen, *Picture Windows*, 164–65; Becky M. Nicolaides, *My Blue Heaven: Life and Politics in the Working-Class Suburbs of Los Angeles, 1920–1965* (University of Chicago Press, 2002), 30–33, 228. Deepdale Gardens family from author's acquaintance.

28. *Report of the Housing Authority of New Orleans, For Year Ending December 31, 1939*, 6, City Archives & Special Collections, New Orleans Public Library, New Orleans, LA; US Bureau of the Census, *U.S. Census of Population: 1950*, vol. III, chap. 37,

140; US Bureau of the Census, "Current Populations Reports, Consumer Income," February 15, 1951, 2; US Bureau of the Census, *U.S. Census of Population and Housing: 1960. Census Tracts*, 181; US Bureau of the Census, *Historical Statistics of the United States, Colonial Times to 1970*, bicentennial ed., pt. 2 (US Government Printing Office, 1975), 296–97; Minutes, Commissioners of the Housing Authority of the City of Los Angeles, July 29, 1954, 7.

29. Interview with Jan Oxenberg, including the quote from Dreyfuss, which comes from a discussion he had with Oxenberg.

30. Sylvie Murray, *The Progressive Housewife: Community Activism in Suburban Queens, 1945–1965* (University of Pennsylvania Press, 2003), 32; US Bureau of the Census, *U.S. Census of Population: 1950*, vol. III, chap. 37, 410.

31. David Grayson, "Parkmerced: A City within San Francisco and Why I Miss Calling It Home," *The Bold Italic*, December 5, 2017, https://thebolditalic.com/parkmerced-a-city-within-san-francisco-e45e9e0ed1b0; "To Me It Will Always Be The Calliope" (video); Minutes, Commissioners of the Housing Authority of the City of Los Angeles, July 29, 1954, 6.

32. *Long Island Star Journal*, January 23, 1957; Lincer, "From Foxholes to Bayside Homes."

33. Joshua B. Freeman, *American Empire: The Rise of a Global Power; the Democratic Revolution at Home, 1945–2000* (Viking, 2012), 126–27; Kenneth T. Jackson, *Crabgrass Frontier: The Suburbanization of the United States* (Oxford University Press, 1985), 234–38; Baxandall and Ewen, *Picture Windows*, 122–39.

34. Because census tract boundaries rarely even roughly correspond to garden apartment boundaries, detailed information on resident incomes and occupations is not available for most of the country. Murray, *The Progressive Housewife*, 32; US Bureau of the Census, *U.S. Census of Population: 1950*, vol. III, chap. 37, 408, 410; US Bureau of the Census, *U.S. Census of Population and Housing: 1960. Census Tracts*, 673, 675.

35. On racial patterns, see chapter 6. Krest, "The Postwar Garden Apartment," 55–56; Murray, *The Progressive Housewife*, 35, 61, 74, 77; Ayala Ben-Yehuda, "Deepdale Gardens Turns 50 with Street Fair Celebration," *QNS*, June 18, 2003, https://qns.com/2003/06/deepdale-gardens-turns-50-with-street-fair-celebration/.

36. Betty Friedan, *Life So Far* (Simon & Schuster, 2000), 77; Budhos, "Summer Nights, Part 1"; Ariel Dorfman, "The Boy Who Taught Me about War and Peace," *CNN Opinion*, November 15, 2018, https://www.cnn.com/2018/11/14/opinions/the-boy-who-taught-me-about-war-and-peace-dorfman/index.html.

37. Chris Smith, "Margaret Trafficante, Who Was Involved in Landmark Fair Housing Case, Dies at 91," *Press Democrat*, August 10, 2016, https://www.pressdemocrat.com/article/news/margaret-trafficante-who-was-involved-in-landmark-fair-housing-case-dies/; Trafficante v. Metropolitan Life Ins. Co., 409 U.S. 205 (1972), https://supreme.justia.com/cases/federal/us/409/205/; Grayson, "Parkmerced."

38. Zenobia, September 30, 2012, Bernadine, June 20, 2013, and Anonymous, January 5, 2014, comments on Williams, "Leclaire Courts: The History of a Community."

39. Betty Friedan, *"It Changed My Life": Writings on the Women's Movement* (Laurel, 1991), 14. See also Frances Schutze, *The Little Bastard* (Anchor & Plume Press, 2014), a short story set in Neighborhood Gardens in its early years, by a resident from that time.

40. Murray, *Progressive Housewife*, 60–88; interview with Paul Milkman, October 17, 2019.

41. Murray, *Progressive Housewife*, 69; Horowitz, *Betty Friedan*, 156–57.

42. Budhos, "Summer Nights, Part 2"; Smith, "Margaret Trafficante."

43. See, for example, interview with Annie Pearl Nelson, in Nelson, *The Combination*, 25; Kaplan-Levenson, "Desire, Louisiana"; Nicole Santa Cruz, "At Nickerson Gardens, 'the Wall' of Names Is Sacred Ground," and comments, *Los Angeles Times*, May 1, 2015, https://homicide.latimes.com/post/nickerson-gardens-wall/; Orissa Arend, *Showdown in Desire: The Black Panthers Take a Stand in New Orleans* (University of Arkansas Press, 2010), 19; "If Those Bricks Could Talk" (video).

44. Leavitt, "Women under Fire"; Arend, *Showdown in Desire*, 17, 26; LaVonna Blair Lewis, "History of Jordan Downs and Nickerson Gardens Housing Projects," *Oxford African American Studies Center*, February 29, 2016, https://doi.org/10.1093/acref/9780195301731.013.50606.

45. [New York City] Landmarks Preservation Commission, "United Workers' Cooperative Colony," Designation List 245 LP-1795, June 2, 1992; Eve Blau, *The Architecture of Red Vienna 1919–1934* (MIT Press, 1999), 2, 6–7; Joshua B. Freeman, *Behemoth: A History of the Factory and the Making of the Modern World* (Norton, 2018), 192–93, 208–10, 250, 254–56; Gail Radford, *Modern Housing for America: Policy Struggles in the New Deal Era* (University of Chicago Press, 1996), 130; Barbara Lamprecht, *Richard Neutra, 1892–1970: Survival through Design* (Taschen, 2021), 48–49.

46. Freeman, *Working-Class New York*, 113; Levy, "Biography of a Building"; Federal Housing Administration, *Planning Rental Housing Projects* (n.p., 1947), 8–9.

47. "Nickerson Gardens Housing Project, Los Angeles, CA," Paul Revere Williams Project, https://www.paulrwilliamsproject.org/index.html.1.113.html; C. Kaye Rawlings, "The Watts Riots, Nickerson Gardens, and Black Lives Matter," July 15, 2020, *Artillery*, https://artillerymag.com/provenance/; "A Place to Play: The First Years of NORD, 1947–1948," City Archives & Special Collections, New Orleans Public Library, New Orleans, LA, https://nolacityarchives.org/2024/03/16/a-place-to-play-the-first-of-nord/#gsc.tab=0.

48. Dolores Hayden, *The Grand Domestic Revolution: A History of Feminist Designs for American Homes, Neighborhoods, and Cities* (MIT Press, 1981), esp. 230–37, 242–43, 255, 258, 282; Freeman, *Behemoth*, 192, 208–10; Landmarks Preservation Commission, "United Workers' Cooperative Colony."

49. Fletcher, "'Where Tenants and Tenets Don't Agree,'" 72–74; Minutes of Regular Meeting of the Commissioners of the Housing Authority of the City of Los Angeles, July 19, 1940, HACLA records (digital); Alison Lefkovitz, "Men in the House: Race, Welfare, and the Regulation of Men's Sexuality in the United States, 1961–1972," *Journal of the History of Sexuality* 20, no. 3 (2011): 597–601; Minutes, Commissioners of the Housing Authority of the City of Los Angeles, July 29, 1954, 7; Levy, "Biography of a Building."

50. Fletcher, "'Where Tenants and Tenets Don't Agree,'" 78–80; Elisabeth Coit, "Notes on the Design and Construction of the Dwelling Unit for the Lower-Income Family—Part I," *The Octagon* 13, no. 10 (1941): quoted passages on 19.

51. Maureen A. Flanagan, *Constructing the Patriarchal City: Gender and the Built Environments of London, Dublin, Toronto, and Chicago, 1870s into the 1940s* (Temple University Press, 2018).

52. Heathcott, "'In the Nature of a Clinic,'"101. For a brilliant discussion of the plight of women during the heyday of garden apartment construction, see Selma James, "A Woman's Place" [1952], reprinted in Selma James, *Sex, Race, and Class—The Perspective of Winning: A Selection of Writings, 1952–2011* (PM Press, 2012). More famously, Betty Friedan wrote about the isolation and unhappiness of housewives in *The Feminine Mystique* (Norton, 1963), published seven years after she moved out of Parkway Village.

53. Gail Gregory Sansbury, "Lincoln Place: A Case Study of a Multi-Family Rental Complex Built in Los Angeles in 1949–50" (master's thesis, University of California, Los Angeles, 1993), 92; Louis Winnick, *Rental Housing: Opportunities for Private Investment* (McGraw Hill, 1958), 285; FHA, *Insured Mortgage Portfolio*, Fall 1953, 6.

54. Krest, "Postwar Garden Apartment," 69; [New York] *Daily News*, September 17, 1986; Ben-Yehuda, "Deepdale Gardens Turns 50"; "About Clearview," Clearview Gardens Corp, http://clearviewgardens.com/84647-about/; Sansbury, "Lincoln Place," 97.

55. Friedan could have tried to get a larger apartment at Parkway Village, but as she later wrote, by then she and her husband "were also succumbing to that dream of a suburban house." *Long Island Star Journal*, January 23, 1957; J. S. Fuerst, *When Public Housing Was Paradise: Building Community in Chicago* (University of Illinois Press, 2005), 26–27; Maria Newman, "Clason Point Gardens Journal: For 50 Years a Home, a Real Home," *New York Times*, August 6, 1992; Peter Guralnick, *Last Train to Memphis: The Rise of Elvis Presley* (Little Brown, 1994), 49; Jonathan Gould, *Otis Redding: An Unfinished Life* (Crown, 2017), 96; Friedan, *Life So Far*, 83–84.

56. Kathleen Lynn, "Garden Apartments Help Shape the N.J. Landscape," *The Record*, August 28, 2016.

57. Lasner, "Bell Park Gardens"; Metzgar to the author, August 27, 2023; Lynn, "Garden Apartments Help Shape the N.J. Landscape."

Chapter 7

1. *FHA Investigation Before the Senate Committee on Banking and Currency*, 84th Cong. 1st sess. (January 6, 1955), 8–9; "Lauds FHA Extension," *New York Times*, October 23, 1949.

2. *FHA Investigation*, 4; Homer Hoyt, "The Housing Market in the United States Since World War II," *Real Estate Issues* 8, no. 1 (1983): 2.

3. Lee E. Cooper, "Realty Men Fear Status of Housing Under '608' Loans," *New York Times*, November 19, 1950.

4. Congress authorized an additional half billion dollars in mortgage insurance commitments, which allowed the FHA to insure an estimated 70 percent of the section 608 applications that came in as the program was set to expire. "Sounds Warning on Rental Housing," *New York Times*, February 24, 1950; "New Rules Check Apartment Work," *New York Times*, May 7, 1950; *FHA Investigation*, 11–12.

5. Robert M. Fogelson, *Working-Class Utopias: A History of Cooperative Housing in New York City* (Princeton University Press, 2022), 45–53, 76; Richard O. Davies, *Housing Reform During the Truman Administration* (University of Missouri Press, 1966), 117–21; Hoyt, "The Housing Market," 2.

6. The difference between the two tax treatments amounted to a $28 million loss of federal revenue. Anthony Leviero, "F.H.A. Chief Out, Frauds Charged; U.S. Opens

Study," *New York Times*, April 13, 1954; "Andrews Asserts Housing Windfall was 65.5 millions," *New York Times*, April 21, 1954. The early warning about mortgaging out appears in E. A. Mattison to B. C. Bovard, February 18, 1942, "Corres. Insurance Companies Title VI" file, Record Group 31, Records Pertaining to Title VI and Title VII of the National Housing Act, National Archives at College Park, College Park, MD.

7. Leviero, "F.H.A. Chief Out, Frauds Charged"; Anthony Leviero, "F.H.A. Aide Invokes Fifth Amendment in Housing Inquiry," *New York Times*, April 20, 1954; "Andrews Asserts Housing Windfall was 65.5 millions"; "21 More Ousted in F.H.A. Scandal," *New York Times*, October 24, 1954. The IRS ultimately lost its claim about the tax treatment of excess mortgage money. In a test case, the United States Tax Court ruled that the Gross-Morton interests, which had built Glen Oaks Village and other developments, did not owe back taxes for treating their windfalls as capital gains. "Levittown Made 5 Million Profit, Glen Oaks More," *New York Times*, July 16, 1954; "U.S. Loses in Test of 'Windfall' Tax on Housing Gains," *New York Times*, February 2, 1955.

8. Holding hearings in Indianapolis probably reflected the desire of the committee chair, Homer E. Capehart, to get some political payoff in his home state of Indiana. *FHA Investigation: Hearings, Part 1, Before the Senate Committee on Banking and Currency*, 83rd Cong. 2nd sess. (1954).

9. Perhaps somewhat ingenuously, the report of the Republican-led committee commented, "We have frequently been told that the building industry will not build multifamily rental housing unless the builder can make a fair profit out of the Government-financed mortgage funds and also continue to own the property without any substantial investment. If that is the only alternative it is better that the Government build such projects itself." *FHA Investigation*, 3, 5.

10. *FHA Investigation*, 50; *FHA Investigation: Hearings, Part 1*, 545; Harry K. Schwartz, "Sin and Section 608: I," *Harvard Crimson*, April 27, 1954.

11. Ironically, the Senate committee found that the "largest and most unreasonable windfalls occurred in 1950–51," mostly at projects not completed until after the termination of the program. *FHA Investigation*, 4; Alan S. Oser, "Perspectives: Conversions; Upgrading Queens Garden Apartments," *New York Times*, May 19, 1985; Gwendolyn Wright, *Building the Dream: A Social History of Housing in America* (Pantheon, 1981), 246–47.

12. Clayton Knowles, "Public Housing Plans Run Into Serious Snag," *New York Times*, May 30, 1954; Gail Gregory Sansbury, "Lincoln Place: A Case Study of a Multi-Family Rental Complex Built in Los Angeles in 1949–50," (master's thesis, University of California, Los Angeles, 1993), 86; Richard M. Flanagan, "The Housing Act of 1954: The Sea Change in National Urban Policy," *Urban Affairs Review* 33 (1997): 265–86 (production figures on 281).

13. Hoyt, "The Housing Market," 2; Joshua B. Freeman, *American Empire, 1945–2000: The Rise of a Global Power; the Democratic Revolution at Home* (Viking, 2012), 126–28.

14. During the first decade after the war, a sixth of all new nonfarm homes were purchased with VA loans. Catherine Bauer, *Modern Housing* (1934; repr., University of Minnesota Press, 2020), 229; Freeman, *American Empire*, 127; Laura McEnaney, *Postwar: Waging Peace in Chicago* (University of Pennsylvania Press, 2018), 34; Rosalyn Baxandall and Elizabeth Ewen, *Picture Windows: How the Suburbs Happened* (Basic Books, 2000), 121–33.

15. R. J. Thomas, *Housing for Defense* (UAW International Education Department, 1942); International Union, United Automobile, Aircraft and Agricultural Implement Workers of America, *Homes for Workers in Planned Communities Thru Collective Action* (International Union, 1943); Morton M. Hunt, "The Battle of Abington Township: A Case History in Cooperative Housing," *Commentary*, March 1950, 234–43.

16. Hunt, "The Battle of Abington Township."

17. Davies, *Housing Reform During the Truman Administration*, 126–28.

18. Amy L. Howard, *More Than Shelter: Activism and Community in San Francisco Public Housing* (University of Minnesota Press, 2014), 17; Thomas S. Hines, "Housing, Baseball, and Creeping Socialism: The Battle of Chavez Ravine, Los Angeles, 1949–1959," *Journal of Urban History* 8, no. 2 (1982): 123–43; National Register of Historic Places Registration Form for Mar Vista Gardens (Draft), National Park Service, United States Department of the Interior, 11–12.

19. Sylvie Murray, *The Progressive Housewife: Community Activism in Suburban Queens, 1945–1965* (University of Pennsylvania Press, 2003), 47, 57; *Long Island Daily Press*, January 25, 1957; Alan S. Oser, "Clearview: A Sense of Cooperative Living in Queens," *New York Times*, March 31, 1978; Lizabeth Cohen, *A Consumers' Republic: The Politics of Mass Consumption in Postwar America* (Vintage, 2003), 203–4, 236–38.

20. *FHA Investigation: Hearings, Part 1*, 89–93, 101–4; Oser, "Perspectives."

21. Oser, "Clearview"; "Garden Apartments Converted," *New York Times*, November 26, 1978; Oser, "Perspectives"; *A Task Force on Garden Apartments* (City of New York Department of Housing Preservation and Development (HPD), 1980), New York City Municipal Archives, New York, 1, 13.

22. Alan S. Oser, "About Real Estate; Garden Apartments in Queens Becoming Private Homes," *New York Times*, February 13, 1981; Oser, "About Real Estate; Condominium Restoring Life to a Queens Complex," *New York Times*, July 16, 1982; HPD, *A Task Force on Garden Apartments*, 1–2.

23. HPD, *A Task Force on Garden Apartments*, 14–17.

24. Oser, "Clearview"; HPD, *A Task Force on Garden Apartments*, 15.

25. HPD, *A Task Force on Garden Apartments*, 18–23, 26–27; "Garden Apartments Converted"; Oser, "Garden Apartments in Queens Becoming Private Homes"; Oser, "Condominium Restoring Life to a Queens Complex."

26. In non-eviction cooperative conversions, current residents were generally offered the opportunity to buy their apartments at lower "insider" prices than the prices offered to "outsiders." New York City Housing Development Administration, "Manual of Operations—Low Income Coop Conversion" [1971?], New York City Municipal Archives; Benjamin Holtzman, *The Long Crisis: New York City and the Path to Neoliberalism* (Oxford University Press, 2021), 58–94.

27. Alan S. Oser, "About Real Estate; Parkway Village in Queens Going Co-op," *New York Times*, October 29, 1982; Oser, "Perspectives"; Diana Shaman, "If You're Thinking of Living in Glen Oaks, Queens; Born in the Postwar Era," *New York Times*, August 22, 1999.

28. The challenges new cooperatives faced can be followed in *N.Y. Habitat* (later renamed *Habitat*), a magazine founded in 1982 for co-op boards and condominium managers. See, also, Federal Reserve Economic Data, "30-Year Fixed Rate Mortgage Average in the United States (MORTGAGE30US)," Federal Reserve Bank of St. Louis,

June 29, 2023, https://fred.stlouisfed.org/series/MORTGAGE30US; Kathryn Farrell, "Georgetown Mews Solar Project Generating Big Savings," *Habitat*, March 31, 2020, https://www.habitatmag.com/Publication-Content/Green-Ideas/2020/2020-March/Georgetown-Mews-Solar-Project-Generating-Big-Savings.

29. Dennis Hathaway, *The Battle of Lincoln Place: An Epic Fight by Tenants to Save their Homes* (Crania Press, 2022), 23–25.

30. This account of the Lincoln Place events draws heavily on Hathaway, *The Battle of Lincoln Place*. See, also, Sansbury, "Lincoln Place"; and Lauren Walser, "California Dream: Lincoln Place Apartments," *Preservation Magazine*, Winter 2016, https://savingplaces.org/stories/california-dream-lincoln-place-apartments.

31. In January 2024, available one-bedroom apartments at Lincoln Place rented from $2,913 to $4,188, while two-bedroom apartments were available from $3,611 to $4,571. Real estate websites had differing figures for averages for all of Venice, ranging for one bedrooms from $2,712 to $3,793 and for two bedrooms from $3,491 to $5,859. Lincoln Place, https://www.lincolnplaceapthomes.com/en/apartments/residences.html; "Average Rent in Venice, Los Angeles, CA," Rental Market Trends, https://www.zumper.com/rent-research/los-angeles-ca/venice; "Rental Market Trends in Venice, CA," Apartments.com, https://www.apartments.com/rent-market-trends/venice-ca/.

32. It took fifteen years and further changes in ownership for the new buildings to be erected. Substantial renovations of the original buildings and of the landscaping left the project in excellent condition. Roberto J. Manzano, "Chase Knolls Residents Meet to Fight Demolition of 53-Year Old Apartments," *Los Angeles Times*, April 6, 2000; Hector Becerra, "Historic Complex Faces New Preservation Fight," *Los Angeles Times*, November 27, 2004; Marianne Love, "Developers fuse old and new with Chase Knolls renovations in Sherman Oaks," *Los Angeles Daily News*, July 28, 2020; "Chase Knolls," Los Angeles Conservancy, https://www.laconservancy.org/locations/chase-knolls.

33. Roger Vincent, "Towering ambitions for Boyle Heights," *Los Angeles Times*, January 11, 2008; "Tenant group speaks out," *Los Angeles Times*, January 22, 2008; Hector Becerra, "For garden complex in Boyle Heights, a season of change," *Los Angeles Times*, December 5, 2009; David Zahniser, "L.A. Councilman Jose Huizer states opposition to Boyle Height development proposal," *Los Angeles Times*, April 1, 2011; Kristopher Fortin, "Residents Protest Demolition of Wyvernwood Apartments, Seek Preservation," *Streetsblog*, February 22, 2013, https://la.streetsblog.org/2013/02/22/residents-protest-demolition-of-wyvernwood-apartments-seek-preservation/; Jesús Hermosillo, "Op/Ed: Saving Wyvernwood is the Environmental Choice," *Streetsblog*, April 17, 2013, https://la.streetsblog.org/2013/04/17/saving-wyvernwood-is-the-environmental-choice/; Jessica Cowley, "Which Wyvernwood?," video, 2009, Center for EthnoCommunications of the UCLA Asian American Studies Center; interview with Jesús Hermosillo, March 8, 2023.

34. Mary Otto, "More Doors Closing on Working Poor," *Washington Post*, August 12, 2003.

35. Edward G. Goetz, *New Deal Ruins: Race, Economic Justice, and Public Housing Policy* (Cornell University Press, 2013), 7, 36, 90. In 1950, the median income for white families was $3,445 and for non-white families $1,869. Those figures rose, respectively, to $5,835 and $3,233 in 1960 and $10,236 and $6,516 in 1970. US

Bureau of the Census, *Historical Statistics of the United States, Colonial Times to 1970*, bicentennial ed., pt. 1 (US Government Printing Office, 1975), 297.

36. The Kennedy order covered all existing residential property owned or operated by the federal government; for other residential property, it only applied to buildings with new federal loans, grants, or mortgage insurance. Goetz, *New Deal Ruins*, 7, 90, 104, 112; Exec. Order No. 11063, 3 C.F.R. (November 20, 1962), text available at https://www.archives.gov/federal-register/codification/executive-order/11063.html; Howard, *More Than Shelter*, 19–20; Luis Ferré-Sadurní, "The Rise and Fall of New York Public Housing: An Oral History," *New York Times*, July 9, 2018.

37. Joseph Heathcott, "The Strange Career of Public Housing: Policy, Planning, and the American Metropolis in the Twentieth Century," *Journal of the American Planning Association* 78, no. 4 (2012): 367; Lawrence J. Vale and Yonah Freemark, "From Public Housing to Public-Private Housing: 75 Years of American Social Experimentation," *Journal of the American Planning Association* 78, no. 4 (2012): 385; Goetz, *New Deal Ruins*, 7, 37–38.

38. Larry Keating and Carol A. Flores, "Sixty and Out: Techwood Homes Transformed by Enemies and Friends," *Journal of Urban History* 26, no. 3 (2000): 284, 287.

39. Goetz, *New Deal Ruins*, 7–8, 38–39; Heathcott, "The Strange Career of Public Housing," 370; Alex F. Schwartz, *Housing Policy in the United States*, 2nd ed. (Routledge, 2010), 128–29, 136–37; LaVonna Blair Lewis, "History of Jordan Downs and Nickerson Gardens Housing Projects," *Oxford African American Studies Center*, February 29, 2016, https://doi.org/10.1093/acref/9780195301731.013.50606; Joseph Heathcott, "Planning Note: Pruitt-Igoe and the Critique of Public Housing," *Journal of the American Planning Association* 78, no. 4 (2012): 450–51; D. Bradford Hunt, "What Went Wrong with Public Housing in Chicago? A History of the Robert Taylor Homes," *Journal of the Illinois State Historical Society* 94, no. 1 (2001): 96–123.

40. Oscar Newman, *Creating Defensible Space*, US Department of Housing and Urban Development, Office of Policy Development and Research, April 1996, 67.

41. Laine Kaplan-Levenson, host, *TriPod: New Orleans at 300*, podcast, "Desire, Louisiana," WWNO 89.9, October 11, 2018, https://www.wwno.org/podcast/tripod-new-orleans-at-300/2018-10-11/desire-louisiana; Orissa Arend, *Showdown in Desire: The Black Panthers Take a Stand in New Orleans* (University of Arkansas Press, 2010), 6–7; Rachael Breunlin, *If Those Bricks Could Talk: A Collaborative Book Dedicated to the Lafitte Public Housing Development in New Orleans* (Neighborhood Story Project, 2016); "If Those Bricks Could Talk," video, produced by Spyboy Production, 25 min., 27 sec., https://www.hano.org/media/; "To Me It Will Always Be The Calliope: The Oral History of a Housing Project," video, directed by Georges Collinet, 2013, 33 min., 6 sec., https://www.hano.org/media/.

42. The Chicago Housing Authority provided a no-down-payment mortgage for the purchase. Residents unable or uninterested in purchasing their apartments were moved to other public housing projects. "Racine Courts," *Chicago Gang History*, https://www.chicagoganghistory.com/housing-project/racine-courts; Devereux Bowly Jr., *The Poorhouse: Subsidized Housing in Chicago*, 2nd ed. (Southern Illinois University Press, 2012), 118–19.

43. Grisel Cornejo, "Wentworth Gardens," *SAH Archipedia*, https://sah-archipedia.org/buildings/IL-01-031-0033; Jacqueline Leavitt, "Women under Fire: Public Housing Activism in Los Angeles," *Frontiers: A Journal of Women's Studies* 13, no. 2 (1993):

112, 120–25; Breunlin, *If Those Bricks Could Talk*; D. Bradford Hunt, "Public Housing in Urban America," *Oxford Research Encyclopedia of American History*, https://oxfordre.com/americanhistory/view/10.1093/acrefore/9780199329175.001.0001/acrefore-9780199329175-e-61.

44. Newman, *Creating Defensible Space.*

45. Keating and Flores, "Sixty and Out," 286–87.

46. Under federal law, HUD could grant waivers allowing the demolition of obsolete public housing buildings or ones that threatened the preservation of the rest of a project. Heathcott, "Planning Note: Pruitt-Igoe and the Critique of Public Housing," 450–51; Hunt, "Public Housing in Urban America"; Edward G. Goetz, "The Transformation of Public Housing Policy, 1985–2011," *Journal of the American Planning Association* 78, no. 4 (2012): 453; John F. Bauman, "Jimmy Carter, Patricia Roberts Harris, and Housing Policy in the Age of Limits," in *From Tenements to the Taylor Homes: In Search of an Urban Housing Policy in Twentieth-Century America*, ed. John F. Bauman, Roger Biles, and Kristin M. Szylvian (Penn State University Press, 2000), 249.

47. Goetz, *New Deal Ruins*, 2 ("discourse"), 43; Leavitt, "Women under Fire," 114–17; Heathcott, "The Strange Career of Public Housing," 370; Goetz, "The Transformation of Public Housing Policy," 454.

48. Goetz, "The Transformation of Public Housing Policy," 459–61.

49. Hunt, "Public Housing in Urban America"; Goetz, "The Transformation of Public Housing Policy," 452–53, 458–59. For examples of statements of elite desire to rid center cities of undesirable residents, see Leigh Graham, "Razing Lafitte: Defending Public Housing from a Hostile State," *Journal of the American Planning Association* 78, no. 4 (2012): 474.

50. Keating and Flores, "Sixty and Out," 275, 284–301; Goetz, *New Deal Ruins*, 100–103.

51. Goetz, *New Deal Ruins*, 76, 93–99; *HUD's Takeover of the Housing Authority of New Orleans: Testimony Before the H.R. Subcommittee in Housing Opportunity and Community Development* (July 8, 1996) (statement of Judy A. England-Joseph), https://www.govinfo.gov/content/pkg/GAOREPORTS-T-RCED-96-212/pdf/GAOREPORTS-T-RCED-96-212.pdf; Breunlin, *If Those Bricks Could Talk*; Graham, "Razing Lafitte"; "To Me It Will Always Be The Calliope" (video).

52. Howard, *More Than Shelter*, 50–51, 85–90.

53. *New York City Housing Authority News*, October 15, 1942; *New York Post*, March 28, 2005; Jan Somma-Hammel, "Some Former Residents of Staten Island's Markham Gardens Not Eligible to Return," *Staten Island Advance*, March 9, 2009.

54. Joi Dukes, "Fifty Years Later, Former Tindall Heights Tenant to Move into New Senior Housing," WMGT, April 3, 2018, https://41nbc.com/2018/04/03/50-years-later-former-tindall-heights-tenant-to-move-into-new-senior-housing/; Stanley Dunlap, "Tindall Heights Transformation to Begin in May," *The Telegraph* (Macon, Georgia), April 30, 2016; Lucia Anaya, "Former LeClaire Courts Residents Are Still Fighting to Go Home," *Chicago Reader*, August 4, 2016, https://www.chicagoreader.com/chicago/leclaire-courts-redevelopment-controversy-cha/Content?oid=23039100.

55. Vale and Freemark, "From Public Housing to Public-Private Housing," 394–95; Hunt, "Public Housing in Urban America"; "Markham Gardens," The Domain Companies, https://thedomaincos.com/portfolio/markham-gardens/; Somma-Hammel, "Some Former Residents of Staten Island's Markham Gardens."

56. Breunlin, *If Those Bricks Could Talk*; Howard, *More Than Shelter*, 87–93.

57. In addition to the listed Markham Gardens units, in a final phase of the project an eighty-unit building for low-income seniors was built, sponsored by the Sisters of Charity of St. Vincent de Paul, with twenty of the apartments reserved for former residents of Edwin Markham Houses. Howard, *More Than Shelter*, 88–89; Schwartz, *Housing Policy*, 147; Eric Deutsch, "Markham Gardens Residents Return—and Now They Can Be Owners," *New York City Housing Authority Journal*, September 2010; Virginia N. Sherry, "Markham Gardens Manor, Staten Island's Newest Low-Income Senior Housing, Nears Completion," *silive.com*, December 29, 2012, https://www.silive.com/northshore/2012/12/markham_gardens_manor_staten_i.html.

58. The number of families at Techwood and Clark Howell who were offered the right of return was far below the one-time occupancy of the projects, since the Atlanta Housing Authority stopped renting out vacant apartments in anticipation of redevelopment. Schwartz, *Housing Policy*, 147–48; Howard, *More Than Shelter*, 89; Keating and Flores, "Sixty and Out," 300–301; Somma-Hammel, "Some Former Residents of Staten Island's Markham Gardens"; Goetz, *New Deal Ruins*, 176.

59. Davis was a quintessential modernist, having studied with Walter Gropius and Marcel Breuer and interned with Eero Saarinen. He designed a host of buildings in New Orleans and elsewhere, including the Superdome. Arthur Q. Davis, "Design Criteria for William J. Guste, Sr. Homes—LA," 1–15, in *Report of the Housing Authority of New Orleans, For Year Ending September 30, 1961*, 9, 35, City Archives & Special Collections, New Orleans Public Library, New Orleans, LA; John Pope, "Arthur Q. Davis, New Orleans Architect, Dies at 91," NOLA.com, December 2, 2011, https://www.nola.com/news/business/arthur-q-davis-new-orleans-architect-dies-at-91/article_b5813f58-082d-5fdf-81ac-b11042dece32.html.

60. Hunt, "What Went Wrong with Public Housing in Chicago?," 103–7.

61. See, for example, Breunlin, *If Those Bricks Could Talk*; "Amenities," Faubourg Lafitte, http://faubourglafitte.com/about/amenities/; Keating and Flores, "Sixty and Out," 302; Howard, *More Than Shelter*, 90, 189–90.

62. Including stores and commercial spaces in some replacement projects was another departure from earlier garden apartment design. "HUD HOPE VI," Congress for the New Urbanism, https://www.cnu.org/our-projects/hud-hope-vi; Goetz, *New Deal Ruins*, 125; Schwartz, *Housing Policy*, 143–44; Howard, *More Than Shelter*, 90, 189–90; Oscar Newman, *Defensible Space: Crime Prevention through Urban Design* (Macmillan, 1972).

63. Hoyt, "The Housing Market in the United States," 2; Schwartz, *Housing Policy*, 14; Carl F. Horowitz, *The New Garden Apartment: Current Market Realities of an American Housing Form* (Center for Urban Policy Research, 1983), 16–17, 20–22. See my introduction, note 18, for Horowitz's methodology.

64. Paul Mitchell Hess, "Rediscovering the Logic of Garden Apartments," *Places* 17 (2005): 30–35; Matthew Gordon Lasner, *High Life: Condo Living in the Suburban Century* (Yale University Press, 2012), 206–9, 221–23, 225.

65. A Google alert for "garden apartment" will bring in a flood of rental and sales offers, renovation and demolition notices, public approval announcements, and crime site stories for a wide variety of types of low-rise, multiunit residences, many quite different from traditional garden apartments, illustrating how loosely the term has come to be used. Horowitz, *The New Garden Apartment*, 22, 24, 70, 76, 87, 90, 101, 116. House cost-to-income ratios calculated from US Bureau of the

Census, "Median Home Values: Adjusted to 2000 Dollars," https://www2.census.gov/programs-surveys/decennial/tables/time-series/coh-values/values-adj.txt; US Bureau of the Census, "Money Income in the United States: 2000," https://www.census.gov/library/publications/2001/demo/p60-213.html; and US Bureau of the Census, *Historical Statistics of the United States, Colonial Times to 1970*, pt. 1, 297. House size from Freeman, *American Empire*, 455. For comparative detached, townhouse, and condo prices, see "United States Housing Market," Redfin, January 19, 2024, https://www.redfin.com/us-housing-market.

66. Though REITs and other larger institutional investors owned tens of thousands of garden apartments, most such units were owned by developers or individuals. Bendrix Anderson, "Multifamily REITs Focus on Garden-Style Apartment Communities," WealthManagement.com, December 27, 2018, https://www.wealthmanagement.com/multifamily/multifamily-reits-focus-garden-style-apartment-communities; Bendrix Anderson, "Garden Apartments Remain Favored Among Multifamily Buyers," WealthManagement.com, August 9, 2022, https://www.wealthmanagement.com/multifamily/garden-apartments-remain-favored-among-multifamily-buyers (includes "giant acquisitions"); Kyle Campbell, "Why Garden Apartments Have Growing Institutional Appeal," PERE, February 22, 2022, https://www.perenews.com/the-growing-institutional-appeal-of-garden-apartments/ (includes "not glamorous"); Blackstone Real Estate Investment Trust brochure, in possession of the author; "Resource REIT to be Acquired by Blackstone Real Estate Income Trust in $3.7 Billion Transaction," Blackstone, https://www.blackstone.com/news/press/resource-reit-to-be-acquired-by-blackstone-real-estate-income-trust-in-3-7-billion-transaction/.

Conclusion

1. Thomas C. Hubka, *How the Working-Class Home Became Modern, 1900–1940* (University of Minnesota Press, 2020), 86–87, 189.

2. For the development of homes during this period, see Jane C. Busch, Mark Edward Braun, and Brenda Kayzar, *The Greenwood Encyclopedia of Homes through American History: Volume Four 1946–Present* (Greenwood Press, 2008).

ILLUSTRATION CREDITS

Figure I.1 Stan Honda/AFP via Getty Images.
Figure I.2 Schlesinger Library, Radcliffe Institute.
Figure I.3 Joshua B. Freeman.
Figure I.4 Robert Evans Alexander Papers, #3087. Division of Rare and Manuscript Collections, Cornell University Library.
Figure I.5 Housing Authority Photo Collection, Los Angeles Public Library.
Figure 1.1 © Garden City Collection (Letchworth Garden City Heritage Foundation).
Figure 1.2 © Garden City Collection (Letchworth Garden City Heritage Foundation).
Figure 1.3 Eve Blau, *The Architecture of Red Vienna 1919–1934*.
Figure 1.4 Museum of the City of New York.
Figure 1.5 Institut für Stadtgeschichte Frankfurt (ISG FFM) Best. S7A (Stadtbilder—Frankfurt bis 1943 (Abzüge/Digitalisate) Nr. 1998-22455).
Figure 1.6 Louis Pink, *The New Day in Housing*.
Figure 1.7 © 2024 Artists Rights Society (ARS), New York/Bildrecht, Vienna. Collection and Archive, University of Applied Arts Vienna, Inv. No. 50/10/FW (© Bildrecht GmbH).
Figure 2.1 Courtesy of the Queens Borough Public Library, Archives, Thomas Langan Collection.
Figure 2.2 Paul Jakubovich, City Clerk's Office, City of Milwaukee.
Figure 2.3 Museum of the City of New York.
Figure 2.4 *Five-year Report of the Michigan Boulevard Garden Apartments Building Corporation*.
Figure 2.5 *Five-year Report of the Michigan Boulevard Garden Apartments Building Corporation*.
Figure 2.6 Liverpool University Press.
Figure 2.7 Clarence Stein Papers, #3600. Division of Rare and Manuscript Collections, Cornell University Library.

Figure 2.8 Regional Plan Association.

Figure 2.9 Regional Plan Association.

Figure 2.10 Buhl Foundation photographs, 1929–1950, MSP 0187, Detre Library & Archives, Senator John Heinz History Center.

Figure 3.1 Courtesy of the Landmarks Association of St. Louis.

Figure 3.2 © *Architectural Record.*

Figure 3.3 Digital Image © The Museum of Modern Art/Licensed by SCALA / Art Resource, NY.

Figure 3.4 Charles F. Palmer papers, box 167, folder 8, Emory University Stuart A. Rose Manuscript, Archives, and Rare Book Library.

Figure 3.5 Courtesy of the Housing Authority of the City of Atlanta Archives. Photographer Carl Dickerson.

Figure 3.6 *The Architectural Forum.*

Figure 3.7 *The Architectural Forum.*

Figure 3.8 *The Architectural Forum.*

Figure 3.9 John Vachon, Library of Congress, Prints & Photographs Division, FSA/OWI Collection, LC-DIG-fsa-8a05184.

Figure 3.10 John Vachon, Library of Congress, Prints & Photographs Division, FSA/OWI Collection, LC-USF34-060121-D.

Figure 3.11 *The Architectural Forum.*

Figure 3.12 *Report of the Housing Authority of New Orleans for the Period March 15, 1937 to December 31, 1938.*

Figure 3.13 Image 261, Housing Authority of New Orleans Photograph Collection, City Archives & Special Collections, New Orleans Public Library.

Figure 3.14a and Figure 3.14b New York City Housing Authority, *Clason Point Gardens.*

Figure 3.15 Photograph by Calder Loth, 1995. Courtesy of the Virginia Department of Historic Resources.

Figure 3.16 Library of Congress, Prints & Photographs Division, HABS, Reproduction number HABS VA, 7-ARL, 13-4.

Figure 3.17 Library of Congress, Prints & Photographs Division, HABS, Reproduction number HABS VA, 7-ARL, 13-9.

Figure 3.18 © *Architectural Record.*

Figure 3.19 FHA Rental Housing Division Architectural Bulletin #1.

Figure 3.20 USC Digital Library. "Dick" Whittington Photography Collection.

Figure 3.21 Clarence Stein Papers, #3600. Division of Rare and Manuscript Collections, Cornell University Library.

Figure 3.22 Avery Architectural and Fine Arts Library, Columbia University.

Figure 4.1 John DeFerrari.

Figure 4.2 Library of Congress, Prints & Photographs Division, Gottscho-Schleisner Collection, LC-G612-T-44299.

Figure 4.3 qwesy qwesy.

Figure 4.4 Library of Congress, Prints & Photographs Division, HAER, Reproduction number HAER PA, 65-NEKEN, 3A—3.

Figure 4.5a and Figure 4.5b Courtesy of Cranbrook Archives, Cranbrook Center for Collections and Research.

Figure 4.6 Louis I. Kahn Collection, the University of Pennsylvania and the Pennsylvania Historical and Museum Commission.

Figure 4.7 Walter P. Reuther Library, Archives of Labor and Urban Affairs, Wayne State University.

Figure 4.8 Library of Congress, Prints & Photographs Division, Farm Security Administration/Office of War Information Black-and-White Negatives.

Figure 4.9 Richard and Don Neutra Papers, 1925–1970, UCLA, Library Special Collections, Charles E. Young Research Library.

Figure 4.10 J. Paul Getty Trust. Getty Research Institute, Los Angeles (2004.R.10).

Figure 4.11 J. Paul Getty Trust. Getty Research Institute, Los Angeles (2004.R.10).

Figure 4.12 J. Paul Getty Trust. Getty Research Institute, Los Angeles (2004.R.10).

Figure 5.1 Courtesy of Joshua B. Freeman.

Figure 5.2 Courtesy of Housing Authority of the City of Los Angeles.

Figure 5.3 Federal Housing Administration, *Insured Mortgage Portfolio*, 4th quarter 1947.

Figure 5.4 Avery Architectural and Fine Arts Library, Columbia University.

Figure 5.5 Federal Housing Administration, *Insured Mortgage Portfolio*, 2nd quarter 1948.

Figure 5.6a Library of Congress, Prints & Photographs Division, HABS, Reproduction number HABS VA, 7-ARL, 13-16.

Figure 5.6b Joshua B. Freeman.

Figure 5.7 Avery Architectural and Fine Arts Library, Columbia University.

Figure 5.8 Federal Housing Administration, *Insured Mortgage Portfolio*, Fall 1953.

Figure 5.9 Courtesy of Gladys Weaver, Queens Memory Collection at the Archives at Queens Borough Public Library, Queens, New York.

Figure 5.10 Robert Natkin, courtesy of Paul Natkin.

Figure 5.11 Googe Earth.

Figure 5.12 The Historic New Orleans Collection, Gift of Edwin Hoffa in memory of Jimmy and Ruth Hoffa, Acc. No. 2006.0025.15.
Figure 6.1 Courtesy of Joshua B. Freeman.
Figure 6.2 Courtesy of Housing Authority of the City of Los Angeles.
Figure 6.3 *Report of the Housing Authority of New Orleans for the Year Ending September 30, 1955.*
Figure 6.4 Courtesy of Housing Authority of the City of Los Angeles.
Figure 6.5 Tina Lincer.
Figure 6.6 Federal Housing Administration, *Insured Mortgage Portfolio*, 4th quarter 1947.
Figure 6.7 Otto Rothschild, Housing Authority Collection, Los Angeles Public Library.
Figure 6.8 City Archives & Special Collections, New Orleans Public Library.
Figure 7.1 Avery Architectural and Fine Arts Library, Columbia University.
Figure 7.2 International Union, United Automobile, Aircraft and Agriculture Workers of America (UAW-CIO), *Homes for Workers in Planned Communities through Collective Action.*
Figure 7.3 Joshua B. Freeman.
Figure 7.4 Historical Perspectives, Inc.
Figure 7.5 Joshua B. Freeman.
Plate 1 © Kerry James Marshall. Courtesy of the artist and Jack Shainman Gallery, New York. Saint Louis Art Museum, Museum Minority Artists Purchase Fund 190:1995.
Plate 2 Joshua B. Freeman.
Plate 3 Joshua B. Freeman.
Plate 4 Ebenezer Howard, *To-Morrow: A Peaceful Path to Real Reform.* Scan courtesy of Avery Architectural and Fine Arts Library, Columbia University.
Plate 5 Budby via Flickr.
Plate 6 © C. Stadler/Bwag.
Plate 7 © Angela-Kroell.
Plate 8 Landesdenkmalamt Berlin, Wolfgang Bittner, 2015.
Plate 9 A. Savin, Wikimedia.
Plate 10 New York City Housing Authority, *Clason Point Gardens.* From The New York Public Library, https://digitalcollections.nypl.org/items/0243d840-4116-0132-aa8e-58d385a7b928.
Plate 11 Beau Cabell.
Plate 12 Joshua B. Freeman.
Plate 13 © 2024 Frank Lloyd Wright Foundation. All Rights Reserved. Licensed by Artists Rights Society.

Plate 14 Joshua B. Freeman.

Plate 15 Patrick Choy, courtesy of Housing Authority of the City of Los Angeles.

Plate 16 Library of Congress, Prints & Photographs Division, WPA Poster Collection, LC-USZC2-1085.

Plate 17 Adrian Scott Fine/L.A. Conservancy.

Plate 18 Joshua B. Freeman.

Plate 19 David Schalliol.

Plate 20 Van Meter Williams Pollack (VMWP).

Plate 21 David Schalliol.

Plate 22 Harry Connolly.

INDEX